Travellers' Visions

French Literary Encounters with Japan, 1881–2004

Contempor ures 4

D1334858

Contemporary French and Francophone Cultures

This series aims to provide a forum for new research on modern and contemporary French and francophone cultures and writing. The books published in *Contemporary French and Francophone Cultures* reflect a wide variety of critical practices and theoretical approaches, in harmony with the intellectual, cultural and social developments which have taken place over the past few decades. All manifestations of contemporary French and francophone culture and expression are considered, including literature, cinema, popular culture, theory. The volumes in the series will participate in the wider debate on key aspects of contemporary culture.

AKANE KAWAKAMI

Travellers' Visions

French Literary Encounters with Japan,
1881–2004

LIVERPOOL UNIVERSITY PRESS

First published 2005 by
Liverpool University Press
4 Cambridge Street
Liverpool L69 7ZU

British Library Cataloguing-in-Publication data
A British Library CIP record is available

ISBN 0–85323–811–1 cased
ISBN 0–85323–730–1 limp

Typeset in Sabon by Koinonia, Manchester
Printed and bound in the European Union by
Bell and Bain Ltd, Glasgow

Contents

Acknowledgements

I would like to thank the Japan Foundation Endowment Committee for their support, which came in the form of two generous travel grants for research in Japan, and the AHRB Modern Languages Panel for awarding me a Research Leave Grant. I am also grateful to *French Studies*, the *Modern Language Review* and the *Forum for Modern Language Studies* for permission to reprint parts of articles first published by them.

Thanks are due to Mark Treharne, Christopher Thompson and Charles Forsdick – among others – for reading and commenting on parts of my manuscript; Gérard and Anne Macé, for their extreme kindness and hospitality; and Andrew Kirk and Robin Bloxsidge of Liverpool University Press for their efficiency, patience and good humour.

This book is dedicated to Paul, who read everything, at least twice; and to Theo, who arrived soon after it was finished.

Akane Kawakami

Introduction:
Modes of Travel, Modes of Seeing

> I must free myself from the remembrance of too many descriptions –
> from those of Marco Polo, deliciously archaic, to the modern and
> sentimental ones of Pierre Loti – in order to re-enter reality, to see
> the much-awaited object with my own eyes.
>
> Guido Gozzano, 'Il fiume dei roghi' (1914)[1]

Gozzano's wish is one common to most travellers, but which few realise. Guidebooks, historical references and cultural prejudices constantly colour what the traveller might hope to see with the 'naked eye'. There is, of course, no such thing, as Wittgenstein has explained: the visual experience is never free of thought, and a sight will not make *sense* to us unless it is framed by a context ('"the echo of a thought in sight" – one would like to say'[2]). This sense, however, is elusive when we are abroad, because the social or philosophical contexts that shape our ways of seeing do not always travel well. The traveller may not have at his disposal the linguistic or cultural codes needed to understand what he sees in the foreign country, and in these cases the visual experience will not correspond to the wider sense of 'seeing' which involves 'understanding'. This book is about the different ways in which French travellers have seen Japan, from the last decade of the nineteenth century to the present day.

Japan has been, over the years, a privileged object of the French gaze, for at least three reasons. After it closed its ports abruptly to the rest of the world in 1640 and opened them again in 1854, Japan re-entered the Western consciousness as a primarily visual entity through the phenomenon of *japonisme*, and through the French Impressionists' appreciation of Japanese art. This situation gave rise to an *aesthetic* way of seeing Japan, which has been practised by successive generations of travellers. The second reason for Japan's unique status in the Western imagination is that it was never colonised, and therefore never imagined by France in the context of the coloniser–colonised relationship. France's vision of Japan cannot, therefore, be considered in the same category as that of her vision of other Far Eastern countries, such as China, Vietnam or Indonesia. The third reason is its postwar economic success, which gave the country a reputation for wealth to rival the Western nations. More recently, of course, we have witnessed the rise of the 'Tiger economies', but in the 1970s and 1980s Japan was Europe's sole serious competitor in the Asian markets, and this marked it out once more as an exceptional case. I will show how, in every age, our French travellers embark on their travels with a collection of inherited images, which they will need to reconcile with their own experiences once they arrive in Japan; and how their accounts, published when they returned home, affect the visions of future travellers. Thus this study will map out a genealogy of literary images of Japan, which interact, at various historical stages, with the popular stereotypes of Japan in France. And the stereotypes, in their turn, develop alongside the colourful history of Franco–Japanese relations during the period, an era which includes the two world wars and charts the development of Japan from 1854, the year of its reopening to the world after 214 years of isolation, to the twenty-first century.

My proposed examination of the images of Japan in French literature and of the historical and social contexts in which they come into being has much in common, methodologically speaking, with the practice of the imagologists.[3] Imagology declares that its goal is 'l'étude des représentations littéraires de l'étranger': it too probes the sociological and intellectual contexts of an era which give rise to the 'imaginaire social' prevailing in the home country, and from which fertile ground the literary image is born. The focus of my project, however, is different. The imagologist is mainly interested in the images themselves, whereas I am pursuing the particular 'ways of seeing' that give rise to those specific images.[4] Different kinds of traveller *see* differently, have different relationships with the other that is Japan. The journalist-type of traveller, for instance, will look at Japan with an eye to writing a good 'story'; the ethnographer, by contrast, will observe the customs in order to systematise them into a coherent vision of 'Japanese society'. And within each category of traveller, every individual has his or her unique relationship with the other, giving rise to a text that is structured according to the traveller's personal vision of Japan.

My study, therefore, will examine each writer as a certain type of traveller,[5] and analyse the frames and methods of their particular ways of seeing. My focus on the writers' individual *visions* of Japan means that my book is methodologically distinct from studies that aim to describe literary images of the Orient in relation to a 'real' Orient, and from there to evaluate the writers' varying degrees of 'error'. The image of a country is always fictional to some degree, whether it is created by a foreigner or a native,[6] and the aim of this study is not to expose the *falsity* of stereotypical or prejudiced visions. This book will describe the ways in which Japan is represented as an other, but the representations will not be evaluated as being either 'true' or false'.

Differences in attitudes towards otherness have been documented in previous literary studies, and I will be making use of some of the categorising terms coined by theorists and critics in the past. Edward Said's term 'Orientalist' is pertinent and still useful;[7] I will be using it to refer to ways of seeing the East that cast it as the inferior opposite of the West.[8] 'Exoticisation', 'assimilation' and 'reduction' are all variations on this attitude towards the other, in which the Westerner subsumes the East's otherness into categories within his own domain. It is an attitude born of fear: as Levinas argues, a completely alien other represents an ontological threat to a self who believes himself to be the source of all meaning and being, and the obvious solution is to reduce the other to 'des jeux de l'intériorité'.[9] We will see how the movement of *japonisme*, in the late nineteenth century, functions as a version of Orientalism specific to Japan. Another concept that I will be using is the version of 'exotisme' invented by Victor Segalen in the early twentieth century. Segalen's 'exote' values the other for his difference from himself, and seeks to 'maintenir cet objet comme différent du sujet, préserver la précieuse altérité de l'autre'.[10] Unlike the Orientalist, he has no desire to conquer the other, but this is because he has no interest in understanding or accepting it. This attitude is characteristic of Loti, for instance, in certain passages of *Madame Chrysanthème*, as well as being the avowed one of Michaux in *Un barbare en Asie*. Finally, the most tolerant attitudes towards the other come under the umbrella of 'universal humanism', although some forms of this position are still fundamentally Eurocentric, based as they are on European notions of humanity and civilisation. Farrère's attempts to embrace the Japanese as the equal of the European are unable, in spite of his good will, to escape the parameters of a Eurocentric vision. However, 'entrer en relation avec l'insaisissable, tout en lui garantissant son statut d'insaisissable'[11] is possible if the self is willing to sympathise with the other to the point of risking its own centrality in the relationship. This attitude is best exemplified by the self's attempts to speak the other's language: we will see how both Loti and Claudel, for instance, encounter the irreducibility of the other when they enter the Japanese linguistic system.

Because they are based on a relationship with another culture, the texts to be studied in this book have in common a *double* vision, their straddling of two cultural contexts. Arthur Koestler describes such texts as bisociative acts, in that they simultaneously inhabit two frames of reference, a situation that is conducive to creative thought.[12] Another way to describe an 'intercultural' text of this sort is to use the metaphor of translation. A translation always harks back to its original, however close to perfection it may be: its very presence indicates an absence, because every lexical and syntactical choice evokes the distance, both temporal and cultural, separating it from its original.[13] This relationship holds as much for the traveller as for the translator. The distance between the self and the other is an integral part of both translations and travel narratives, and the traveller's attempts to translate his foreign experiences into his home language are always, in a fundamental sense, metaphorical. These 'intercultural' texts thus constitute a unique genre in the history of French literature: they are all attempts to contain, in a single text, a double knowledge of – or a double 'way of seeing', 'understanding' – otherness. In what follows, we will examine the effect of this new kind of vision on the writers' styles and generic choices. The attempt to understand Japan often leads the writers in question to venture into formally unfamiliar territory, as I will show, and at times produces some of the boldest and therefore most interesting effects in that writer's oeuvre.

At this point it might be objected that, instead of discussing 'ways of seeing' and 'intercultural texts', I should rather have categorised these texts as instances of 'travel writing'. I have not done this for two reasons. First, the texts with which I am concerned cannot all be classified as travel narratives. Proust's novel could not be considered a travel narrative, except in the most metaphorical sense; neither can Goncourt's *La Maison d'un artiste*, and the postwar texts are also difficult to place unproblematically into that category. The second reason why I have not started by invoking the category of travel writing is that this genre is not a particularly useful one for discriminatory purposes, because of its all-inclusiveness: it is a genre 'composed of other genres, [...] a genre that confronts, at their extreme limit, representational tastes proper to a number of literary kinds'.[14] I will have recourse, where pertinent, to methods adopted from studies of travel narratives, and make use of the generic category when it is appropriate. In the meantime, I prefer to call these works 'intercultural texts', and to concentrate on the ways of seeing that they embody.

The chapters of the book are roughly chronological, beginning with the introduction. In the second half of this introduction, I sketch out a brief history of travellers and texts prior to the period in question, that is to say those from the seventeenth century to the mid-nineteenth century, with a view to giving historical perspective to what is examined in the main body of the book. Chapter 1 focuses on the phenomenon of *japonisme*, which flourished in the late nineteenth century, and examines the effects of the movement on the works of Edmond de Goncourt, Proust, and Pierre Loti. Chapter 2 moves into the first half of the twentieth century, during which various wars fought by Japan provided an effective antidote to its *japoniste* image, replacing the image of the *geisha* with that of the Yellow Peril: Anatole France, Claude Farrère and Henri Michaux analysed and contributed to the dissemination of this new, warlike image of the country. Chapter 3 is devoted to Claudel, whose unique and evolving vision of Japan was based on an acquaintance with the country that began during *japonisme* and went on until the end of the Second World War. Chapter 4 gives an account of a select number of post-1945 French writers on Japan, whose vision is filtered through that quintessentially modern instrument for seeing, the camera. As will be clear from this brief synopsis, I am not aiming to provide a comprehensive history of French encounters with Japan: the book analyses a series of chosen texts, selected for their singular or representative 'ways of seeing'. But these works constitute, in themselves, a history of inherited images and visions that create a narrative which would be valid, I believe, for a more comprehensive history. The interactions between the different travellers, as well as their interactions with Japan, create inter-writerly as well as inter-cultural tensions within the works, as we will see at the end of this study.

The first Westerners to set foot on Japanese soil were sixteenth-century Portuguese sailors, who were swiftly followed by merchants, adventurers, scientists and missionaries from Portugal, Spain, Holland and

England. Many of them wrote down their impressions of this strange new country, and their different accounts attest to their particular modes of seeing: Japan as the object of missionary zeal, for instance, is in sharp contrast with the scientist's systematic classification of the country's botanical, animal and human features. Nineteenth-century visitors to Japan did not always make use of the observations of their predecessors, as we will see, but the images and stereotypes created by the earlier travellers were most influential, often at a subconscious level, in determining the starting point for the later accounts. I therefore propose, in the following pages, to sketch out an extremely brief history of Western encounters with Japan – and the resulting representations – before 1881.

> I can tell you the quantity of gold they have is endless [...]. I will tell you a wonderful thing about the Palace of the Lord of that Island [Japan]. You must know that he hath a great Palace which is entirely roofed with fine gold, just as our churches are roofed with lead, insomuch that it would scarcely be possible to estimate its value. Moreover, all the pavement of the Palace, and the floors of its chambers, are entirely of gold, in plates like slabs of stone, a good two fingers thick; and the windows also are of gold, so that altogether the richness of this Palace is past all bounds and all belief.
>   They also have pearls in abundance, which are of a rose colour, but fine, big, and round, and quite as valuable as the white ones.[15]

Japan first entered the Western imagination through the fourteenth-century words of Marco Polo, to be found in *The Travels of Marco Polo, the Venetian, concerning the Kingdoms and Marvels of the East*. Marco Polo's accounts of his travels were not universally believed, and in the case of Japan he certainly deserved his readers' suspicions as he had never set foot on Japanese soil, although he had heard much about it during his time at the court of Kublai Khan. His fictional description, however, firmly put Japan in that class of countries that made up the stuff of a sixteenth-century sailor's dreams: exotic, faraway lands of fabulous wealth, with friendly natives and beautiful women. The combination of distance and strangeness has certainly stayed with images of Japan ever since: 'in the earliest European literature it was actually thought to be the Antipodes'.[16] As for the roofs covered in gold, it was left for the first real travellers to arrive in Japan to disprove their existence: until then, 'Japan' was a name without a known referent that conjured up colonialist fantasies in the same way as any number of exotic place names.[17]

Nanban screen

   The first Europeans to set foot on Japanese soil were Portuguese sailors blown off course on their way to Macao.[18] They were driven ashore by a contrary wind on a small island off the coast of Kyushu, the southernmost of the four main islands that make up Japan. This first encounter between the Japanese and a European race, which took place in 1542 or 1543, was cordial and highly satisfactory for both sides. The Portuguese reported back home about their astonishment at the high degree of civilisation of the Japanese: the Japanese, on the other hand, dubbed this race represented by tanned and unshaven sailors Nanbanjin, or 'southern barbarians'. They borrowed this term from the Chinese, who had coined it to describe the non-Chinese people in the South China Seas and the Indo-China peninsula. The Japanese, however, had to acknowledge that these barbarians far outstripped them in at least one area. Firearms had hitherto been unknown to the Japanese, and when the Portuguese showed them their collection of muskets, the lord of the region was greatly impressed and bought a large quantity.

This first encounter was soon followed by many more: adventurers, traders, sailors and missionaries from Portugal, Spain, Holland and England. They mainly arrived, and stayed, on the island of Kyushu, especially in and around the port of Nagasaki. There was soon a growing community of merchants in Deshima, a small island off the coast of Nagasaki designated for foreign dwellings and warehouses. From the very start there was rivalry and animosity amongst the foreigners, between the Protestant nationalities of Holland and England and the Catholic ones of Spain and Portugal. The latter countries also sent travellers of a different kind: missionaries, mostly Jesuits, arrived in large numbers. Francis Xavier, one of the founding fathers of the Society of Jesus, came to Japan as early as 1549, and set up a number of educational establishments and novitiates which flourished. Xavier was delighted with the Japanese, and wrote enthusiastically back to the Society:

> Firstly, the people whom we have met so far, are the best who have yet been discovered, and it seems to me that we shall never find among heathens another race to equal the Japanese. It is a people of very good manners, good in general, and not malicious; they are men of honour to a marvel, and prize honour above all else in the world.[19]

The conversion of Japan progressed apace, so much so that in 1582 four young Japanese Catholic princes set off on a visit to the Vatican, by way of a number of European countries, accompanied by their Jesuit mentors. They arrived in Rome in 1585, were received warmly by the Pope, and returned to Japan in 1588. Unfortunately for them, the situation for Catholics and missionaries had changed drastically during their absence: in 1587 there had been an edict issued expelling missionaries, and although Japanese Christians were not yet being persecuted at this stage, being of this foreign faith was not what it had been when they left Japan just six years previously.

To understand the rapid rise and fall of Christianity and Westernisation in sixteenth- and seventeenth-century Japan, it is necessary to look briefly at the domestic situation.[20] In 1542, when the Portuguese sailors first arrived, Japan was still not effectively united under one central government: it was coming to the end of the Sengoku period, during which local feudal lords, each reigning over their own fiefdoms, were constantly at war with each other. The emperor resided in Kyoto, but with no political power: and the three great leaders who were to build Japan into a nation, the third of whom would call himself the shogun and establish the Tokugawa dynasty, had not yet appeared on the political stage. Oda Nobunaga, the first of the three, succeeded in uniting the greater part of the warlords under his rule; Toyotomi Hideyoshi, who followed him, came to power in 1587 and had effective control of the whole of Japan. It was Hideyoshi who issued the edict against missionaries in 1587, after having learned from Protestant Europeans that Christianity in the West was in fact divided and that Catholic priests had a reputation for scheming against governments. But it was under his successor, Tokugawa Ieyasu, that the persecution of Christians began in earnest. Ieyasu became ruler of Japan in 1598 and established the shogunate, or *bakfu*, in Edo. His persecution of Christians was based on a good understanding of the religion: he felt that a religion which allowed any commoner or peasant direct access to God would ultimately lead to the downfall of the Japanese political system, in which the emperor was the symbolic head of both the religion and the state. The greater number of Protestant clergy who arrived in 1609 and 1613 also contributed to his general mistrust of divided and divisive Christianity. In 1614 the general persecution of Christians began, with both Japanese Christians and foreign missionaries being required to apostasise: when they did not, they underwent various forms of torture, and were usually put to death. The persecution of the missionaries led eventually to a complete rejection of foreigners and all things foreign in 1640, when Ieyasu took the unprecedented decision to close down his realm to the rest of the world. In 1624 all Spaniards, missionaries or otherwise, were expelled from Japan on pain of death: in 1639 it was the turn of the Portuguese, and in 1640

Japan's period of *sakoku* officially began. The Dutch were the only Europeans allowed to remain, in extremely reduced numbers, on the condition that they refrained from missionary activities.[21] This they did, and from 1640 onwards theirs was the only route to trade with Japan until 1852.

During this period of closure, several fearless Europeans travelled to Japan in spite of the still-fresh tales of martyrs and tortures. In 1708 Sidotti, an Italian missionary, asked a boat from the Philippines to deposit him on the coast of Japan. Once he had arrived he made no attempt to hide, but gave himself up to the authorities, who did not execute him immediately, given that he had arrived on his own and professed no allegiance to any European nation or religious order. Sidotti was placed under house arrest, but when his guards – a married couple – confessed to having been converted by him, he was made to listen to them being tortured, then incarcerated until his death. Records of his dialogues about Christianity with an intelligent and well-informed Japanese official survive in the memoirs of the official, Arai Hakuseki. There were several other European travellers to Japan during the period of *sakoku*, however, who returned to tell their tales, often doctors serving the small Dutch trading station of Deshima. Engelbert Kaempfer (1651–1716), for instance, was a German doctor who wrote an encyclopaedic account of his time in the country: his *Histoire naturelle, civile et ecclésiastique du Japon*,[22] a remarkable work compiled on the basis of materials gathered during his two years on Deshima at the end of the seventeenth century as physician to the Dutch community, became the basis for the entry on Japan in the second edition of the *Encyclopaedia Britannica*. But although he was important in the history of European studies of Japan, his account was 'quite marginal in Europe itself'.[23]

A later eighteenth-century traveller who wrote on Japan was Carl Peter Thunberg, a Swedish botanist, who was given safe passage to and from Japan by a group of Dutch merchants. Thunberg's intentions were purely scientific: the record of his travels, published in 1780 and translated into French in 1794, is a detailed study of the geography, flora (he was a botanist, after all) and people of the country. The first volume of *Voyage en Afrique et en Asie, principalement au Japon, pendant les années 1770–1779* is a travelogue, tracing the narrator's steps from his arrival in Nagasaki, through customs (there is a chapter on 'formalités humiliantes qu'éprouvent les Hollandais') to his visit to 'Jeddo', not omitting the various types of pine that he encounters on the way. The later volumes are thematically organised, touching on subjects such as 'Description géographique et physique du Japon', 'température', 'superstition', 'habillement', 'le gouvernement', 'nourriture'. There is even a lexicon of Japanese words at the end of the work. The overall impression that he gives his reader is one of a civilised, frugal and honest people. Judging by the forewords to the reprints, however, the book appears to have been read most eagerly by French men of science to uphold their racialist theories. Thus in 1796 a new edition of the *Voyage* was reprinted with the scientist Lamarck reviewing the scientific sections; and by 1824, Thunberg is being used to justify a racialist science by J. J. Virey in his *Histoire naturelle du Genre Humain*. Racist theories (justifying colonialism) had become very popular in the nineteenth century, with promoters such as Gobineau, and the little information about Japan that had been gleaned by men such as Thunberg and Kaempfer were put to use in global theories proclaiming the superiority of the Western races.[24]

In the meantime, various Western countries such as Britain, America and Russia (all of whom, by this stage, had embarked on the exploitation of the crumbling Chinese Empire) had been trying to encourage Japan to open her ports once more to the rest of the world. Holland had put a formal request to Japan in 1844: an American ship and a Russian ship, on the other hand, had each made the threatening move of sailing into the ports of Uraga and Shimoda, in 1846 and 1852 respectively, although they were not allowed to land. In 1853, the American Commodore Perry decided to force the issue by sailing his 'black ships', as they came to be known, bristling with cannon and other firearms, into the bay of Tokyo. Japan ceded to the pressure and signed trade agreements with America, England and France in the following two years. The reopening of the country and the threat of potential colonisation precipitated the imperial restoration, what is known in Japan as the *Meiji-ishin*: traditionalists and modernisers had been battling over the issue of transferring sovereignty from the shogunate to the emperor. The modernisers won, the emperor became the actual rather than symbolic head of the country for the first time since the ninth century, and the Meiji period – synonymous with rapid modernisation – began in 1868.

The travellers who arrived in this newly opened Japan in the second half of the nineteenth century were not very different in kind from those who had made the same journey in the seventeenth century. The merchants, adventurers and missionaries came again, and their accounts of the country can almost be seen as extensions of the earlier narratives. Yet there were, of course, differences. Thomas Glover, an exemplary adventurer-entrepreneur from Scotland, made a huge fortune in Japan during the upheavals, but having done so he married a Japanese woman and settled there, and contributed greatly to the growth of Nagasaki's industries through his wealth. As for the missionaries, this time it was the fathers of the Missions Etrangères de Paris (MEP) who were chosen to undertake the reconversion of Japan. Their reports and letters to their superiors show that they, like the missionaries two hundred years previously, found the Japanese receptive and eager to learn.

But there was another narrative of Japan that these missionaries wanted to write, based on the work of their seventeenth-century predecessors. One of the specific aims of the nineteenth-century mission was to find out whether there were any descendants left of the Christians baptised in the seventeenth century. What actually happened was more wonderful than anything they had dared hope for. On 17 March 1865, Father Petitjean found some peasants in the newly built Oura church of Nagasaki. This was still a time when the freedom of religious belief had not been fully established, and although the missionaries were not persecuted, they were not permitted to mingle freely with the Japanese people, and vice versa. The priest was therefore greatly astonished when one of the peasants asked him where the statue of 'Santa Maria' was, and even more surprised when the peasant knelt before the statue he had pointed out to him. The peasants identified themselves as Christians, and a report went out duly across the seas to France.

There was, and is, much discussion as to whether these descendants of Christians could be considered to have kept the faith for two hundred years, whether the Church was really brought *back* to life in nineteenth-century Japan. Father Francisque Marnas of the MEP certainly thought so, describing his task in the preface to his book, *La 'Religion de Jésus' (Yaso Ja-kyo) ressuscitée au Japon dans la seconde moitié du XIXe siècle*, in the following words:

> J'ai eu à rapporter de quelle manière l'Eglise fondée au XVIe siècle par saint François Xavier, puis renversée et comme anéantie au commencement du XVIIe, fut, dans la seconde moitié du XIXe relevée de ses ruines. J'ai eu à montrer les chrétiens que le glaive de la persécution avait épargnés, gardant avec un soin jaloux, au milieu

de leurs ennemis et de leurs dénonciateurs, la foi de leurs pères et se la transmettant fidèlement dans l'ombre à travers sept ou huit générations; les apôtres, attendant sans se lasser aux portes du Japon fermé, y entrant à la fin et découvrant la postérité des anciens martyrs; par eux la sainte doctrine prêchée et les sacrements administrées tout d'abord dans un profond secret; [...] enfin la paix triomphant et, après tant de combats soutenus, tant de souffrances endurées, tant de larmes et tant de sang versés pour le nom de Jésus-Christ, la première et la plus sainte de toutes les libertés, la liberté religieuse, solennellement proclamée.[25]

It is a wonderful story, and it is hardly surprising that the MEP historian fashioned the facts into a phoenix-narrative, the tale of another resurrection. The missionaries 'on the ground' might not have been quite so convinced that their discovery was in fact the completion of the circle as suggested by their historian.[26] But this representation of Japan as a Christian country, or at least as a proto-Christian country, is an important one to add to our collection of early images of Japan, and one which was to be kept alive by later writers, for instance the Catholic Claudel.

So what were the images of Japan current in France before 1887, the year of Loti's *Madame Chrysanthème*? It is extremely difficult to establish such things with any degree of accuracy, but judging from the historical events and published writings, we might reasonably conjecture that the image of the Antipodes – with all the connotations of topsy-turvy morals and manners – was still dominant. Japan was clearly not a country of golden roofs, unlike some South American discoveries, but it remained gratifyingly *strange*, and the racialist theories of Gobineau and his colleagues would also have contributed to the general impression of difference. The image of the proto-Christian country, on the other hand, would only have had a select audience:[27] also, Western Christians would have remembered in the same thought the tales of the Japanese martyrs, and therefore by extension those of the cruel persecutions and tortures inflicted upon them by the 'pagan' Japanese. All things considered, the knowledge of Japan in the West was still extremely limited at the end of the nineteenth century: there were a number of accounts for those who wished to inform themselves, but these were not known to the public at large.[28] There was not even a stereotypical discourse to describe Japan until *japonisme* and Loti, through the immense success of *Madame Chrysanthème*, created one: and where there are no stereotypes, there is no 'presence' of the other in a culture. *Japon-isme*, prejudiced and erroneous though many of its assumptions were, may be said to have been responsible for giving 'Japan' an existence *tout court* in the French imagination.

CHAPTER ONE

Travels through Objects: Marcel Proust, Edmond de Goncourt, Pierre Loti

After Japan re-opened to the West in 1854, it was through *japonisme* that it travelled to France. France's rediscovery of Japan in the final quarter of the nineteenth century took place largely in the context of *japonisme*, a fashion for all things Japanese and Japanese-like: the movement had a crucial and lasting influence on contemporary French art and music, but on a more popular level it was simply a fad for collecting Japanese objects, known as *japonaiseries*. The 'Japan' to which the sophisticated consumers of *fin-de-siècle* Paris travelled through the medium of these *japoniste* objects was an imaginary place which they saw as an aesthetic utopia: *japonisme* was the lens through which they saw a domesticated, aestheticised image of Japan, as easily assimilable into the display cabinets of society hostesses as into the *fin-de-siècle* aesthetic.

Japonisme certainly qualifies as an 'Orientalist' movement in that it offered Parisians a view of Japan refracted by an aestheticising agenda, but its strong artistic bias made it a peculiar form of Orientalism especially appealing to artists and writers. The primarily aesthetic nature of this 'Japan' clearly differentiates it from, for instance, the sexual utopias of the Near East in mid-nineteenth-century French literature. The colonialist context is also absent, and with it the hierarchising gaze that made the Near East the inferior other of Europe. Writers of the period who made use of the *japoniste* discourse in their works would certainly have been attracted to it by the connection it made between the exotic and the aesthetic. However, the subsequent creative process whereby a French writer might adapt and apply the discourse of *japonisme* to his or her own narratives is a complex undertaking that is not, I believe, most usefully described as an act of cultural appropriation. In this chapter I explore the complicated nature of three such cases, relationships built between *japonisme* and the works of three writers: Edmond de Goncourt, Marcel Proust and Pierre Loti. In each case I will distinguish between any 'outright' Orientalism that might exist in their work, and their more subtle use of the interplay between 'Japan' and *japonisme*, by focusing on the place of the Japanese object, the *japonaiserie*, in their works.

The *japonaiserie* is a highly effective medium for the imagined and imaginary travel that can constitute a text, and a writer's attitude towards it often indicates his particular way of seeing Japan. Of the three, Edmond de Goncourt is most guilty of an 'Orientalist' attitude to the *japonaiserie*, which results in a knowledge-based, but ultimately reductionist, view of Japan. Loti's decision to write a 'japonaiserie' of a book in *Madame Chrysanthème* was financially motivated, and he paid for it with his posthumous reputation as a facile crowd-pleaser: but the tension between his private experience of Japan and his desire to fulfil his readers' expectations results in some beguilingly ambivalent views of Japan and of himself. And in Proust, the *japonaiserie* enters the novel as part of a semiotic system recognisable to contemporary Parisians, but develops into an object laden with private connotations and desires: it functions as a trope related to desire and memory, the most celebrated instance of this being the role that a *japonaiserie* plays in the narrator's first experience of involuntary memory.[1] I will begin this chapter, however, with an introduction to the cultural climate in which *japonisme* flourished.

The term 'japonisme' was first used in print in 1872, in an article by the art collector Philippe Burty, but by then the phenomenon of *japonisme* had been an integral part of the Parisian artistic scene for a good ten years.[2] In 1858, France signed a commercial treaty with the newly opened Japan, and by the early 1860s the collecting of *japonaiseries* had become fashionable amongst artists and high-society art lovers, such as members of the Princesse Mathilde's circle.[3] Artists such as Millet, Fantin-Latour and Bracquemond, and literary men such as the Goncourts and Baudelaire, flocked to Madame Desoye's *japonaiserie* boutique in the Rue de Rivoli. This shop, according to Edmond de Goncourt, was the effective birthplace of 'le grand mouvement japonais qui s'étend aujourd'hui de la peinture à la mode':[4] he claimed that he and his brother Jules had been its very first clients. As for more direct contact with Japan, Philippe Burty, Emile Guimet, Félix Régamey, Henri Cernuschi, Charles de Chassiron and Samuel Bing were sent by the French government to the Far East soon after Japan's opening to study Japanese art and culture;[5] on their return they contributed in diverse ways to the dissemination of

Claude Monet (1840–1926), *La Japonaise (Camille Monet in Japanese Costume)* (1876, oil on canvas), © Museum of Fine Arts, Boston, Massachusetts, USA, 1951 Purchase Fund/ Bridgeman Art Library 2005

knowledge about Japan. Guimet, whose main interest was in Eastern religions, set up a library of religious texts and a museum of religious artefacts;[6] Samuel Bing would found a high-quality monthly magazine called *Le Japon artistique*, whose well-informed contributors wrote learned essays designed to introduce Japanese art to the public. Burty, artist, influential critic and editor of the 'curiosités' section of the *Gazette des Beaux Arts*, promoted Japanese art in print. One of his most celebrated converts was Mallarmé: the poet's interest in *japonaiseries* can be dated roughly from the beginning of their friendship. Mallarmé's study in Valvins was decorated entirely with *japonaiseries*, where his most precious manuscripts and notes for 'le Livre' accumulated 'in the lacquer drawers of a Japanese cabinet'.[7]

Japan fever did not spread to the public at large until after the Exposition universelle of 1867, whose success led to a general craze for *japonaiseries*. According to Goncourt, it was after 1870 that the purveyors of *japonaiseries* became more respectable: Madame Desoye's shop had been known as a 'rendez-vous des couples adultères',[8] but in the 1870s *japonaiseries* became available in Samuel Bing's shop in rue Chauchat, or in that of Philippe Sichel, a middle-class merchant friend of the Goncourts', in rue Pigalle. The clientele was not always well-informed: not all customers would have been clear about the distinction between *japonaiseries* and *chinoiseries* (Madame Desoye's shop, specialising in *japonaiseries*, was nevertheless called 'la Porte chinoise'). The less discerning certainly bought *japonaiseries* that were in fact no more than cheap trinkets, whose value lay wholly in their exotic provenance. In other words, they were not being bought for any artistic merit, but simply for the fact that they were 'choses du Japon'. As a discerning art lover Bing deplored this state of affairs, in which all manner of objects were uncritically accepted and then given 'un nom générique comme celui de "japonerie" et on s'en tient là'.[9] For this he blamed the major state museums, which would not exhibit Japanese artworks alongside the established classics of Western art. If *japonaiseries* were only ever to be seen in shop windows as opposed to museum displays, he argued in his manifesto-like essay in the first edition of *Le Japon artistique*, how could they achieve their rightful status as art? Bing's concerns about the status of Japanese art may be extended logically to that of the 'Japan' that came to be represented chiefly through these items that were *for sale*. Such a status would have been far from unique in the second half of the nineteenth century: indeed, treating the rest of the world as a vast exhibit,[10] and therefore a potential shopping display, was a characteristic of the European 'age of the world picture'.[11] That it is only a short step from putting an object on display to treating it as an object on sale is confirmed by the fact that 'the first Arabic account of a world exhibition, describing the next Paris exposition in 1867, was entitled, simply and accurately enough, "the Universal Exhibition of Commodities" '.[12]

But possession was not the only way in which the passion for *japonaiseries* manifested itself: Japanese art was much imitated, chiefly by artisans of the decorative arts. Some of these cases of imitation were more or less exact copying: 'ils ont fouillé les albums [of Japanese prints] pour les décalquer et en reporter les motifs sur leurs bronzes et leur faïences', reported Chesneau.[13] Others were cases of inspiration rather than imitation. Decorative artists of the Art Nouveau movement certainly used many a motif 'd'inspiration japonaise', while some of Debussy's works[14] and a number of popular plays produced in the 1870s (Camille Saint-Saëns' operetta *La Princesse jaune*; *La Belle Saïnara* by Ernest Hervilly) were also linked to *japonisme* by the looser thread of inspiration. On the side of knowledge rather than imitation or inspiration, the first attempts at scholarship in the field of Japanese art history appeared after the second Exposition universelle of 1878. They tended, however, to concentrate on *ukiyo-e*, a nineteenth-century art form, as if it were the major or even the sole achievement of Japanese art. Louis Gonse, who published two volumes entitled *L'Art japonais* in 1883, was criticised by the American scholar and mentor of Ezra Pound, Ernest Fenollosa, writing from Yokohama, for precisely this shortcoming.[15] Edmond de Goncourt appears to have been more careful about historical perspective when writing his books on *Utamaro* (1891) and *Hokusai* (1896).[16] Although scholarly interest continued to develop, *japonisme* as a fashion began to decline in the 1890s, roughly in tandem with the advent of more substantial knowledge about the hitherto mysterious Japan.[17] Fashionable *japonisme* had certainly reached its peak before the turn of the century, although the Japanese section of the Exposition universelle of 1900 was a great success. For this occasion, the Japanese government had offered a wide selection of national treasures and masterpieces: it has been suggested that this had an adverse effect on the bibelot craze, alerting the collectors to the true worth of their fans and prints.[18]

Writing about *japonaiseries*

At first sight, the craze for *japonaiseries* in *fin-de-siècle* Paris may appear to have been an unprecedented opportunity for making Japan familiar to the masses. In effect, however, popular *japonisme* probably did more to hinder, rather than aid, the dissemination of any real knowledge about Japan. Through the *japonaiserie*, which became the stereotypical and predominant symbol of Japan in Paris, *japonisme* offered Parisians a 'bite-size' image of Japanese otherness: in possessing these small objects, exotic enough to titillate but not substantial enough to threaten the authority of the French aesthetic, Parisians were able to experience the strangeness of Japan as a harmless frisson of exoticism. Roland Barthes has analysed exoticism as a containing reaction to otherness:

> Parfois – rarement – l'Autre se dévoile irréductible [...]. Comment assimiler le Nègre, le Russe? Il y a ici une figure de secours: l'exotisme. L'Autre devient pur objet, spectacle, guignol: relégué aux confins de l'humanité, il n'atteint plus à la sécurité du chez-soi.[19]

The stranger, when labelled and stowed away mentally in a category labelled 'the exotic',[20] immediately becomes unthreatening, a spectacle to be gazed at rather than an 'other' requiring interaction. The *japonaiserie* goes one crucial step further in its domestication of the otherness of Japan in that it is *literally* an object, a small knick-knack that can be put away in a box: it is physically assimilable into the cabinets of Parisian salons as a curio.[21] The *japoniste* 'Japan' was thus an imaginary space peopled by a collection of small porcelain figures, paper lanterns and other pretty *bibelots*.

It is also significant that these objects were *commodities*, available to all for money. Only in such a particular climate, in which the essence of a country had come to be represented by saleable objects, could a book dealing wholly and solely with the buying of *japonaiseries* in Japan have been written and published. *Notes d'un bibeloteur au Japon* (1883) by Philippe Sichel, with an approbatory preface by Edmond de Goncourt, is an account of his recent shopping trip to Japan. Sichel makes it clear that the purpose of his visit was to 'dévaliser le Japon', and in his preface he tells his readers that 'ce pays était entièrement nouveau pour moi; je dois cependant le dire franchement, je ne prêtai aucune attention aux choses de la rue: les laques du bazar étaient ma seule occupation'.[22] The narrator does, of course, describe some 'choses de la rue', but only those that he encounters in his relentless search for merchandise: the bulk of the narrative is a list of objects and prices, relieved by only brief touches of local colour. The objects are described in the tone and detail of a sales catalogue,[23] and indeed the book is a catalogue of artistic objects masquerading as a travelogue. The sheer decadence of his choice of subject, even in the age of *A rebours*, could only have been justified by the inordinately important place that the *japonaiserie* had come to occupy in French views of Japan.

Thus the *japonaiserie* craze gave momentum to a popular view of Japan that was primarily art-related and commodified, and this came to take precedence over scholarly, historical or otherwise more comprehensive views of this newly rediscovered country. Historical perspectives, in particular, tended to be neglected.[24] It was not as if there were no other sources of information on Japan from past centuries, but relatively few writers on Japan in this period appear to have consulted the Jesuit archives, for instance,[25] or to have read the numerous eighteenth- and nineteenth-century accounts of travels to Japan by the Dutch (many of which were available in translation).[26] There were honourable exceptions. At least one member of the earliest French diplomatic mission to Japan, sent to negotiate the 1858 treaty, had read Siebold and Kaempfer on Japan.[27] Guimet was highly knowledgeable about Far Eastern religious practices, and Félix Régamey wrote *Le Japon pratique* in the encyclopaedic fashion adopted by writers on Japan in the sixteenth, seventeenth and eighteenth centuries,[28] with sections devoted to 'l'alimentation', 'moeurs et coutumes' and even a 'petit vocabulaire' of elementary Japanese terms. Yet even in his volume, the artistic bias dominates. Of the eight main sections, five are clearly of greatest relevance to a reader interested in Japanese arts and crafts: 'Le Japon vu par un artiste', 'Décoration de la maison européenne' (a description of a house in Paris decorated with *japonaiseries*), 'Midori no sato' (about the same house), 'Produits naturels et procédés de fabrication' (with subtitles such as 'la céramique', 'les tissus' and 'la laque'), and 'Arts graphiques'. Moreover, one of the greatest attractions of the book is the fact that it contains 'cent dessins par l'auteur' of the Japanese and of various Japanese objects, drawn in a 'Japanese style': in other words, the book itself is much more of a *japonaiserie* than the author would perhaps have cared to admit, both in its choice of subjects and in its destined readership.

Even within literature devoted to art, history seems to have been a weak point. Ernest Fenollosa's criticisms of Louis Gonse's work have already been mentioned. Albert Jacquemart, master engraver, so eloquently (and knowledgeably) deplores his contemporaries' lack of historical perspective when considering Japanese art that he deserves to be quoted at some length:

> Loin d'étudier ce qu'avaient écrit les Portugais et les missionnaires accueillis un moment à Nippon, de rechercher les documents publiés par Koempher, Titsingh, Siebold et Hoffman, on a jeté dans le public les appréciations les plus fantaisistes, mis l'engouement à la place de la vérité, créé un Japon presque aussi idéal que fut la Chine pour les curieux du XVIIIe siècle. Les albums modernes, importés à profusion, ont été la cause principale de ces aberrations; on s'y est attaché, on les a loués tous, au lieu de distinguer entre les chefs-d'oeuvre et la pacotille, puis on a conclu de leur abondance même que l'art japonais avait une origine peu ancienne. Nous n'insisterons pas sur l'inanité de ces assertions.[29]

Historical ignorance was not as dangerous, however, as the sheer confidence of 'l'homme de goût' in the realm of Art. Where Beauty is concerned, the distinction between personal taste and objective standards has often been notoriously weak, and Japan's absorption into the realm of art through *japonisme* seems to have sanctioned, in the minds of certain writers, a licence to employ personal taste to evaluate all manner of things pertaining to Japanese culture. In an introduction to the catalogue for the Goncourt brothers' collection after the death of Edmond, the usually scrupulous Bing referred to Goncourt as one of these men of superior taste: 'les élus qui portent en eux l'instinct du Beau, ce guide plus sûr que tout l'acquis des longues études'.[30] Bad luck to the scholars, then. Of course, this was a special occasion in which it was important for Bing to shift as much merchandise as possible, and his hyperbole was certainly opportunistic. Even so, the statement relies on a general acceptance of an aestheticised view of Japan that reduces the country to a work of art: an insidiously Orientalist view, because it has a tendency to sound more flattering and therefore more acceptable an image than, say, the view of a foreign country as a sexual utopia. The view of Japan as an artistic paradise was one subscribed to by many a collector of *japonaiseries*, of whom the most famous is Edmond de Goncourt himself.

Edmond de Goncourt

The elder Goncourt was an assiduous scholar of Japanese art, of which he was also a devoted and discerning collector. The author of well-researched works on two *ukiyo-e* artists, he was no amateur *japoniste*. Yet when he came to write *La Maison d'un artiste* (1881), the sections of the work which deal with Far Eastern art objects betray an uneasy tension between his scholarly and 'collectorly' personae.

La Maison d'un artiste is a generically singular work, an immense catalogue (in two volumes of over 300 pages each) of the objects in his house, listed lovingly from wall to wall, room to room. Alternatively, it might be described as a travelogue around the rooms of his house: containing many objects from abroad, especially from Japan and China (and not only in the 'Cabinet de l'extrême-orient'), it takes the reader from country to country through the objects that it examines. Goncourt's prose does not always discriminate, however, between knowledge of an object and knowledge of the culture from which it hails. The *japonaiserie* often ends up 'representing' Japan to such an extent that statements about it become indistinguishable from statements about Japan itself. The work thus embodies, in a very real sense, the problematic nature of a *japonaiserie*-centred vision of Japan.[31]

Goncourt painstakingly acquaints us with the Far Eastern subdivision of his collection over the course of 114 pages:[32] his descriptions constitute an astonishing collection in themselves. He generally begins by describing a particular type of object, which he then follows with a *catalogue raisonnée* of the instances of that object in his possession. Object follows object in each of the categories, in no discernible order and relentless detail. After a section on *netsuké* come similar sections on 'porcelaines de la Chine', miscellaneous objects in crystal, jade and bronze, bowls from Satzuma, a carved wooden desk, samurai swords of varying sorts, a Japanese brazier, Chinese tobacco-pouches and lacquerware.

Goncourt does not describe the objects out of context: for each, he supplies a minimal but sufficient quantity of information which makes it possible even for the relatively uninformed reader to appreciate its qualities. For instance, describing the variety of porcelain known as 'craquelé' – whose cracks are deliberately created – Goncourt gives a brief explanation of the origins of this particular aesthetic, helping his reader to appreciate its sophisticated beauty in the appropriate framework (*MA*, p. 204). Where these contexts tend towards general comments about Japanese culture, however, it becomes increasingly clear that the process is circular: that is to say that the facts about 'Japan' which are used to explain the *japonais-erie* seem to have been derived from the very object in question. For instance, having described an impressive array of miniature objects, Goncourt tells his reader in conclusion that 'Les ouvriers japonais ont eu, comme les ouvriers de l'antiquité grecque et romaine, l'imagination des bijoux-joujoux lilliputiens' (*MA*, p. 271). This statement about Japanese artisans may well be accurate, but the manner of its obtaining can surely not be recommended as a general method for arriving at truths about Japanese art. Or again, can it be true that all Japanese objects possess the attribute of quirky fantasy, the *japoniste* characteristic *par excellence* according to Goncourt: '[ils] possèdent une qualité que n'a pas l'objet chinois, l'amusant' (*MA*, p. 283)? Perhaps all of *his* collectables did, but if so, that would be much more likely to be a function of his taste than a quint-essentially 'Japanese' characteristic.

Even more damagingly for his scholarly reputation, however, Goncourt claims, towards the end of the collection, that 'l'art japonais n'a pas d'antiquité' (*MA*, pp. 275–76). A *japoniste* who examined Goncourt's collection at the time of its sale explained this astonishing claim by pointing out that Goncourt's collection suffered from the fact that he started collecting *japonaiseries* relatively early, that is to say before Japanese antiques began to be available any-where in France, which meant that Goncourt never developed an eye or a taste for true antiques.[33] The truth of the matter is, as the same *japoniste* suggests, probably a combination of lack of opportunity and Goncourt's conscious decision to rely on his celebrated taste as a collector with an innate sense of 'le Beau'. This is his verdict on Japanese antiques:

> Au fond, parmi les vieilles choses du Japon qui ne sont pas des objets chinois ou des imitations imparfaites de chinoiseries, qu'est-ce que vous trouvez? Des bronzes, sans conteste, inférieurs aux bronzes chinois, des peintures d'un primitif baroque, des laques que je crois, jusqu'à preuve du contraire, inférieurs aux laques de choix des dix-sept et dix-huitième siècles, et en dernière ligne cette porce-laine or, rouge et gros bleu, ce *vieux Japon* qui n'est pas sans mérite, mais d'une monotonie désespérante. Mais tout ce que j'aime, tout ce que je vois aimer par *ceux dont j'estime le goût* [...] est moderne, [...] appartient au dix-neuvième siècle. (*MA*, p. 279, my italics)

Goncourt's thoughts here certainly appear to be personal generalisations about Japanese art based on his own collection and those of other 'hommes de goût', rather than being based on any historical or scholarly source. He will very occasionally cite Thunberg, or some other pre-nineteenth-century authority on matters Japanese, but it is usually in order to strengthen a case upon which he has already pronounced. Goncourt's 'Japan' is deduced from the *japonaiserie*, and that 'Japan' is then used to qualify the *japonaiserie*: the process is a self-fulfilling hermeneutical arc which never fails to satisfy, the voyage to 'Japan' starting and ending at the object.

A closer reading of some of the entries confirms the curiously circular and circumscribed nature of the knowledge put to use in this work. The following are two examples of his *netsuké* collection:

> Un jongleur japonais, tout en dansant, fait tomber à terre, d'une gourde tenue au-dessus de sa tête, les grands dés triangulaires d'un jeu de chô-ghi. Cet ivoire est signé; Tomô tada.
>
> [...]
>
> Une Japonaise, tout en mordillant un bout flottant de son kirimon, de sa robe, se pique une épingle dans les cheveux; un petit Japonais, blotti dans sa jupe, touche avec une palette d'ivoire le sam-sim, la guitare nationale à trois cordes. (*MA*, p. 176)

In describing the objects, Goncourt wisely takes great care not to overload the reader with information, but his selection of the details is telling in itself. The reader knows already that *netsukés* are 'de petites sculptures d'ivoire ou de bois' (*MA*, p. 169). The first is a dancing 'jongleur', a universally recognisable figure, holding a 'gourde' (another familiar common noun, although with Eastern connotations) and involved in 'un jeu de chô-ghi'. The only Japanese word in this description is the name of the game. Games are useful in intercultural descriptions because they do not require much in the way of justification: whatever is happening in a game can be justified by the fact that it is a game, so to speak, and therefore it is a word that renders further discussion superfluous. In this case Goncourt himself does not know enough about the game to supply further information, as is evident from his description of the falling objects as 'les grands dés triangulaires'. *Chô-ghi* (to retain Goncourt's transcription) is a board game similar to chess, and so the triangular objects function as chess pieces would, rather than dice. It would seem that Goncourt, when examining his *netsukés*, had deduced –

Netsuké, tsuge wood, 4.1 cm wide. Minkoku, early nineteenth century.

erroneously in this particular case – that *falling* objects in a *game* must be related to dice: his mistake reveals that he arrived at this conclusion through examination of the object rather than reliance on external sources. The description of the second *netsuké* raises the question of why Goncourt bothers to specify the nationality of the figures ('une Japonaise', 'un petit Japonais'). It is possible that some of the *netsukés* might represent Chinese figures, but surely, in a bunch of Japanese carvings, the 'default' nationality would be Japanese? The reason why Goncourt uses 'Japonaise' here is not so much to do with the denotative meaning of the word as with its connotations for the Parisian reader. 'Japonaise' signifies something more than a woman of a certain nationality: it has connotations of daintiness, prettiness and smallness that all come from the *japonaiserie*, and that are here reflected precisely back onto a specific *japonaiserie*.[34] 'Kirimon' and 'sam-sim'[35] add exotic allure but no confusion, as they are immediately followed by apt translations. Goncourt is careful not to tax the reader with an excessive quantity of foreign words in this text: his attitude is not that of a teacher, but that of a collector who wishes his readership to fall in love with the objects that he loves.

   This textual evocation of his beloved objects is both a means of *re*confirming his ownership of them, and giving them a lease of life beyond his own lifetime: the collection will thus survive its own dispersal, the dispersal that was bound to occur (and in fact occurred) after Goncourt's death when the objects were put on sale. This immortalising power of the catalogue is evoked at the end of *La Maison d'un artiste* when Goncourt includes a catalogue – the catalogue of a collection of *Chinese* objects belonging to a seventeenth-century *Japanese* collector in Osaka – in his own collection. Goncourt prefaces his inventory of this catalogue's contents thus:

> l'on peut se rendre compte du nombre d'objets chinois que *contenait*, que *contient* une collection japonaise, par ce curieux inventaire d'objets d'art possédés au dix-septième siècle par Yodoya Fatsgro, l'un des plus riches marchands d'Osaka, inventaire si renseignant sur les goûts d'un bibeloteur exotique. (*MA*, p. 277, my italics)

Revealingly, having referred to the collection in the past tense (*contenait*), Goncourt here corrects himself and changes the verb into the present tense (*contient*). With this change of tense, Goncourt appears to be indicating that the collection of this seventeenth-century Japanese merchant still exists, in a textual world, whatever tragedies may have befallen the objects in the physical world: and surely this is one of the reasons for his painstaking enumeration of his own treasured objects.[36]
   In spite of this common cause, however, Goncourt establishes a clear distance between the Japanese collector and himself by referring to him as 'un bibeloteur exotique', and describing his inventory as 'curieux'. He shows no collectorly solidarity: rather, he transforms the Japanese collector into yet another exotic object, to be marvelled over like an item in his own collection. Perhaps Goncourt adopts this attitude so that he can plunder the Osaka merchant's collection without compunction, for as far as the reading experience is concerned, the Japanese merchant's collection effectively merges into that of Goncourt. This means that the reader can *take possession* of both sets of objects, in the same way that Goncourt can take possession of the Japanese collector's objects through their textual evocation. By adding to his own collection in this way, Goncourt initiates the reader into the pleasures of vicarious possession. He also unfolds in front of his eyes the possibility of an endless series of collections, an 'infinite regression' effect of precious objects in his textual space:

reading can be a continuous act of appropriation if the text is in the form of a *catalogue raisonnée*. Given that the objects in Goncourt's text have come more and more to stand for Japan, this kind of reading leads the reader closer and closer to the act of appropriating – in textual guise – Japan itself.

The scholar is thus revealed to be very much subordinate to the collector in *La Maison d'un artiste*. The vision of Japan that emerges from this work remains resolutely at 'object-level': it is as though the collector, whose favourite occupation is a tête-à-tête with his possessions, keeps his head down to avoid seeing the scholarly vistas beyond his glass cabinets. At various points in *La Maison d'un artiste*, Goncourt seems to want to discuss his cherished objects simply *as* objects, putting aside any knowledge he possesses about the culture they have come from. His relationship with his porcelain bowls, for instance, is intensely physical, and his knowledge of them has a visceral quality to it:

> Ici, à propos du poli, de la douceur, de l'onctueux pour ainsi dire, des choses parfaites dans les mains: un aphorisme. Le toucher, c'est la marque à laquelle se reconnaît un amateur. L'homme qui prend un objet avec des doigts indifférents, avec des doigts *bêtes*, avec des doigts qui n'ont pas l'enveloppement amoureux, cet homme n'est pas un passionné d'art. (*MA*, p. 205)

There is a certain truth to this sort of claim about taste, about an innate 'feel' (literally, in this case) for artistic quality, and in any case Goncourt pre-empts any criticism of his elitist statement by playfully introducing it as an 'aphorisme' (which, evidently, it is not). Most people would accept this sort of claim from a connoisseur. But Goncourt allows personal 'taste' to dominate excessively in his evaluations and pronouncements, ignoring contextual knowledge whenever convenient.[37] He is determined to dwell only briefly, if at all, on any knowledge that does not relate directly to the objects: their function, for instance, is usually considered to be extraneous. There is no mention of tea in the section of Satsuma bowls, no discussion of food or drink in the section on lacquerware. The sword section contains a reference to the tradition of ritual suicide as part of the description of the *waki-zashi* ('le hara kiri est presque de l'histoire ancienne, en ces jours'), but only briefly. In other words, the *japonaiseries* are given meaning purely in the context of their existence in Goncourt's collection, as objects-on-display, not in their previous existence as objects-in-use: the object is not allowed to take us out of the glass cabinet and into its country of origin.[38] In the case of the *netsuké*, there is a particular irony in practising this way of seeing. The *netsuké* is a miniature carving, 'originally attached to the cord of a small purse or pouch and then *tucked into* the sash of a kimono'.[39] That is to say that they were never meant to be seen, let alone be on display: a *netsuké* was a secret pleasure for the owner and user. Antique *netsukés* were prized as collectables in Japan also, and were not alone among formerly utilitarian objects in having been thus transformed. However, their fate in Goncourt's text is in line with the fact that Goncourt treats all of his collectables *as* collectables and nothing else.

The collector is of course a classic type of traveller, who searches for curios in faraway lands in order to fill a museum or his private collection back home.[40] The context of vision for this kind of traveller is, of necessity, the home country, because potential specimens – especially if they are to be sold – need to be assigned a recognisable value within the traveller's own culture. There will be discrepancies between the local and 'home' values: for instance, an object carved out of a single piece of stone is often of great worth in Japan because of the artistry required, whereas in Europe the baseness of the material might make it less highly prized. The traveller-collector would have to decide how the object's value could be translated into the terms of his home country, and this is the point at which transmission of knowledge becomes crucial. If French buyers could be educated to appreciate the local value of such an object, then the traveller would not have to engage in acts of evaluative translation.[41] Goncourt was not a travelling collector, but he certainly possessed sufficient knowledge to estimate the value of his own *japonaiseries*. However, his knowledge, crucially, is limited to what is necessary for estimating the value of the object: the collector's knowledge, unlike the scholar's, is the knowledge of the *owner*. It is knowledge circumscribed by interest, and therefore does not extend beyond the boundaries of the need-to-know, does not take the collector beyond his *japonaiseries* into Japan, Japanese history and culture.

Writing about Japanese objects in a style based on personal taste and 'feel' is a very different matter from writing about a Japanese person, as in fact Goncourt would do ten and fifteen years later in his studies of Utamaro and Hokusai. Attempting to understand another human being, one of genius at that, involves moving from one's own set of cultural references to a foreign one, or at least trying to negotiate a balance between the self and the other. Dealing with objects, on the other hand, is not so risky: Goncourt can sit quietly at home, literally as well as metaphorically, contemplating the *bibelots* that do not object to his characterisations of them. In the postface to the second edition of *La Maison d'un artiste*, Pol Neveux describes the relationship between the Goncourts and their collection as being almost human: 'dès qu'un objet a été choisi par les Goncourt [...] le voilà promptement leur familier, leur parent' (*MA*, p. 320). This positive spin on the relationship between objects and sentient beings is often evoked in order to suggest a depth of humanity in the person involved. In reality, however, people and objects do not form the same kind of relationship as two people do, for the simple reason that objects do not force people to comply with their own terms. This contrast will become more pertinent later in this chapter when I turn to the relationship between one person and another person who takes on the attributes of a decorative but mute object: in the meantime, I will conclude this section on *La Maison d'un artiste* by pointing out that the travelling collector's attitude towards Japan is the easiest kind of relationship to have with a foreign country, being based on the limited level of knowledge that comes with possessing an object. The Japanese object, which comes to function as a kind of signifier for Japan, overshadows its signified so completely that it eventually *becomes* 'Japan', or at least a *japoniste* version of Japan. The *japonaiserie* in Goncourt's text thus becomes a self-reflecting sign, referring back – ultimately – to *japonisme* rather than to Japan.

Marcel Proust

Unlike the Goncourts, Proust was not a collector: in spite of his wealth and his fine artistic taste, he never accumulated collections. Proust's relationship with *japonaiseries* was one which made use of their place in the semiotic system of fashionable Paris. From being simple signifiers of certain trends and fads, however, they gradually grow into a complex web of associations – of which collecting is an aspect – within the economy of Proust's symbolic universe.

It was in the 1890s that Proust first began to develop a taste for Japanese art. His entry into high-society circles brought him into contact with collectors and artists of a slightly older generation who

were imbued with the *japoniste* aesthetic.[42] He sent *bonsaï* and bou-
quets of enormous Japanese chrysanthemums to Madame Strauss,
and like Mallarmé before him, had a 'meuble japonais' in which he
stored his precious papers. At a time when the public's enthusiasm
for books on Japan as well as for *japonaiseries* had begun to wane, in
spite of annual exhibitions at the Musée des Arts Décoratifs from
1909 through to 1914, Proust's was only beginning: his long
friendship with Marie Nordlinger, Reynaldo Hahn's English cousin
who was working for Samuel Bing and who became central to
Proust's knowledge of *japonisme*, only began around 1904. The
result was that, for this latecomer, *japonisme* possessed the added
allure of nostalgia.

In *A la recherche du temps perdu*, Proust places Odette in this
period of his elders. When Swann is invited for the first time *chez*
Odette, he sees 'une grande lanterne japonaise suspendue à une
cordelette de soie' hanging in the corridor. Inside her drawing room,
the décor is a mish-mash of *japonaiseries* and *chinoiseries*:

> Elle l'avait fait asseoir près d'elle dans un des nombreux retraits
> mystérieux qui étaient ménagés dans les enfoncements du salon,
> protégés par d'immenses palmiers contenus dans des cache-pot de
> Chine, ou par des paravents auxquels étaient fixés des photo-
> graphies, des noeuds des rubans et des éventails. [...] [Elle] avait
> installé derrière la tête de Swann, sous ses pieds, des coussins de soie
> japonaise [...]. (*Du côté de chez Swann*, II, pp. 10–11)

Proust here takes full advantage of the fact that *japonisme*, as a social
phenomenon, is a semiotic system *legible* to his readers. For instance,
the modish and uninformed arrangement of Odette's trashy bibelots
('des paravents auxquels étaient fixés des photographies, des noeuds
des rubans et des éventails') characterises her immediately as a woman
whose taste is neither refined nor discerning, and positions her firmly
in a certain caste of the period.[43] Furthermore, the *japoniste* décor
fulfils a chronological function: the profusion of *japonaiseries* places
Un Amour de Swann unmistakably in the 1880s.[44] Proust makes use
of *japonisme* as a subtle yet effective dating mechanism in a novel
which, at least until *Le Temps retrouvé*, completely avoids the insertion of dates into its narrative. This relation to a recent but clearly
defined past, the past of Swann and Odette's amours, also bestows
upon *japonisme* an aura that has nostalgic value in the young
narrator's eyes:

J'aurais voulu pouvoir aller finir la journée chez une de ces femmes, devant une tasse de thé, dans un appartement aux murs peints de couleurs sombres, comme était encore celui de Mme Swann (l'année d'après celle où se termine la première partie de ce récit) et où luiraient les feux orangés, la rouge combustion, la flamme rose et blanche des chrysanthèmes dans le crépuscule de novembre [...] Mais maintenant, même ne me conduisant à rien, ces instants me semblaient avoir eu eux-mêmes assez de charme. Je voudrais les retrouver tels que je me les rappelais. Hélas! Il n'y avait plus que des appartements Louis XVI tout blancs, émaillés d'hortensias bleus. (*Du côté de chez Swann*, II, p. 279)

The narrator here describes a past that he himself never knew, when women dressed elegantly and décors were mysterious and alluring, in an overtly nostalgic tone. This is a rare occurrence in a novel which is normally extremely careful to avoid nostalgia. It may be that the narrator is allowed to sound nostalgic here precisely because his longing is for a past *that is not his own*: he is not evoking a 'real' memory but an imaginary past, a *fantasy*. It is of course generally accepted that Swann is a proto-Marcel figure (as Odette is the proto-Albertine): if the narrator's future is prefigured in Swann's, there is a possible logic in his adoption of Swann's past also. But it remains a logical possibility, not a true memory, which may well be why the banned mode of nostalgia is exceptionally allowed into its narration.

Japonisme in Proust, however, is not only linked to this imagined 'memory' of a sentimentalised past, but is tightly woven into one of the most important moments of remembering that occur in the whole novel, the narrator's first experience of involuntary memory:

Et dès que j'eus reconnu le goût du morceau de madeleine trempé dans le tilleul que me donnait ma tante, aussitôt la vieille maison grise sur la rue, où était sa chambre, vint comme un décor de théâtre s'appliquer au petit pavillon donnant sur le jardin [...] Et comme dans ce jeu où les Japonais s'amusent à tremper dans un bol de porcelaine rempli d'eau de petits morceaux de papier jusque-là indistincts qui, à peine y sont-ils plongés s'étirent, se contournent, se colorent, se différencient, deviennent des fleurs, des maisons, des personnages consistants et reconnaissables, de même maintenant toutes les fleurs de notre jardin et celles du parc de M. Swann, et les nymphéas de la Vivonne, et les bonnes gens du village et leurs petits logis et l'église et tout Combray et ses environs, tout cela qui prend forme et solidité, est sorti, ville et jardins, de ma tasse de thé. (*Du côté de chez Swann*, I, pp. 68–69)

In his discussion of this celebrated passage, Luc Fraisse shows how Proust, who first received these Japanese 'flowers' in 1904 from Marie Nordlinger,[45] incorporates the image into his revised text of 1910.[46] Yet Japan had been crucial to this resuscitation of the past even before Proust had hit upon the image of the paper flowers: an earlier description of involuntary memory in *Contre Sainte-Beuve*, which was reworked by Proust into the definitive version, concludes with a reference to 'ces petites fleurs japonaises qui ne reprennent que dans l'eau'.[47] In Proust's novel, Japanese objects, or *japoniste* ones, are consistently identified with the all-important act of remembering: Fraisse cites numerous instances of the way in which 'le *japonisme* [...] fournit au héros d'abord, mais principalement au narrateur, des objets qui serviront d'éléments conducteurs à la mémoire'.[48]

Proust himself possessed a 'meuble japonais' that takes on a similarly memory-related function in one of his letters.[49] Writing to Lionel Hauser, his friend and consultant on matters financial, Proust refers to a letter stored in the 'meuble japonais': 'une fois où je serai moins fatigué que ce soir, je me lèverai et irai jusqu'à mon petit meuble japonais chercher la lettre'. The 'meuble japonais' becomes a metaphorical box of memories, storing precious facts to be remembered: referring to a vague estimate he made for the benefit of a visitor, Proust specifies that he made this 'sans aller jusqu'au petit meuble japonais c'est-à-dire très vaguement'. The trouble with this box – or perhaps it is its alluring quality – is that it is never immediately to hand, but requires Proust to travel, if only from his bedroom to an adjacent room: quoting from a book recently published by Hauser, Proust specifies that he is able to do this because 'ton livre, lui, est près de moi et non dans le meuble japonais'.

The 'meuble japonais' appears only once in Proust's writings, in a single letter, but even then the Japanese object is associated with precious objects that necessitate some form of travel, either through space or time, as in the case of involuntary memory. Indeed *japonisme* functions as a topos of desirability and distance or even unattainability throughout *la Recherche*, a realm of mysterious and attractive otherness. As such, it is the natural décor for mysterious and desirable people:[50] Odette, as has already been noted, but also Charlus and Albertine. Significantly, Odette is only surrounded by *japonaiseries before* her marriage with Swann (after becoming Mme Swann, 'c'était plus rarement dans des robes de chambre japonaises qu'Odette recevait ses intimes, mais plutôt dans les soies claires et mousseuses de peignoirs Watteau'[51]): this indicates that her desirability diminishes for Swann once they are married. It is the sexually available, almost disreputable Odette de Crécy, not the respectable Odette Swann, who is associated with *japonisme*.[52] Similarly Albertine, desirable, mysterious and again not entirely respectable (the narrator tells us that his mother finds it 'bizarre, choquant, qu'une jeune fille habitât seule avec moi', an implicit condemnation of her morals), is clothed by the narrator of *La Prisonnière* in a 'kimono'.

The suggestion of dubious morality that attaches to the attraction of both Odette and Albertine, and which is signalled in their *japoniste* tastes, is carried over to Charlus. In his first encounters with the Baron, the narrator is repeatedly bewildered by the bizarreness of Charlus's character: in his mind, the strangeness of the Baron is inextricably linked to his eclectic taste, his love of art, his exclusivity in friendship. When the narrator's *cognitive* view of Charlus undergoes a 180-degree turn after witnessing his encounter with Jupien, he continues to associate him with the same qualities of artistic sensitivity, eclecticism, and a fondness for secrecy and exclusivity, simply adding homosexuality to the list of attractive and exclusive tastes that lead men like Charlus to take part in certain kinds of gatherings:

> Ils ont vite découvert d'autres jeunes gens que le même goût particulier rapproche d'eux, comme dans une petite ville se lient le professeur de seconde et le notaire qui aiment tous les deux la musique de chambre, les ivoires du moyen âge; appliquant à l'objet de leur distraction le même instinct militaire, le même esprit professionnel qui les guide dans leur carrière, ils les retrouvent à des séances où nul profane n'est admis, pas plus qu'à celles qui réunissent des amateurs de vieilles tabatières, d'estampes japonaises, de fleurs rares, et où, à cause du plaisir de s'instruire, de l'utilité des échanges et de la crainte des compétitions, règne à la fois, comme dans une bourse aux timbres, l'entente étroite des spécialistes et les féroces rivalités des collectionneurs. (*Sodome et Gomorrhe*, I, p. 29)

It is suggested here that these various interests, ranging from a love of chamber music to the collection of Japanese prints, are analogous to homosexuality. This comparative method has the logically dubious but affectively compelling result of linking, in the reader's mind, sexual strangeness with artistic sensitivity, superior intelligence and exclusivity. Proust is of course not the first to have suggested such links: collecting, in particular, has been associated with moral dubiousness since the eighteenth century, when its private and self-indulgent nature made it vulnerable to moral censure and accusations of sexual obsession.[53] What is new here is the specific inclusion of *japonisme* in this list of attractive and dangerous interests, and this in turn may provide a clue to what they have in common.

The artist, the collector and the homosexual are all solitary, exclusive and excluded *others*, and this is symbolised by their link to objects from an *other* land, both *japonaiseries* and *chinoiseries*. Furthermore, like their vices, their exoticism is something of a secret: it is only when we see them in private that they are explicitly linked to *japonaiseries*. As noted earlier, Swann sees Odette in a kimono for the first time when he visits her at home: Albertine, in *La Prisonnière*, is enfolded in a kimono, but only in the narrator's house. The *japoniste* kimono,[54] used as a dressing-gown, is a garment for indoors that befits the private nature of these women's attractions and activities. The same equation operates for Charlus: when the narrator visits him late at night after the dinner at the Duchesse de Guermantes', the Baron is 'en robe de chambre chinoise, le cou nu, étendu sur un canapé' (p. 207). In the privacy of his own home, Charlus is thus immediately characterised by exoticism ('robe de chambre chinoise'), eroticism ('le cou nu') and latent lasciviousness ('étendu sur un canapé'). His transformation, effected through his donning of the Chinese dressing-gown,[55] is symbolic of the distance travelled by the narrator that night: by taking just a short carriage ride away from the society dinner of the duchess, the narrator has travelled thousands of miles in terms of sexual *moeurs* and potential intimacy with Charlus.

The *japonaiserie* in Proust is thus an object which transports the narrator into a private, precious and secret world, never more so than in his intimate life with Albertine in *La Prisonnière*. In this volume, Albertine is not only clothed in *japonaiseries* (kimonos, and also the 'derived' kimono that is the 'robe de Fortuny'[56]), but she also becomes a *japonaiserie* herself, the most treasured object in the narrator-collector's possession. Collectors have traditionally hidden away their treasured objects in boxes,[57] their curios in richly lined and carefully guarded cabinets. The narrator in *La Prisonnière* not only enfolds Albertine in precious fabrics, but jealously and secretly keeps her concealed ('je l'avais cachée à tout le monde') in his parents' house: the room assigned to her is like a jewellery box, the richly *lined* 'cabinet à tapisseries de mon père'.[58] He often refers to her in non-human terms, and likes to watch her when she is asleep, that is to say when she is more object than subject.[59] He also touches her as he would a precious object, an object entirely in his power and at his disposal, as the use of the verb 'pouvoir' here indicates: 'je pouvais bien prendre Albertine sur mes genoux, tenir sa tête dans mes mains; je pouvais la caresser, passer longuement mes mains sur elle'. However, unlike Edmond de Goncourt, Proust's narrator is not a collector by nature. The above sentence continues:

> [mais], comme si j'eusse manié une pierre qui enferme la saline des océans immémoriaux ou le rayon d'une étoile, je sentais que je touchais seulement l'enveloppe close d'un être qui, par l'intérieur, accédait à l'infini. Combien je souffrais de cette position où nous a réduit l'oubli de la nature qui, en instituant la division des corps, n'a pas songé à rendre possible l'interpénétration des âmes (car si son corps était au pouvoir du mien, sa pensée échappait aux prises de ma pensée). Et je me rendais compte qu'Albertine n'était pas même, pour moi, la merveilleuse captive dont j'avais cru enrichir ma demeure, tout en y cachant aussi parfaitement sa présence, même à ceux qui venaient me voir et qui ne la soupçonnaient pas, au bout du couloir, dans la chambre voisine, que ce personnage dont tout le monde ignorait qu'il tenait enfermée dans une bouteille la Princesse de la Chine; m'invitant, sous une forme pressante, cruelle et sans issue, à la recherche du passé, elle était plutôt comme un grande déesse du Temps. (*La Prisonnière*, II, p. 230)

In this passage, the narrator confesses both his desire and his failure to be a collector. His wish to 'enrichir ma demeure' with Albertine's presence is precisely that of a collector, of the kind that we have encountered earlier: his delight in secretly possessing her is aptly compared with the fairy tale about the man who kept the Princess of China in a bottle (a fairy tale that is itself based on the equation between exoticism and desirability). Yet the narrator is unable, in the end, to possess Albertine as if she were an object, not so much because she is a human being with thoughts of her own, as because he cannot stop wondering about her thoughts. Paradoxically and perhaps ironically, he compares her unknowable aspect to that of an inanimate object with a transcendental dimension: 'comme si j'eusse manié une pierre qui enferme la saline des océans immémoriaux ou le rayon d'une étoile, je sentais que je touchais seulement l'enveloppe close d'un être qui, par l'intérieur, accédait à l'infini'. This comparison with the elements (the sea, the heavens) emphasises the otherness of Albertine, and at the same time points to her independent existence as a human being. There have been plenty of cases in and outside literature where one person possesses another without worrying about the thoughts of the possessed person, but Proust's narrator is not one of them. In this attitude, as we will see, Marcel resembles the hero of Loti's *Madame Chrysanthème*: unable to retain the detached perspective of the collector, the self wonders about the other, the subject about the object.

Marcel, of course, is aware of the limitations of the collecting life:

> Mais si j'avais mené la vie de collectionneur que me conseillait Swann (que me reprochait de ne pas connaître M. de Charlus, quand, avec un mélange d'esprit, d'insolence et de goût, il me disait: 'Comme c'est laid chez vous!'), quelles statues, quels tableaux longuement poursuivis, enfin possédés, ou même, à tout mettre au mieux, comtemplés avec désintéressement, m'eussent – comme la petite blessure qui se cicatrisait assez vite, mais que la maladresse inconsciente d'Albertine, des indifférents, ou de mes propres pensées, ne tardait pas à rouvrir – donné accès hors de moi-même, sur ce chemin de communication privé, mais qui donne sur la grande route où passe ce que nous ne connaissons que du jour où nous en avons souffert, la vie des autres? (*La Prisonnière*, II, p. 231)

Although he has 'collected' Albertine in order to spare himself the pain of jealousy, and to 'enrichir ma demeure', Marcel knows that there is a different kind of richness, a painful but more instructive one, to be gained from accepting an other subject into his life. The collector, surrounded by mute objects, never needs to leave his own solipsistic world, whereas Albertine, when she is truly herself, forces Marcel to confront 'la vie des autres'. The Japanese object plays a complicated role in the drama of Albertine's otherness, and Marcel's gradual realisation of it. The *japonaiserie* that is her kimono starts off as a signifier of her otherness and sexual desirability, carried over from the same associations in the cases of Odette and Charlus. Albertine is then gradually turned into a *japonaiserie* herself, and Marcel into her 'collector'. But Albertine eventually eludes both the narrator and object status, and this, with the narrator's complicity. Albertine sometimes takes off her kimono in her sleep and throws it on the armchair: in its pockets are all her letters. Although he is greatly tempted, Marcel never reads the letters:

> Quand je sentais le sommeil d'Albertine bien profond, quittant le
> pied de son lit [...] je faisais un pas, pris d'une curiosité ardente,
> sentant le secret de cette vie offerte [...] je restais longtemps à
> regarder le kimono comme j'étais resté longtemps à regarder
> Albertine. Mais [...] jamais je n'ai touché au kimono, mis ma main
> dans la poche, regardé les lettres. (*La Prisonnière*, I, p. 89)

Marcel never explains why he does not take this decisive step which
would give him access into Albertine's 'vie d'autre'. Why not?
Perhaps it is in order to free Albertine from her status as collected
object: one area of her life is thus left unpossessed by Marcel. This is
also a sacrifice made by the narrator *as* narrator, for Albertine's
kimono is perhaps the object that is filled with the greatest number of
possible stories in the whole of *la Recherche*: its mere appearance can
'thicken' the narrative with the promise of alternative plots, stuffed
full as it is – literally – with sources of secret stories. But the narrator
chooses not to delve into this treasure trove of narratives. Like the
precious 'meuble japonais' in Proust's letters to Hauser which contain crucial – but unattainable – information, the kimono contains a
multitude of narratives that might be harnessed to the overarching
narrative of the search for lost time: but they are not.

   Thus Albertine's kimono undergoes a gradual but radical transformation in the course of *La Prisonnière*. From being a symbol of
Albertine's object status, it begins to symbolise (because it contains)
everything about her which eludes his narrative grasp. The kimono is
a constant reminder to the narrator of Albertine's irrepressible
otherness which means that she can never be wholly possessed by
him: and this is a state of affairs that the narrator himself has col-
luded in, by not reading her letters. This qualified independence,
however, is followed by her disappearance and sudden death, which
together constitute a radical escape which makes her desirable but
inaccessible again, forever.

Pierre Loti[60]

In Loti's *Madame Chrysanthème* (1887), the relationship between
the collection of *japonaiseries* and the view of women as precious
objects finds its fullest expression, featuring as it does a traveller to
Japan who there acquires his woman-*japonaiserie*.[61] In spite of the
fact that he actually goes to Japan, Loti's narrator continues to travel

through objects, as we shall see. The fact that he thus continues to make use of the filter of *japonisme*, notwithstanding his direct experience of the foreign country, attests to the dominant role of the *japonaiserie* in writings on Japan in this period, and its function as a communicating device between the work and the reader.

Pierre Loti has been much reviled over the years for his pernicious and persistent influence on French images of Japan. *Madame Chrysanthème*, his first 'Japanese' novel, attracted particularly virulent comment. One contemporary reviewer, an anonymous Chinese journalist, was scathing: 'si l'on me demandait de nommer le livre qui montre le degré le plus bas de la civilisation européenne, je nommerais sans hésiter *Madame Chrysanthème*', he wrote in the *Japanese Mail*.[62] Félix Régamey, filled with righteous indignation at the passive depiction of the Japanese woman in Loti's novel, wrote a version of *Madame Chrysanthème* from the point of view of the eponymous heroine.[63] Some later critics have been no less indignant: one critic has accused Loti of inventing the 'colonial novel', the 'novel of desertion' and 'the novel of sexploitation', all in the single work of *Madame Chrysanthème*.[64] Such accusations are a little unfair, both to Loti and to his much-maligned novel. *Madame Chrysanthème* has indeed had the effect of perpetuating certain stereotypes, and Loti was aware that it would: thence to dismiss the work as a straightforward piece of cultural stereotyping, however, would be to misread it, in the way that too many of his contemporary readers obviously did. *Madame Chrysanthème* is a more ambiguous work than has previously been recognised, in which Loti embeds anti-*japoniste* indications for the connoisseur while maintaining, overall, a crowd-pleasingly *japoniste* demeanour.

Madame Chrysanthème appears, at first sight, to be the living-out of a *japoniste* fantasy, making ample use of *japoniste* references to characterise Japan in general and Japanese women in particular: in view of the fact that the author had had direct experience of Japan, having actually travelled there, this use of *japonisme* would certainly seem to indicate an unhealthy reliance on stereotype. The narrator, called *Loti*,[65] is a French naval officer who is stationed in Japan for a number of months. These are his thoughts as the ship approaches the Bay of Nagasaki, corresponding precisely to the presumed fantasies of the French (male) reader about to start Loti's novel:

> – Moi, disais-je, aussitôt arrivé, je me marie… […] avec une petite femme à peau jaune, à cheveux noirs, à yeux de chat. – Je la

choisirais jolie. – Elle ne sera pas plus haute qu'une poupée. Ça se passera dans une maison de papier, bien à l'ombre, au milieu des jardins verts.[66]

We have encountered the figure of the woman-as-object already in this chapter, in Albertine, but what is specifically *japoniste* in this fantasy is the size of the woman: 'elle ne sera pas plus haute qu'une poupée'. The woman is thus immediately linked to the toy, the bibelot, the *japonaiserie*, and the fantasy is therefore revealed to be as aesthetic as it is sexual. This is why *Loti* places such importance on the setting of his fantasy: like a precious object that needs special packaging, again like Albertine, the woman is placed in 'une maison de papier, bien à l'ombre, au milieu des jardins verts'. All of *Loti*'s initial fantasies are of this aesthetic kind, and both he and his reader begin the novel with a set of *japoniste* images which they expect the reality of Japan to corroborate. And it does: *Loti*'s vision is so powerfully shaped by his *japoniste* notions that he finds what he is looking for. Even nature obliges, offering unmistakably 'Japanese' trees and rocks to the visitor from France:

> Toute cette nature exubérante et fraîche portait en elle-même une étrangeté japonaise; cela résidait [...] dans l'invraisemblance de certaines choses trop jolies. Des arbres s'arrangeaient en bouquets, avec la même grâce précieuse que sur les plateaux de laque. De grands rochers surgissaient tout debout, dans des poses exagérées. (*MC*, p. 49)

Moreover, he 'recognises' the women: 'Ah! mon Dieu, mais je la connaissais déjà! Bien avant de venir au Japon, je l'avais vue, sur tous les éventails, au fond de toutes les tasses à thé' (*MC*, p. 72). As with Goncourt describing Japan in *La Maison d'un artiste*, *Loti*'s point of reference is the *japonaiserie*, but given that he is actually in Japan as he speaks, the 'knowledge' provided by the objects he remembers seeing in France is even less likely to be relevant for understanding Japanese reality.

This style of pseudo *déjà-vu*, while managing to say nothing about the 'real' Japan, would be immensely satisfying to the *japoniste* reader. By confirming a stereotype instead of describing Japan, the narrator gives the reader the illusion that information has been transmitted; but in reality the stereotype stands between the text and what it refers to. This happens each time that the narrator 'describes' something with reference to a stereotype, or by using the tautological 'japonais', or 'japonerie'. For instance, we are told that a Japanese man, in his excitement at striking a bargain, forgets 'toute sa japonerie' (*MC*, p. 74). This statement makes no logical sense, but is satisfying on another plane of discourse, that of stereotype-confirmation. However, at the very heart of this *japoniste* 'description', Loti has installed a discreet disclaimer, a sign indicating that he is aware of his own pandering to its stereotyping language. If 'japonerie' is intrinsic to the Japanese, it is clearly not possible for a Japanese to 'forget' it. By indicating thus the illogic of this terminology, Loti quietly subverts the terms of his own description. What is more, the man is called 'Monsieur Kangourou'. This choice may seem simply to confirm the ridiculous nature of the character, and of the Japanese in general (everything is 'amusant', 'pas sérieux' or 'saugrenu' in Loti's Japan): here again, however, Loti has concealed an instance of subversion. 'Kangourou', apart from being the French for kangaroo, sounds strikingly similar to 'Kangôrô', a Japanese man's name very much in keeping with the social class and period in question.[67] As his Parisian reader delighted in the choice of 'kangourou' with its resonances of fantasy, ridicule and exoticism, Loti would have enjoyed his own little joke, his quiet insertion of an authentic Japanese name under the guise of a French word.

Most of the names in Loti's Japanese novels, however, are French words: Chrysanthème, Jasmin, Neige, Prune. Yet, paradoxically, they contrive to 'sound Japanese' to the *japoniste* ear: they are not so much Japanese as Japanese-like, conforming to a vague idea of exoticism, prettiness (flower names) and ephemerality. This paradox results from the nature of proper names. Most philosophers of language agree that names are denotative, not connotative; a name *refers* to a person, but does not *describe* him. For example, 'Socrates' is a name that refers to a certain philosopher, but does not describe him, for it can also refer to a Brazilian footballer. But what happens when a Japanese name is translated into a French word that is not a name-word? 'Chrysanthème' then becomes *descriptive* of an exotic content which does not exist in the original; the sound becomes imbued with a meaning, that of 'Japaneseness', for the Parisian reader. Translation here also has the effect of taming the threatening foreignness of the word; 'Chrysanthème' is exotic, but is also a word that we recognise. Thus Chrysanthème the woman is reduced, by the exoticising power of the descriptive name, to an unthreatening existence through the act of translation. Not only is she unthreatening:

named after an object, a recognisable *japonaiserie*, her status is a
little less than human. The strangeness of the 'mousmés', the young
girls who surround Chrysanthème and who are all named after
flowers and fruit in Loti's translated renditions of their names, is
partly due to this onomastic association with the vegetable kingdom.
The non-human nature of their names is enhanced by frequent
comparisons to non-human beings:

> Elles se prennent par la main toutes les cinq, comme des petites filles
> à la promenade. Et nous suivons par-derrière, avec des airs détachés.
> Ainsi vues de dos, elles sont très mignonnes, les poupées, avec leurs
> chignons si bien faits, leurs épingles d'écaille si coquettement mises.
> Elles traînent, en faisant un vilain bruit de sabots [...] A toute minute
> on entend leurs éclats de rire. Oui, vues de dos, elles sont mignon-
> nes; elles ont, comme toutes les Japonaises, des petites nuques
> délicieuses. Et surtout elles sont drôles, ainsi rangées en bataillon.
> En parlant d'elles, nous disons: 'Nos petits chiens savants', et le fait
> est qu'il y a beaucoup de cela dans leur manière. (*MC*, pp. 96–97)

Loti is careful to eliminate as much of the human as possible from
this description. Not only are the young women likened to dolls and
dogs, but the enumerated attractions are all superficial, devoid of any
suggestion of interiority, 'leurs chignons si bien faits, leurs épingles
d'écaille [...], les petites nuques délicieuses': and the noises they make
are non-verbal (the sound of their clogs, and laughter). Even more
significantly, they are described as a *view*, the standpoint of the
viewer crucial as if they were objects in a display cabinet: 'ainsi vues
de dos' (twice), and 'ainsi rangées en bataillon'. Looking at the
women from behind robs them of yet another humanising factor,
their faces, but it also creates the strong sense that they are not so
much live women as life-size *japonaiseries*.

Loti spends most of the novel insisting thus on the strangeness of
Japan, and its people ('*parce que nous ne sommes pas les pareils de
ces gens-là*', *MC*, p. 148), chiefly by superimposing a *japoniste* view
on what he sees. At a key point in his relationship with Chrysanthème, however, *Loti* decides to call Chrysanthème, and the objects
around her, by their Japanese names:

> Jusqu'à présent j'avais toujours écrit sa guitare, pour éviter ces
> termes exotiques dont on m'a reproché l'abus. Mais ni le mot
> guitare ni le mot mandoline ne désignent bien cet instrument mince
> avec un si long manche, dont les notes hautes sont plus mièvres que
> la voix des sauterelles; – à partir de maintenant, j'écrirai chamécen.

Et j'appellerai ma mousmé Kihou, Kihou-san; ce nom lui va bien
mieux que celui de Chrysanthème, qui en traduit exactement le sens,
mais n'en conserve pas la bizarre euphonie.

Donc je dis à Kihou, ma femme:

– Joue, joue pour moi; je resterai là toute la soirée, et je t'écouterai.

Étonnée de me voir si aimable, [...] elle s'assied dans la pose des
images [...]. A cette tombée de nuit, je me sens presque chez moi
dans ce coin de Japon, au milieu des jardins de ce faubourg; – et cela
ne m'était jamais arrivé encore... (*MC*, pp. 203–204)

By calling her 'Kihou' and his wife in the same breath, *Loti* restores
both name and status to her, making her into a legitimate being on
the same level as himself. She still conforms to the *japoniste* image of
the pretty Japanese woman ('elle s'assied dans la pose des images'),
but in spite of this *Loti* here appreciates her as a real human being
worthy of being listened to ('je t'écouterai'), rather than a living
japoniste fantasy, or a non-human specimen in a glass cabinet.

It is crucial that *Loti*'s communion with Chrysanthème, her music
and her country comes in a moment of linguistic generosity – that is,
when Loti decides to allow Japanese words into his French text. This
generosity, however, is fraught with dangers. Opening oneself up to
the other may result in the fragmentation, or even the loss, of the
self.[68] Proust's narrator speaks of 'la petite blessure qui se cicatrisait
assez vite, mais que la maladresse inconsciente d'Albertine, des
indifférents, ou de mes propres pensées, ne tardait pas à rouvrir', as if
otherness were a constant, painful reminder of the incompleteness of
the self: it is certainly responsible for wounding him.[69] For Loti, it is
in the realm of language that the risks are most evident. The linguistic
intrusion of the other that Loti accepts is potentially threatening to
his sense of identity. In *Japoneries d'automne*, Loti describes what
happens to him when he speaks Japanese: 'je ne reconnaissais plus le
son de ma voix dans ces mots nouveaux que je prononce, il me
semble n'être plus moi-même'.[70] The relationship between language
and identity, the source of the fear that may be at the heart of his
apparent espousal of *japonisme* in *Madame Chrysanthème*, is dealt
with more openly in *Japoneries d'automne* and in *La Troisième
Jeunesse de Madame Prune* (1905).

Read as sequels, these works shed much light on the motives
underlying the narrative strategies of the first work. For instance, the
stereotype-induced vision which caused *Loti* to see *japoniste* trees
and rocks in *Madame Chrysanthème* is echoed, with a difference, in

Japoneries d'automne. Although the Japanese rock formations may *appear* artistically arranged to the Western eye, here it is concluded that they are the work of nature: 'deux rangées de collines symétriques la bordent, collines japonaises, ayant toujours des formes *qui ne semblent pas* naturelles' (*JA*, p. 122, my italics). This trope of false recognition, which is so effectively used in *Madame Chrysanthème* as part of a discourse of stereotype-confirmation, is similarly deconstructed in *La Troisième Jeunesse de Madame Prune*. Upon returning to Nagasaki, the hero is delighted to rediscover his 'Japan' through his beloved Japanese objects: 'il existe encore, mon Japon de jadis, celui du temps de Chrysanthème, et du temps de ma jeunesse; je reconnais tout cela, les tasses minuscules, les bâtonnets en guise de fourchette...'.[71] The rhythm of the phrasing, the vocabulary, the objects beloved of a *japoniste* imagination are all powerfully reminiscent of *Loti*'s bogus 'recognition' of Japan in *Madame Chrysanthème*. The difference, however, is that in the later works the recognition is real: he has seen these things before, and so he is truly recognising them, not just seeing his fantasies materialise. With this realisation, the reader recognises an older, disabused narrator for whom travel has become almost entirely an act of nostalgia.

Loti in Japan falls prey to two distinct kinds of nostalgia, which are both specifically related to the experience of exotic travel. The kind that I will call real nostalgia is based on memories of his own past in France. The other kind, imaginary nostalgia, consists of Loti's imagined 'memories' of Japan's past: a form of exoticism anticipating that of Segalen, but also echoing Proust. Loti's nostalgic musings about his childhood are frequently triggered by his experiences in Japan:

> Ces mousses, ces feuilles jaunes [...] j'ai beaucoup connu jadis des choses analogues... C'était dans les bois familiers à mon enfance, dans ces chers coins où, depuis tant d'années, je n'ai plus revu l'automne. (*JA*, p. 168)

> Mon empressement joyeux à m'habiller pour aller courir [dans Nagasaki] est comme un regain de ce que j'éprouvais, tout enfant, chaque fois que je venais d'arriver chez mes cousins du Midi, où se passaient mes vacances. (*MP*, pp. 291–92)

The above examples seem to indicate a natural connection between Japanese present and French past, the one observation (about autumn, or about his eagerness to go out) slipping effortlessly into the other. The notion of exoticism appears to be on the same wavelength as that of nostalgia for childhood. That is, the self's relationship with the exoticism of Japan is analogous to the self's relationship with its past, which is why 'cette notion d'exotisme extrême [...] avive ma nostalgie' (*MP*, p. 116). Exoticism in space seems to set off exoticism in time:[72] geographical distance is translated into temporal distance, as if the traveller's displacement in space had triggered a mental displacement in time. For the two worlds of childhood and Japan, both so foreign to the adult Loti, share a number of characteristics. They are both worlds in which he is linguistically limited, often reduced to gestures and grimaces. They are also both sources of freshness, youth and vivid sensation: 'J'y reviens beaucoup trop à mon enfance [...] Mais il me semble que je n'ai eu des impressions, des sensations qu'en ce temps-là' (*MC*, p. 140). The cliché of the world-weary traveller, constantly in search of new stimuli as a way of recapturing lost youth, is a familiar trope in *fin-de-siècle* literature. This may be one reason why Japan relates so naturally to childhood for Loti: Japan becomes the space in which he can deploy his child-hood memories, being a land untainted by his own ageing. The effects of ageing are followed through: Loti is like an Alzheimer's patient whose disease cuts him off from his present, but who can accede effortlessly to his more distant past. Thus the travelling Loti – cut off from his Frenchman's present by geographical distance – can evoke his French childhood with a freedom which would perhaps not be available to him in France. This is why Loti's real nostalgia for his past accompanies his present voyage in Japan: the exotic other occasions his frequent returns to his past self.

Loti also makes use of the rhetoric of nostalgia in an imaginary context. That is, he expresses nostalgia for something that he never knew, something whose existence he can only imagine: ancient, pre-industrial Japan. All three 'Japanese' works are full of nostalgic references to a Japan before its opening to the West, a Japan of noble samurai and expert craftsmen. Sheltering from the rain in an old and beautiful temple, *Loti* muses of the latter that 'ils ne devaient pas ressembler aux Japonais d'aujourd'hui, les hommes qui ont conçu tous ces temples d'autrefois' (*MC*, p. 140). The Japan that *Loti* encounters in *Madame Chrysanthème* has confirmed him in many of the *japoniste* notions with which he had arrived, but what truly attracts him is the Japan of the past, Japan before its colonisation by its vulgarised persona of *japonisme*. Like Proust's narrator nostalgically evoking the elegant ladies in the Bois de Boulogne that

he never knew, Loti uses the mode of nostalgia to evoke the noble samurai he came too late to meet. His search for this Japan is chronicled in detail in *Japoneries d'automne*, in which he travels to various historic sites within Japan. At times, in recounting his trips, the rhetoric of travel through space slowly translates into that of travel through time, as in this pilgrimage to Nikko through a darkling autumn evening: 'De village en village, il semble que le caractère du vieux Japon s'accentue plus fortement' (*JA*, p. 165). Similarly, his journey to a temple in Kamakura to see the ancient robes of a second-century empress is as much a journey through time as through space. When he gets to Kamakura, the ancient capital of Japan, Loti discovers that it is now a ruin: '[L]es temples seuls sont restés debout, par-ci, par-là sous l'envahissement vert, et les avenues se voient encore, à peu près tracées, mais vides et silencieuses à présent' (*JA*, p. 120).[73] The spatial distance covered seems to have been translated into a temporal one; Loti feels as if he has arrived in ancient Japan. Of course this is no more than a fantasy, as he realises soon enough when he is allowed access to the mysterious 'toilette de l'impératrice' with dispiriting ease (*JA*, 135).

In *Japoneries d'automne*, Loti the traveller has become a collector of experiences, specifically of experiences which will amount to *evidence* that ancient Japan used to exist. The impulse behind this collecting seems to be nostalgia. The relationship between collecting and nostalgia has been noted by a number of critics, most recently by John Elsner in this discussion of Sir John Soane's collections of ancient Roman and Etruscan artefacts:

> while collecting, obviously, is a movement of desire and acquisition, it is also a process of nostalgia. Collecting is inherently a cult of fragments, a sticking together of material bits that stand as metonyms and metaphors for the world they may refer to but *are not*. [It is] a dream lying wistfully *behind* the collecting impulse, namely, the urge to evoke [...] a complete ancient world.[74]

There is of course a difference between collecting artefacts and collecting experiences, but both kinds of collecting may be driven by nostalgia, either real or imaginary. In the cases of both Loti and Soane, the nostalgia is imaginary in that the men obviously had no direct experience of ancient Japan or ancient Rome. We might add to the list the nostalgia of Proust's narrator for the 1890s, and conclude that in all three cases, the nostalgia is for an idealised, unreal world.

Like the unreal 'Japan' evoked by Goncourt's *japonaiseries*, Loti's 'ancient Japan' is a romanticised vision based on a collection of experiences that may be accurate in parts but are essentially 'metonyms and metaphors for the world they may refer to but *are not*'.

It is essential that this ancient world be unreal, for the most precious aspect of ancient Japan, for Loti, is its mystery, its unknowability, its essential alterity to himself. As in Proust's 'Japan', where mystery is an integral part of the attraction of *japonaiserie*-clad Odette, the nostalgia that Loti experiences for the ancient Japan he never knew is based on its undiscovered secrets: he writes joyfully of his entrance into the palace of Taiko-sama in Kyoto that 'j'ai l'impression de pénétrer dans le silence d'un passé *incompréhensible*' (*JA*, p. 27, my italics). In this case, he fails even to imagine the banquets that took place there so many centuries ago (*JA*, p. 32). It is vital for Loti that these things remain inaccessible to him, a Westerner, and that the truly foreign retain its independence and mystery. Such an exalted view of ancient Japan is no more helpful towards a real understanding of the other than the *japoniste* vision of pretty porcelain figures and laughing mousmés. But there is a qualitative difference. The *japoniste* vision is one that seeks to reduce the otherness of Japan by subsuming it into the system of the self, through putting it into the category of the 'exotic' which can then be stored away:[75] we may call this vision that of the *dominating* collector, who believes that he *understands* his collectables. Loti's love of ancient Japan differs from this in that it sets up the otherness of Japan as something that is ultimately unknowable: it is the *fact* of its difference from France, not the substance, which constitutes its value. In other words, Loti does not seek to understand ancient Japan, but only to marvel at its alienness; he is a *romantic* collector who wants to luxuriate in its 'étrangeté rare et exquise'. Indeed, his attitude towards Japan's past is governed by a Segalenian sense of the exotic, a delight in 'la perception du Divers; la connaissance que quelque chose n'est pas soi-même',[76] deployed in the dimensions of both time and space: Segalen, had he noticed, would have approved.[77]

At times, this exoticism is also cultivated with regard to Japan's present. There are several instances in *Madame Chrysanthème* where *Loti* opts for difference over comprehension, in the manner of Segalen's 'exote', and these are often highlighted by a contrast with Yves, his close friend who accompanies him on his Japanese adventure. In chapter 23, *Loti*, Yves and Chrysanthème meet a funeral procession, which *Loti* begins to describe as a strange, exotic event. He then realises that both Yves and Chrysanthème react differently from him: 'Chrysanthème tout à coup prend un air de circonstance; Yves se découvre. C'est pourtant vrai, que c'est la mort qui passe! Moi qui oubliais...' (*MC*, p. 113). For Yves, the universality of the situation leads to his immediate understanding of it, and an appropriate response. *Loti*, however, rejects the universal humanist option of reacting to the funeral as a funeral, and persists in differentiating the Japanese ceremony from the French equivalent. In a forced attempt to maintain a distance between the two cultures, he predicts that the procession will return from the cemetery 'moitié riant, moitié pleurnichant. Demain, on n'y pensera plus' (*MC*, p. 114). Here, Loti has adopted Segalen's position of detached incomprehension.

However, in the main Loti's position of neutrality towards the other is only precariously maintained, because his hero is much more susceptible to the two classic forces of attraction: women and money. It is often forgotten that *Madame Chrysanthème* is the story of a customer and the product he has purchased. *Loti* himself is painfully aware that, when he entered into a business contact with Chrysanthème, he destroyed then and there the possibility of a normal relationship with her (*MC*, pp. 177–78). Once money enters the equation, Chrysanthème collapses into becoming a *japonaiserie* again, if only because she is *Loti*'s possession. From this point of view, *Loti*'s tendency to denigrate Chrysanthème at every turn in the novel can be explained as the frustrated attitude of the man who has bought a woman, but has thereby made it impossible to obtain anything genuine from her. This is why he persists in seeing her not as a human being but as a plaything, a *japonaiserie*.

Less obvious, however, is the fact that this is the same situation that holds between Loti, the author of this novel, and his public. In a letter to a friend, written during the composition of *Madame Chrysanthème*, Loti complains: 'Travaille énormément, écris roman japonais que dois livrer en août; grosse affaire d'argent. Roman sera stupide. Le deviens moi aussi'.[78] Loti the colonialist, the dominant Westerner who buys a young Japanese woman for his pleasure, has in turn sold himself to a Parisian publisher; like Chrysanthème, he has prostituted his talents to become a *japonaiserie*.[79] His book requires the narrator to maintain a *japoniste*, reductive attitude towards Japan and Chrysanthème, for the simple reason that this is what will sell it. He does maintain this attitude, alternating it occasionally with the 'differential', Segalenian attitude of wonder at the exotic, except in the few cases I have mentioned where he begins to develop something of a human relationship with Chrysanthème. The fact that 'Loti' is the name of the author (although a nom de plume), as well as of the hero of this novel, makes his betrayal even more personal; the misrepresenter of Japan is now the misrepresented, as indeed he has been for many years by his critics who have continued to condemn him for the callous sale of his experiences. I have tried to suggest that Loti was aware of his betrayal; that he embedded a number of discreet hints of this in his book, principally destined though it was for a *japoniste* readership who would make him the money that he needed. There is a delicate irony in his stance vis-à-vis this readership, as he moves deftly between the roles of authentic witness and fellow-*japoniste*. Having ridiculed, in the name of authenticity, the Parisian salons where *japonaiseries* are arranged in a most un-Japanese fashion ('je souris en moi-même au souvenir de certains salons dit japonais encombrés de bibelots et tendus de grossières broderies d'or sur satin d'exportation' [*MC*, p. 157]), *Loti* subsequently portrays himself as being no better than the owners of such salons, burdened with his spoils on the night of his departure: 'Dix-huit caisses ou paquets, de bouddhas, de chimères, de vases' (*MC*, p. 218). These, we are made to feel, will be arranged in exactly the way that he condemned earlier, upon his return to France.[80] In *La Troisième Jeunesse de Madame Prune*, with a similarly weary cynicism, *Loti* accepts a recent change in vocabulary on his ship: 'on nous a tant traités de pillards, dans certains journaux, que nous avons admis la dénomination "pillage" pour toute chinoiserie ou japonaiserie' (*MP*, p. 96). Money has corrupted his language, his book, and his relationship with Chrysanthème.

This last, however, remains an area of ambiguity, as an analysis of the following passage, in which *Loti* finds her asleep, will show:

> Elle dormait à plat ventre sur les nattes, sa haute coiffure et ses épingles d'écaille faisant une saillie sur l'ensemble de son corps couché. La petite traîne de sa tunique prologeait en queue sa personne délicate. Ses bras étaient étendus en croix, ses manches déployées comme des ails et la longue guitare gisait à son côté.
>
> Elle avait l'air de fée morte. Ou bien encore elle ressemblait à quelque grande libellule bleue qui se serait abattue là et qu'on y aurait clouée.
>
> [...] Quel dommage que cette petite Chrysanthème ne puisse pas

toujours dormir: elle est très décorative, présentée de cette manière, – et puis, au moins, elle ne m'ennuie pas. – Peut-être, qui sait? Si j'avais le moyen de mieux comprendre ce qui se passe dans sa tête et dans son coeur... (*MC*, pp. 108–109)

The sleeping Chrysanthème has been compared with the sleeping Albertine, and this parallel is a mutually revealing one.[81] Both Chrysanthème and Albertine are likened by their lovers to a specimen of the non-human kingdom: Chrysanthème is 'quelque grande libellule bleue', while Albertine exhibits 'l'air d'une longue tige en fleur'.[82] Metamorphosis has occurred in both cases, emphasising the exoticism of the woman. Marcel confers upon the sleeping Albertine a 'vie plus différente de la mienne, plus étrange'.[83] From exoticism both men veer into sheer reductionism. Chrysanthème is described as if she were a *japonaiserie* herself ('très décorative'), whilst Albertine, as has previously been mentioned, is clothed in one, a kimono. Finally both men arrive at a curious psychological state precariously poised between a lover's desire to know the woman's thoughts, and a strange preference for her to be asleep. *Loti*'s reluctance to give in to his very human curiosity, retaining it as a merely hypothetical possibility ('si j'avais le moyen de...'), is deeply symbolic of the ambiguity of his desires. Marcel's state of mind is very similar.[84] Both *Loti* and Marcel derive a mixed pleasure from watching the woman asleep, wondering about, but not acting to obtain her innermost thoughts: from watching her when she is, in a sense, not there. Why is this so? *Loti* tells us that in this state, 'elle ne m'ennuie pas'. But 'ennuyer' does not only mean 'to bore': it can also mean 'to worry'. In what way is Chrysanthème a source of worry to him when she is awake?

In the cases of both Marcel and *Loti*, perhaps it is the lack of balance in their relationships which makes them uneasy, although they themselves are responsible for the existing arrangement: unconsciously, or semi-consciously, the man is aware that his power over his captive makes a relationship of equals impossible. The portrayal of Albertine as 'la charmante captive', and that of Chrysanthème with her arms 'étendus en croix' and resembling a dragonfly 'qui se serait abattue là et qu'on y aurait clouée' (a specimen in the lepidopterist's collection) only serve to emphasise their status of victim. To this situation of ownership without true consent, human beings bought like so many *japonaiseries*, sleep provides a welcome (if temporary) respite, through *freeing* the woman. Sleep, traditionally, brings freedom from care:[85] so in sleep, the captive woman is temporarily free from – and of – the man. The freedom thus obtained is not absolute, and this too coincides with the fragile and limited nature of Chrysanthème's – or Albertine's – freedom. But limited though it may be, their freedom gives them an equality with the man, and this in turn sets the man free from the nagging consciousness of his power over her, giving him a temporary sense of peace. On an equal footing with her at last, he dares to wonder about her thoughts and feelings, safe in the knowledge that she will not respond: faced with otherness at rest, in the guise of the feminine and the Japanese, he desires to come to know this other.

There is another moment in *Madame Chrysanthème* in which *Loti*'s desire to understand his mistress overcomes his habitual pose of indifference, within the context of a certain kind of equality, temporarily constructed, between the two. In this case the equality comes not through sleep, but through an object: not a Japanese bibelot, but an English one.

> Parmi les affaires de Chrysanthème, ce qui m'amuse à regarder, c'est la boîte consacrée aux lettres et aux souvenirs: elle est en fer-blanc, de fabrication anglaise, et porte sur son couvercle l'image coloriée d'une usine des environs de Londres. – Naturellement c'est comme chose d'art exotique, comme *bibelot*, que Chrysanthème la préfère à d'autres mignonnes boîtes, en laque ou en marqueterie, qu'elle possède. [...] Cela m'amuserait bien de lire ces lettres d'amies, et surtout les réponses que leur fait ma mousmé... (pp. 126–27)

In this passage *Loti* deliberately challenges the one-sided point of view that calls the East exotic and and the West home: the very English tin is an exotic *bibelot* for the Japanese woman, and treasured 'comme chose d'art exotique'.[86] In this rare instance of understanding, *Loti* goes further and admits – albeit without an unseemly show of longing – that '[C]ela m'amuserait bien de lire ces lettres d'amies, et *surtout* les réponses que leur fait ma mousmé...' (my italics). *Loti*'s adoption of the other's point of view, however temporarily, helps the reader to realise that Chrysanthème also has a tale to tell. Simply by mentioning the existence of Chrysanthème's letters to her friends, *which he cannot read*, Loti weaves into the fabric of his apparently *japoniste* novel the possibility of counter-narratives which frustrate the reader in exactly the way that *Loti*, the character, is frustrated by his inability to communicate with her. Régamey, in his well-intentioned attempt to give us Chrysanthème's 'side of the story', was only able to give her the voice of a nineteenth-century French romantic heroine, and in so doing perhaps suffocated her otherness even more effectively than Loti's frustrated narrative did.[87] Instead of trying to give Chrysanthème a voice, Loti preferred to leave a number of metaphorical blank spaces in his text, surrounded by traces of his desire to come to know her. Unlike Segalen's 'exote', he was too weak to savour forever the aesthetic pleasure of 'une incompréhensibilité éternelle', particularly when it came to dealings with the opposite sex. This weakness has given us some of the most beautiful passages of *Madame Chrysanthème*.

Loti's attitude is weaker than that of the exote, but more human. Like most human beings, he had to deal with contradictory commitments: to his *japoniste* readership, to his Segalenian delight in difference, but also to his simple desire for intimacy. In *Madame Chrysanthème*, we can trace his awareness of these competing allegiances, and of his own historical position between them. Loti is only too aware that the story of his relationship with a Japanese woman, to a Parisian readership in 1887, is bound to be read within the context of *japonisme*: that is, fated to be *mis*read. Given this historical and cultural context, perhaps Loti's blatant pandering to his readers constituted a kind of self-sacrifice. By risking being misread and offering up his reputation to posterity as having written 'les livres les plus inexacts, les plus superficiels, les plus frivoles, les plus malséants'[88] on Japan, only daring to hint covertly at his deeper knowledge of Japan in well-concealed references and private jokes, perhaps Loti had a sense of atoning for that greater act of misreading, that of Japan by *japonisme*.

The impact of *japonisme* on late-nineteenth-century French culture was widespread and enduring,[89] and this in turn made the *japonaiserie* a stable currency in the metaphorical economy of *fin-de-siècle* literature. In some cases, this meant that the *japonaiserie* became a subject – and an object – worth writing about for itself, as in the case of *La Maison d'un artiste*. We have seen how the *japonaiseries* in *La Maison d'un artiste* invariably ended up 'representing' Japan, the statements about them becoming indistinguishable from statements about Japan itself. The *japonaiserie* here becomes a signifier for 'Japan' that overshadows its signified so completely that it eventually *becomes* the signified: a self-reflexive sign that signifies only itself, like a neon sign by a conceptual artist. Having thus become the sole source of Goncourt's information about Japan, the *japonaiserie* then subsides – in Goncourt's text – into muteness: that is to say that its opacity and silence encourage Goncourt to rely on his own 'aesthetic' sense to decipher it for the reader. Objects are not 'legible', do not make sense, until they are put in a semiotic context: but the collector, emboldened by possession, may attempt to read them notwithstanding. The result, as we have seen, is Goncourt's erroneous understanding of 'Japan'. 'Japan', imagined through *japonisme*, is a multivalent topos in Proust's novel. Its semiotic value is acknowledged and harnessed as the narrator makes use of the *japonaiserie* for its connotations. The simple connotations of these objects, however, are slowly developed into a metaphorical language capable of describing the most intimate desires of the narrator. It offers privileged access to the past, but it is also the realm of exoticism and sexual desire: the *japonaiserie* links exoticism to the collector's mentality ('la vie de collectionneur' advocated by Charlus), and thus comes to denote secrecy, sexual otherness and desirability. As the narrator is seen practising, then rejecting, the 'collection' of Albertine, the inevitable transformation takes place: Woman becomes the *japonaiserie*, acquiring all the concomitant connotations of exploitation, exoticism and commodification.

The 'public' connotations of the *japonaiserie* – its values as accepted in the Parisian semiotic system – could thus be built upon and developed, or, as in the case of Loti, exploited and subverted. In spite of his first-hand experience of Japan, Loti made liberal use of the distorting lens of *japonisme* in writing *Madame Chrysanthème*, allegedly in order to fill his coffers. However, he also drew attention to his own exploitation of the *japoniste* discourse by *over*-using it: by describing Japanese objects in Japan as possessing the quality of 'japonerie', or as being *japonaiseries*. Loti's use of the objects that symbolised 'Japan' to describe the real Japan creates a surfeit of signification that ultimately points to the artificial nature of the sign. In *Madame Chrysanthème*, the French sign for Japaneseness – the *japonaiserie* – is gradually revealed to be a hollow construct, an empty sign that refers only to itself and never to the actual Japan.[90] In this way, the possession of a *japonaiserie* comes to signify the absence of the real thing, in all three of the authors examined in this chapter: whether it is an absence of real knowledge about Japanese art, of Albertine, or of a satisfactory relationship with Chrysanthème. The collector-traveller is, in the last instance, cheated of his object.

CHAPTER TWO

Journalists and Barbarians: Anatole France, Claude Farrère, Henri Michaux

The greatest antidote to the *japoniste* vision of Japan was the Russo-Japanese War of 1905. Following the unprecedented victory of an Asian nation over a European power, Japan came to be perceived as an exception and a threat: the pretty *mousmé* of Loti fame was replaced by the indomitable Japanese soldier, descendant of the samurai but also a constituent of the Yellow Peril, as the dominant symbol of Japan. This warlike image of Japan had first emerged in 1895, after the Japanese victory in the Sino-Japanese War, but for Europe it was Japan's 1905 victory against Russia that was decisive. Thereafter, until the eve of the Second World War, the image of Japan in the West underwent extensive developments, being transformed and revised by commentators who variously wished to recuperate the Loti-based image, admire the new, military one, or fan anti-Japanese sentiment for economic or racist reasons.

These commentators were, in the main, journalists, statesmen, economists, and historians. Writers of fiction also also rushed to write about this unpredictable and atypical Asian country. Emile Driant's *L'Invasion jaune*, published in 1905, sold well in a climate fuelled by fear of an Asian military bloc headed by the Japanese, whilst Claude Farrère's *La Bataille* was a bestseller that benefited from setting a typical war romance in exotic waters. There was indeed much to analyse in Japan's new persona as a military power, which developed at astonishing speed after 1905, taking on an increasingly darker hue as the nation began its invasion of China in the 1930s.

This chapter will discuss, in historical context, texts by contemporary literary figures that contributed to the fashioning and establishment of this new, anti-*japoniste* image of Japan. Although I have chosen to examine, in the main, texts by 'literary' writers such as Anatole France, Claude Farrère and Henri Michaux, I will be analysing them as instances of *journalistic* writing, given that their purpose was to inform the public of the nature of political events in the Far

East. The type of traveller to be examined in this chapter, therefore, will be classed broadly as the journalist. The texts have in common a way of seeing that aspires to tell the truth, a gaze that intends primarily to observe but which differs from the scientist's in that it also seeks to understand human motives, and to make judgments and predictions for the future from a limited, human point of view. A journalist's job is to report the 'truth' about a situation, be it corruption in domestic politics or the mistreatment of POWs in a war abroad: and France, Farrère and Michaux were all interested, in these writings, in reporting objectively on the political situation of Japan.

The journalist cannot aspire to objectivity of the 'scientific' kind,[1] because he is limited by the human nature of his facts and methods, and the constraints of time. Therefore his vision will always be flawed to a certain extent, constrained within the framework of his own culture and prejudices, however sincerely he wishes to 'see' the truth of the matter. But for the journalist, this limited vantage point is not necessarily a disadvantage: given that his primary purpose is to situate and educate his readership with regard to the events he is reporting, it is important, even desirable, for him to stay within his own cultural framework, while endeavouring to be as well informed and factually reliable as possible about the foreign country. Indeed, from an epistemological perspective, the journalist's search for knowledge might be said to be circular: seeking to report back on events in faraway places, his ultimate aim for the reader at home is self-knowledge through knowledge of the other.

I start this chapter by examining a French socialist's account of the Russo-Japanese War. Anatole France's novel offers an almost abstract image of Japan, a product of his socialist and humanist principles and his thoughts on decolonisation, and from which he hopes that the West will learn some lessons. Claude Farrère, by contrast, offers us the vision of a typically 'civilised' *homme de lettres* of his time, who through his visits to the country aspired to paint a truthful picture of Japan, free of the myths of *japonisme*. As for Henri Michaux, also travelling in Japan in the 1930s, his goal was to achieve a radically different kind of objective vision: that of the 'barbarian', free of the civilising and prejudicial influences of both European and Asian culture, which would allow him to observe the other unfettered by any culturally induced way of seeing. His account of Japan in the thirties is in startling contrast to Farrère's political essays. Seen together, the work of the three writers traces the development of the new image of Japan between 1895 and 1939, within the historical context of a complicated series of conflicts, of which I will now give a summary account.

East beats West

Japan had already made a name for itself as a military power before the Russo-Japanese War. The Sino-Japanese War was waged over the question of influence in Korea, a sovereign country but under Chinese protection, and 'traditionally' coveted by Japan.[2] A revolt in Korea in 1894, followed by the arrival of Chinese troops to assist the Korean king, gave Japan the opportunity for armed intervention. This developed into a full-scale naval battle against China in which the Japanese were so successful that not only did they drive the Chinese troops out of Korea, but went on to capture Port Arthur and the Liaotung peninsula in south Manchuria. The Treaty of Shimonoseki, signed in 1895, ratified these spoils and also gave Japan Formosa and the Pescadores. A French commentator, describing this war as 'l'un des faits politiques les plus considérables des temps modernes', predicted 'la formation dans l'extrême-Asie d'une grande puissance maritime', as well as that Japan would, in time, spearhead the rise of 'un concert de peuples jaunes qui [...] feront à l'Europe et jusque chez elle une concurrence redoutable'.[3]

The war even had an effect on the slumbers of the Kaiser. In April 1895, Kaiser Wilhelm II dreamt that a yellow peril would rise in the East, invade and devastate Europe: deciding that it had been a prophetic dream, he had a drawing of it made and sent it to his friend, Tsar Nicholas II. This was the origin of the concept of the Yellow Peril, which went on to be used 'as an ideological justification for the tripartite intervention of Russia, Germany and France into Sino-Japanese negotiations following Japan's victory in the Sino-Japanese War'.[4] That is to say, the Treaty of Shimonoseki was revised after the three European powers 'advised' Japan to surrender the Liaotung peninsula and Port Arthur in the interests of peace in the region. Japan, with no allies to speak of, was forced to comply. This was humiliating enough, but the fact that within five years of the Treaty the same European powers gained control over the territories that the Japan had returned to China made for a bitterness that the Japanese did not forget. Until the Sino-Japanese War, Chinese sovereignty had been nominally respected by the colony-hungry European powers, Hong Kong and Macao being the main exceptions. But after it, there was a scramble for concessions and spheres of influence: and in 1901, Russia, France, Germany, Great Britain and the United States occupied Peking and openly divided up the country between them. For Japan, it was the expansion of Russia that was particularly galling and worrying. Having obtained the Liaotung peninsula and Port Arthur, Russia's growing proximity cast a shadow over Japan like the bear of its emblem. Russia's ambitions were to dominate North China, Manchuria and, crucially for Japan, Korea. It was Korea again that sparked off the Russo-Japanese War in 1904.

During the actual war, the governments of continental European countries favoured Russia, broadly speaking, as did the general public: 'la guerre russo-japonaise a permis à la grande majorité des Français de faire éclater ses sympathies spontanées pour la Russie'.[5] Even the more moderate commentators picked up on and reiterated the argument voiced by Villenoisy after the Sino-Japanese war, that a strong Japan would unite and lead the Asians to attack Europe. The image of the yellow peril seemed to be turning into reality:

> Quoi qu'on en pense, le 'péril jaune' apparaît, dès maintenant, dans l'imagination des peuples, tel que l'a représenté dans son fameux dessin l'empereur Guillaume II: dans un décor d'incendie et de carnage, les hordes japonaises et chinoises se répandent sur l'Europe, foulant aux pieds les ruines de nos capitales, détruisant nos civilisations anémiées [...] le monde civilisé s'est toujours organisé en face d'un adversaire et contre lui: pour le monde romain, ce fut le 'barbare'; [...] il se pourrait que, pour les sociétés de demain, l'adversaire fût le 'jaune.'[6]

The theme of Asian armies invading Europe, based on the notion of the Yellow Peril, was quickly taken up by popular novelists. Emile Driant's *L'Invasion jaune* (1905), for instance, the story of a Japanese-Chinese army wreaking havoc in France, was a bestseller. This notion of Asian hordes menacing Europe, of which the Kaiser's dream was one influential instance, did not originate in the nineteenth century: it was a reformulated version of Europe's age-old fear of Asia, dating back to the Persian wars against ancient Greece or Attila the Hun's devastation of central Europe.[7] The Kaiser's unconscious was clearly inhabited by a typically European collective memory.

The outcome of the war was a truly shocking one for Europe: for the first time in history, an Eastern nation had triumphed over a

Caran d'Ache, The Russo-Japanese War, from *Le Figaro*, Mansell
Collection © Getty Images

Western one. The event was seen as apocalyptic by many commentators. After the Russo-Japanese War, the image of Japan as the new
Yellow Peril was to become more widespread in Europe, although set
against it was the image of 'the plucky little Japs'[8] who had fought
and won against the great Russian bear, a modern David against a
Goliath who was not, when all had been said and done, especially
popular with any European country apart from France. Britain, in
particular, had signed a treaty with Japan – the Anglo-Japanese
alliance – in 1902, and in so doing had tacitly agreed to give Japan a
free hand in Korea. On both land and sea the Japanese had been
victorious, and tales of their great valour and generosity towards
civilians gave them good press, especially in Britain and the United
States. One battle that caught the imagination of many Europeans
was the Battle of Tsushima, a dramatic and decisive sea battle which
destroyed the Russian Baltic fleet and led them directly to the negoti-
ating table. The Americans were asked to mediate, and the Treaty of
Portsmouth in 1905 gave the Liaotung peninsula, as well as much of
south Manchuria, 'back' to the Japanese, and recognised Japan's
'special interests' in Korea thereafter.

European reactions to the Russo-Japanese War were much more
various than the reactions to the Sino-Japanese War had been, and

resulted in a series of modifications to perceptions of Japan in Europe. Historians recognised that the war signalled an irrevocable shift in the balance of power: 'la guerre qui vient de s'achever en Extrême-Orient est assurément l'événement le plus considérable qui se soit produit dans le monde depuis 1870 [...] ses répercussions euro-péennes ont détruit le système de forces qui depuis trente-cinq années assurait la paix du vieux monde',[9] wrote André Chéradame in the introduction to his in-depth analysis of the balance of power in Europe and the world before and after the events of 1905. For other writers, however, the issue was not so much the emergence of Japan as a political power as its potential threat to Europe's domination of Asia. Works such as *Pays de Mousmés, Pays de Guerre!*, by Charles Pettit, correspondent for *Le Temps*, harnessed the racism inherent in the Kaiser's vision of the East to their appraisal of the Russo-Japanese conflict. Thus the sight of Russian prisoners of war in Osaka was described by Pettit from a powerfully physical point of view: 'J'avais complètement oublié que ces captifs étaient des Russes; [...] je ne voyais plus en eux que des représentants de la même famille humaine, que des êtres faits comme moi, ayant le même coeur et le même cerveau, tandis qu'un abîme me séparait des triomphateurs.'[10] Having whipped up racist resentment against these alien beings, the author went on to fuel it with France's fear of losing her colonies: 'Le Japon est la seule puissance qui soit vraiment à craindre pour notre empire d'Indochine [...] il est à souhaiter que les peuples européens fassent tous leurs efforts pour rester d'accord entre eux et permettre à la race blanche de garder sa suprématie dans tout l'Extrême-Orient.'[11]

Not all Frenchmen, of course, were pro-Russia and anti-Japan after 1905. Indeed the nascent Socialist and related movements in Europe tended to see Japan not so much as the Yellow Peril as a Yellow Hope.[12] For them Japan became the symbol of an anti-colonialist force, struggling valiantly against European domination in the East. Of course, being pacifist, it was difficult for these move-ments to approve unreservedly of Japan: a 1904 meeting of socialists in Paris condemned both Russia and Japan. But Jean Jaurès, an outspoken pacifist, was heard to admit that he hoped Japan would win, now that the war had started.[13] It was in *L'Humanité*, a socialist periodical edited by Jaurès, that Anatole France's thoughts on the Russo-Japanese conflict were first published in serialised novel form, starting in the inaugural issue (April 1904) of the journal.

Anatole France, *Sur la pierre blanche*

In 1904, Anatole France was a well known socialist *homme de lettres* and a member of the Académie Française. *Sur la pierre blanche* was subtitled 'dialogues philosophiques' in the serialised version. France's novel is indeed a dialogue, but made up of chapter-long monologues by 'humanists' of various types (the section on the Russo-Japanese war is to be found in the monologue of Nicole Langelier), and ending with the description of a socialist utopia. This structure follows that of Thomas More's *Utopia*, whose narrator Hythlody begins by attacking the injustices of European society. The utopia that he goes on to describe is, like that of *Sur la pierre blanche*, not a garden of leisure and delights but a rational, sober and egalitarian society.[14] On the way to Anatole France's utopia the reader encounters a number of assessments of the past and present, and one of these concerns the Russo-Japanese war. Using the character of the humanistically educated Nicole Langelier as his mouthpiece, France begins by specifying that he thinks of this war as a colonial war. He then goes on to describe, with the well-poised sarcasm that he would employ again to effect in *L'Ile des Pingouins*, what this means for the capitalist European:

> C'est une guerre coloniale [...] Or, le principe fondamental de toute guerre coloniale est que l'Européen soit supérieur aux peuples qu'il combat; sans quoi la guerre n'est plus coloniale, cela saute aux yeux. [...] En se battant mieux que des Européens, ils [les Japonais] n'ont point égard aux usages consacrés, et ils agissent d'une façon contraire, en quelque sorte, au droit des gens. En vain des personnes graves, comme Monsieur Edmond Théry, leur démontrèrent qu'ils devaient être vaincus dans l'intérêt supérieur du marché européen, conformément aux lois économiques les mieux établies.[15]

Théry was a distinguished economist who, prior to the Russo-Japanese War, had described the Yellow Peril as not so much a military worry as an economic one, a 'rupture violente de l'équilibre économique international sur lequel le régime social des grandes nations indus-trielles de l'Europe est actuellement établi, rupture provoquée par la brusque concurrence, anormale et illimitée, d'un immense pays nouveau' (consisting of a Sino-Japanese territory).[16] Easy game for France's rapier wit, but fair game also, given that Théry's thesis was widely read and respected. As for the overall sense of European superiority that was offended by Japanese military success, France accurately traces its origins back to the racist 'scientific' beliefs still prevalent in the early twentieth century, exploited by Pettit in the text quoted earlier, which had functioned for decades as an unassailable justification for colonialism:

> En vain le docteur Charles Richet leur représenta [aux Japonais], une squelette à la main, qu'étant prognathes et n'ayant pas les muscles du mollet suffisamment développés, ils se trouvaient dans l'obligation de fuir dans les arbres devant les Russes qui sont brachycéphales et comme tels éminemment civilisateurs, ainsi qu'il a paru quand ils ont noyé cinq mille Chinois dans l'Amour. 'Prenez garde que vous êtes des intermédiaires entre le singe et l'homme', leur disait obligeamment monsieur le professeur Richet, 'd'où il résulte que si vous battiez les Russes ou finno-letto-ougro-slaves, ce serait exactement comme si les singes vous battaient. Concevez-vous?' Ils ne voulurent rien entendre.

Sur la pierre blanche is useful in being a precisely dated testimony to the change of image undergone by Japan since *Madame Chrysan-thème*. Smallness and yellowness are perhaps the only characteristics attributed to the Japanese that are recognisably present in both of these works, and in *Sur la pierre blanche* they are embodied in the bee, a creature betokening danger and efficiency: 'et tandis que la bête énorme [the Russian bear] allongeait indolemment le museau sur la ruche nippone, les abeilles jaunes, armant toutes à la fois leur ailles et leurs aiguillons, la criblèrent des piqûres enflammées'.[17] The traditionally pejorative use of 'jaune' to distinguish non-European from European is also transformed by France into a relatively positive description when he compares 'le péril jaune' favourably with 'le peril blanc':

> Il ne parait pas toutefois, à première vue, que le péril jaune, dont les économistes européens s'épouvantent, soit comparable au péril blanc suspendu sur l'Asie. Les Chinois n'envoient pas à Paris, à Berlin, à Saint-Pétersbourg, des missionnaires pour enseigner aux chrétiens le foung-choui et jeter le désordre dans les affaires euro-péennes. [...] L'amiral Togo n'est pas venu avec douze cuirassés bombarder la rade de Brest, en vue de favoriser le commerce japonais en France. [...] Les armées des grandes puissances asiatiques n'ont pas emporté à Tokio et à Pékin les tableaux du Louvre et la vaisselle de l'Elysée.[18]

The 'douze cuirassés' is clearly a reference to the 'black ships' that the American admiral Perry threatened Japan with in 1854. Anatole

France, who refers to the United States as 'l'Europe nouvelle', here acknowledges the opening of Japan as a European blunder, its subsequent industrialisation and development – and by implication its military might – the result of European interference: in other words, he suggests that Europe has no one but itself to blame for Japan's frighteningly well-trained army and navy. 'Nous avons enseigné aux Japonais le régime capitaliste et la guerre', laments Nicole Langelier. This assumption of blame for the opening of this hitherto idyllic land – at least in the imagination of the West – and its corruption through technical advancement was a common theme amongst anti-colonialist intellectuals of the day, and is, as we shall see, at the heart of Claude Farrère's writings. Also to be found in Farrère's works is the rhetorical device here used by France, that of retaining the formula of a relationship and swapping the variables, recasting for instance the looting of the Winter Palace by European armies into the imaginary rape of the Louvre and the Elysée by Asian armies: 'les armées des grandes puissances asiatiques n'ont pas emporté à Tokio et à Pékin les tableaux du Louvre et la vaisselle de l'Elysée'.[19] It is an obvious but effective anti-colonialist mode of discourse, transforming the experience of the colonised into that of the coloniser, so that the self is forced to 'exchange places' with the other. In this way an 'objective view' of the act (of pillaging museums, or turning up fully armed at a port with no provocation) is obtained, and the smooth substitution of 'Louvre' for 'Winter Palace' creates an objective viewpoint, for the French reader. France thus brings his reader to a realisation of his nation's self-centred actions, and to a humanist understanding of the evils of colonisation.

But in the end, France wants to argue the case, as a humanist and socialist, for world peace, and according to his character Nicole Langelier this is where Japan has, unwittingly, been of use:

> Mais si le Japon rend les jaunes respectables aux blancs, il aura grandement servi la cause de l'humanité et préparé à son insu, et sans doute contre son désir, l'organisation pacifique du monde.[20]

Military victory, although unappealing to the pacifist, forces governments to respect the victorious nation, and as such it will have had a salutary effect on Europe's vision of Asia. But most of all, France hopes that Japan will develop and strengthen China, because 'les peuples forts concourent à l'harmonie et à la richesse du monde'.[21] France thus moves his readers from self-understanding and the philosophical indictment of colonialism to a plan for world peace. A strong China will contribute to a better balance of power, and therefore lead to the ultimate goal of the socialist, peace amongst the nations.

Written before the end of the war, France's text is a masterpiece of journalistic writing that attempts to goad his country into recognising its guilt and responsibility as a Eurocentric colonial power. In exemplary 'objective' style, he analyses the facts of the war even-handedly, recontextualising events occurring in Asia into a European framework. But because his ultimate aim is to educate his readers, his writing is turned inwards, back onto Europe from Japan. In the final analysis, this European viewpoint adopted by France gives rise to a somewhat abstract image of Japan as the embodiment of the role it is asked to play within the socialist equation.

Claude Farrère, *La Bataille*

The Russo-Japanese War proved to be the source of a very different kind of inspiration for Claude Farrère, already a novelist of note and recipient of the third Prix Goncourt for *Les civilisés*. *La Bataille* is a romantic 'war novel' set in Nagasaki, depicting the story of a young, Westernised Japanese couple whose life is torn apart by their country's war with Russia. It is also a successful attempt to recuperate the old image of Japan by connecting it to the new one, to fuse the aesthetic, nineteenth-century image with the image of the brave and noble soldiers who vanquished the Russians. Published in 1909, *La Bataille* quickly became a bestseller, not only in France but in England following its translation in 1912: the translated version was even broadcast on BBC radio. In 1921 it was dramatised by Pierre Frondaie, premiering at the Théâtre Antoine that same year: in 1934 it was made into a film by Nicolas Farkas, shown in both London and New York. A long-running sensation,[22] it exerted much influence on the French public's vision of Japan in the 1920s and 1930s. And Claude Farrère, as if to keep up with the various reincarnations of his novel, continued to champion the case of Japan through other, non-fictional writings right up until the start of the Second World War.

Claude Farrère was the *nom de plume* of Charles Bargone, another man of letters and the sea who admired Loti's writings: he served under Loti as a naval officer, and as a literary figure too he is usually placed in a subordinate position to the author of *Madame*

Chrysanthème. If the truth be told, *La Bataille* owes much to *Madame Chrysanthème* where décor and detail are concerned. Written in 1908, the depiction of the eponymous naval battle came from Farrère's own research, but for the scenes on land he had to reach back to the memories of his three-day stay in Nagasaki in 1899, or to reach for his copy of Loti's novel. As a result *La Bataille* contains many a feature from the Nagasaki of *Madame Chrysanthème*, but the rest of the work – its dramatic plot, and its characters driven by honour and the spirit of self-sacrifice – is very much Farrère's own.

Farrère's most recent and most exhaustive biographer describes *La Bataille* as a novel that attempts to 'mettre en scène le national-isme japonais'.[23] It certainly aspires to present Japanese nationalism in 1905 from the Japanese perspective, a Japan fighting for its honour and independence against the more experienced Russians: the third-person narrative seems designed to give the characters plenty of scope for voicing their opinions and explaining their Japanese points of view. Farrère even makes use of quotations from actual conversations on at least two occasions, as he specifies in his footnotes.

The action takes place during the spring of 1905, when the Japanese are already at war with the Russians. Jean-François Felze, a celebrated French society painter, arrives in Nagasaki during a luxury tour of the world. There he meets the marquess of Yorisaka and his wife Mitsouko, both descended of noble samurai families but now a flawlessly westernised couple, together with their friend and Mitsouko's lover, the British naval officer Fergan. Felze himself is in thrall to a beautiful but unfeeling American millionairess, a Mrs Hockley, but derives spiritual sustenance from an old Chinese friend, the sage Tchéo-Pei. Whilst painting Mitsouko's portrait, Felze comes to know her better: in the meantime, the decisive Battle of Tsushima takes place, and the Japanese are victorious. Both the marquess of Yorisaka and Fergan are killed in action. Upon hearing this, Mitsouko forgoes her Western ways and friends to retire to a convent in Kyoto, to mourn her husband in the traditional fashion.

Rachilde, a novelist friend of Farrère's, described the novel in glowing terms as a work which did the Japanese justice, finally, after the ill-effects of *Madame Chrysanthème*:

> Voici qui nous console des Japonais de carton que nous servent les journalistes s'étant fait une opinion dans les comptes rendus de *Madame Chrysanthème*. Il y a un Japon de surface, verni et prétentieux, mignard et trop spirituel comme les porcelaines de

collection; mais il y a un Japon sauvage, un Japon d'antiques traditions qui n'oublie rien de ses goûts primitifs. Malgré une apparente européennisation [sic], il y a toujours un Japon qui sait s'ouvrir le ventre à propos pour certifier sa noblesse et nourrir ses enfants de son propre sang répandu pour la cause des beaux gestes.[24]

Quoting Rachilde, Quella-Villéger calls *La Bataille* 'en quelque sorte [...] un anti-*Madame Chrysanthème*',[25] but this is not quite the case: the novel is a much more diplomatic manoeuvre, culturally speaking, which seeks to bridge the chasm between the world of *japonisme* and that of twentieth-century military Japan, to reconcile the geisha with the modern Japanese naval officer. The 'bridging' function is usually carried out by Felze, the French character through whose eyes we first encounter Nagasaki and the other characters: the fact that he is an artist attaches him securely to the world of *japonisme*. Early on in the novel we find him 'vaguement déçu dans ses goûts d'exotisme' when he is shown into Madame Yorisaka's 'boudoir de Parisienne, très élégant, très à la mode',[26] and consoled when he opens the velvet curtains to see that 'la ville, et les villages, et les temples, et les collines portaient ineffaçable la marque ancienne, et ressemblaient toujours [...] à quelque vieille estampe du temps des vieux shôgouns, à quelque kakemono minutieux'.[27] Felze is clearly a character who would be at home in *Madame Chrysanthème*, well-versed as he is in the *japoniste* discourse of Loti and his readers: in other words, through him Farrère caters for the *japoniste* readership. The presentation of the *japoniste* Japan as a fast-disappearing phenomenon makes it even more attractive to the reader, by giving it a patina of nostalgia. Significantly, Felze is in his fifties, almost thirty years older than the other main characters, and this age-gap justifies his old-fashioned expectations of Japan: whereas he would prefer to paint Madame Yorisaka in traditional Japanese dress, her husband, as well as the Englishman Fergan, much prefer her in her Parisian haute couture. Thus Felze exists in the novel to ease the reader over the bridge between the older Japan and the new, guiding him or her into the Japan of 1905 from that of 1887.

Many of the *japoniste* touches in *La Bataille* can be traced straight back to *Madame Chrysantheme*: as mentioned earlier, Farrère's knowledge of Nagasaki was based on a three-day visit, roughly nine years previous to the time of writing. Local colour often appears to be borrowed outright from Loti's work. The Donko-chaya, for instance, a pretty teahouse next to an archery place that features in several scenes of *Madame Chrysanthème*, appears in *La Bataille*: 'une chaya était là, à côté d'un tir à l'arc' (p. 104): in a linking scene of the novel, Yorisaka and Fergan come upon Felze sitting at this chaya by himself. Significantly, these symbols of the new Japan greet Felze but do not sit down in the *japoniste* teahouse with him, and walk on busily discussing naval strategy.

Farrère's descriptions of Djou Djen Dji, a residential quarter of Nagasaki, are also clearly derived from *Madame Chrysanthème*, as is his transcription of the name. Here are their respective descriptions of this hilly area:

> En continuant de suivre le chemin qui monte et passe devant chez nous, on trouve une dizaine de vieilles maisonnettes encore, quelques murs de jardins, – puis, plus rien que la montagne solitaire, les petits sentiers qui s'en vont vers les cimes à travers les plantations de thé, les buissons de camélias, les broussailles et les roches. Et ces montagnes tout autour de Nagasaki sont pleines de cimetières; depuis des siècles et des siècles, on monte là des morts. (*Madame Chrysanthème*, p. 111)

> L'escalier, usé, moussu, branlant, grimpait tout droit au flanc de la colline, entre deux petits murs japonais, interrompus çà et là par des maisonnettes de bois, toutes obscures et silencieuses. Et le quartier endormi, avec ses jardinets déserts et ses chaumières muettes, semblait une avant-garde de l'immense ville des morts, du cimetière touffu et confus dont les tombes innombrables descendent en rangs serrés de tous les sommets d'alentour, et cernent, et pressent, et assiègent la ville, moins vaste, des vivants. (*La Bataille*, p. 37)

Farrère has borrowed much here from Loti – the 'maisonnettes', the gardens, the overall topography of the hill in relation to the city – but his description does not contain the telling details of 'les plantations de thé, les buissons de camélias, les broussailles et les roches' which bring Loti's description to life. His prose style is much more heavy-handed than Loti's, closely following 'maisonnettes' with 'jardinets' (whereas Loti is careful to use 'jardins'), and above all making far too much of the atmosphere of the cemetery, whose tombs 'descendent [...], et cernent, et pressent, et assiègient la ville, moins vaste, des vivants'. Description was never Farrère's strong point,[28] and his adaptations of Loti's finer attempts show up his comparative lack of skill, and interest, in this aspect of writing.

Another description which Farrère appears to have 'borrowed' from Loti's work is that of a Japanese musical instrument, the *koto*.

Farrère's description of the eerie sound of the *koto* precisely echoes that of the *chamécen* (to retain Loti's transcription) in *Madame Chrysanthème*, down to its evocative comparison with the winter wind:

> Des phrases sans commencement ni fin s'ébauchèrent, des rêveries, des tristesses, des plaintes lamentables frémirent, parmi d'étranges grincements sinistres, qui rappelaient le bruit des bises d'hiver et le cri des oiseaux nocturnes. Sur tout cela, une mélancolie désespérée planait... (*La Bataille*, p. 122)

> Cela [the sound of the *chamécen*] devient rapide, avec un tremblement de fièvre [...] Cela se change en bruit de vent, en rires affreux de masques, en plaintes déchirantes, en pleurs [...] (*Madame Chrysanthème*, p. 204)

That this is Loti paraphrased is clear not only from the similarity of the imagery and the vocabulary, but from the fact that in reality a *koto* does not sound quite as much like the *chamécen* as Farrère's description suggests. In his haste to write up the drama of the Battle of Tsushima, Farrère clearly skimped somewhat on his research, gambling on the ignorance of his readers where the finer points of Japanese music were concerned, and making astute use of Loti's earlier work. Farrère's 'borrowings' from Loti of these *japoniste* elements are useful to the critic because they make clear Farrère's priorities in his writing practice, but also because they create intertextual connections between the two works, and help to situate Loti's Japan within Farrère's imaginary system. The older, more beautiful Japan of *Madame Chrysanthème* is neither rejected nor foregrounded in *La Bataille*, but offered as a delicate backdrop to the contemporary drama of the war, and this means that the contrast between Loti's and Farrère's Japan can be said to mirror the dilemma of the Japanese characters who are forced to live with the contradictions between their traditional values and inevitable Westernisation.

There is one obvious difference, structurally speaking, between the Japanese novels of Loti and *La Bataille*: Loti's are first-person narratives, while *La Bataille* is in the third person, which allows Farrère to give a voice to the Japanese characters in his novel, unlike Loti in *Madame Chrysanthème*. What these voices reveal, according to Rachilde in the previously quoted description, is genuine 'Japaneseness' as opposed to Lotiesque nonsense. What exactly is this genuine Japan? '[Un] Japon sauvage, un Japon d'antiques traditions qui n'oublie rien de ses goûts primitifs'. Rachilde's vocabulary is itself revealing of certain prejudices which, as I will show, match those of the novelist. First, it makes the usual connection between the old and the genuine: but more interestingly, its preference for 'un Japon sauvage' echoes an older ideal, that of the noble savage of Rousseau-ist lineage, beloved of all civilised peoples who feel that they have become too civilised for their own good. But even more attractive than the image of the noble savage – which, in actual fact, does not work too well for Japan, with its age-old civilisation – is that of the feudal, traditional Japanese, bound by codes of honour and self-sacrifice, 'un Japon qui sait s'ouvrir le ventre à propos pour certifier sa noblesse et nourrir ses enfants de son propre sang répandu pour la cause des beaux gestes'. This older Japan, unearthed by Farrère beneath that of Westernised Nagasaki as well as that of *japonisme*, has the glamour of knights and battles, the honour-driven romances of *Le Cid* and other Corneillian tales:[29] the attraction of a civilisation that France itself had cultivated in medieval times, and can now only find in romantic novels – that is to say, in fiction.

Indeed, if the contemporary setting of the Russo-Japanese War is abstracted from *La Bataille*, the story – and the characters – can be seen to belong very much within the generic conventions of the romantic, and historical, novel. A young, attractive couple separated by war; an adulterous affair that turns to tragedy; a glorious death in battle: all of these are conventional elements of the popular novel of the day, recognisable from the plots of Dumas père and fils, for instance, or the best-selling works of Ponson du Terrail. War itself, of course, has been the stuff of fiction since the *Iliad*, as has been the male camaraderie of soldiers, bound to each other by a rigid code and brothers-in-arms in life and death. In the mid- to late nineteenth century, the three musketeers embodied this soldierly ideal, as well as those of nobility and patriotism: these were still valid and attractive values in the popular fiction of Farrère's day.[30] All of these elements are present in *La Bataille*, and the result is that the characters would have been immediately and satisfyingly recognisable, *as novelistic types*, to the contemporary reader: there would have been nothing particularly 'other' about the marquess of Yorisaka, a fine young officer of noble lineage, who sacrifices his life and happiness for his country, nor indeed about Madame Yorisaka's reaction to her husband's death, which is to 'vivre dans le couvent bouddhiste des filles de daïmios, – pour y vivre sous le cilice et pour y mourir, – honorablement' (p. 320). The Japanese characters are thus appropriated in *La*

Bataille by the Western gaze, not as *japoniste* stereotypes, but as *novelistic* types: conventional characters from a recognisable fictional family. When seen in this light, the nominally 'Japanese' gestures or behaviour of the characters turn out to be much less foreign than they may have appeared at first sight. They are not exotic characters: unlike Chrysanthème in Loti's novel, they are given a voice and elicit the readers' sympathy in the traditional manner, by explaining their noble motives. The exoticism comes from the décor, not from the human beings in the foreground, who behave according to values such as honour and self-sacrifice; values that are universally recognisable, if tinted with a shade of temporal or novelistic exoticism for the early-twentieth-century reader, who would be more likely to associate such values with historical figures or fictional stories.

Farrère acknowledges implicitly in his preface that the Japanese characters in *La Bataille* are stereotypes, not *japoniste* stereotypes but novelistic ones, when he describes them as being 'beaucoup moins des portraits en quelque sorte photographiques que des peintures très générales, brossées à la ressemblance approximative de toute une caste japonaise dont les traits essentiels ont seuls été choisis et grossis, pour rendre le tableau mieux perceptible aux yeux européens'. The marchioness, in particular, is described as a symbol of the spirit of sacrifice that Farrère believes to have been widespread in Japan in 1905. But such selection and generalisation inevitably leads to stereotyping. This is true of the other nationalities in the novel also, not just the Japanese characters. Fergan, being British, is 'peu enclin aux rêveries et aux spéculations de la pensée' (!), but is formed and bound by a gentleman's rules of honour: indeed it is essential to the plot that he possess this stereotypical trait, as the marquess depends upon it to force him to take part in the naval battle. The British, although allies of the Japanese in accordance with the Anglo-Japanese alliance, were nominally neutral in the Russo-Japanese War (although they had helped greatly with the construction of the Japanese fleet): however, Fergan is shamed into collaboration at a crucial point in the battle when Yorisaka reveals that he has been cognisant all along of Fergan's adulterous affair with his wife. 'Un gentleman doit payer, – murmura Fergan.'[31] Similarly, Tchéou-Pei embodies the stereotype of the Chinese mandarin and sage, as an opium-smoking philosopher of exquisitely formal manners who is completely indifferent to the ups and downs of individual human fortune. The Frenchman is himself something of a stereotype: an artist, and therefore much more interested in beauty than in politics, he is the perfect character to assume the role of observer that allows him – and us, through him – to attain a relatively 'objective', outsider's overview of the political situation.

Farrère's proviso about the 'peintures générales' that are his characters comes alongside a claim of complete fidelity to reality where the historical facts of the battle are concerned: indeed the primary reason for this preface, specially written for the 1911 'édition définitive' of his novel, is to vaunt the 'valeur documentaire' of his work. Farrère names his sources for the Battle of Tsushima, French naval officers who were present at the event, and cites a number of naval specialists who have commended the novelist's accurate portrayal of the event. In the body of his text, before starting the tale of the battle, he reminds us that everything in the account, apart from the fictitious characters and their ship, 'est d'une exactitude historique rigoureuse'.[32] Even the fictional Japanese characters are given more 'reality' once the account of the battle has begun, through the adoption of one strangely literal change in appellation: Farrère consistently calls the marquess of Yorisaka 'Yorisaka Sadao', that is to say by his Japanese name in the correct order (surname followed by given name), from the start of the battle until his death in combat. The effect is striking, immediately lessening the degree of Westernisation to which the character had been subjected up until that point, and presages the 'metamorphosis' of his wife, the elegantly Parisian marchioness of Yorisaka, into a traditional Japanese widow.

It is not only the naval details that are noteworthy for their 'valeur documentaire': the Chinese puns that Felze exchanges with Tchéou-Pei, and several of the patriotic declarations that Farrère has put into the mouths of his lesser Japanese characters, are all scrupulously footnoted as having been taken from reality. This insistence on the reality of the facts used within the fictional frame of *La Bataille* complicates our analysis of Farrère's 'way of seeing' Japan in this work. As we have seen, *La Bataille* makes use of a number of generically recognisable discourses, such as *japonisme*, heroic war romances and nostalgia for the past, but it fits into this scheme contemporary and 'real' facts from a recent event of great political significance. Readability and relevance: a recipe for a bestseller, it is also the result of a 'double' way of seeing, the journalist's vision 'embedded' into that of the novelist for its easier consumption. In other words, *La Bataille* is a romantic novel, but it is also a novel of contemporary relevance, a text in which certain issues are discussed within a novelistic framework which allows for easier access to difficult or sensitive issues.

One contemporary issue that is discussed in the novel is colonialism, or more specifically, the problem that arises when the East meets a technologically superior West. Is it better to defend one's country at the risk of becoming Westernised, by assimilating Western technology and culture as the Japanese have done, or to reject all that is foreign at the expense of freedom, in the Chinese way? Faced with the two opposing examples of Japan and China, Farrère dramatises the choices and their consequences. The Chinese position is embodied in Tchéo-Pei's calm indifference to the invasion of his country. In his first meeting with Tchéou-Pei in Japan, Felze had asked whether it would not have been better for the Chinese to have defended themselves against the European powers, comparing the Chinese empire to a precious vase. Tchéou-Pei responds thus to Felze:

> Vous avez très ingénieusement comparé l'Empire à une vase enfermant la précieuse liqueur des anciens préceptes. Et vous avez, non sans raison, redouté pour la liqueur inestimable la fragilité du vase impérial. Si l'Empire est en effet subjugué, qu'adviendra-t-il des anciens préceptes? [...] L'immortalité des anciens préceptes n'est pas liée à la vie périssable de l'Empire. L'Empire peut être subjugué: pourvu que le Fils du Ciel ait fait son devoir jusqu'au bout, [...] il n'importe en rien que l'Empire soit vaincu ou soit vainqueur. Il n'importe en rien que tous ses habitants soient morts ou soient vivants.[33]

The Chinese position supersedes merely human temporality, elevating the moral excellence that is intrinsic to Chinese identity above and beyond the lives of the Empire's subjects, even that of the 'Fils du Ciel' himself. The Japanese position leads to the tragedy of the marquess of Yorisaka, who is seen, at the end of the novel, to have learned avidly from the West in order to defend his country, but who has therefore ended up becoming irretrievably Westernised: 'votre cervelle a cessé d'être japonaise pour devenir européenne'. These are the words of Hirata, the uncompromisingly 'Japanese' naval officer who speaks no French or English, who predicts that after the victory, all the Japanese in Japan will follow Yorisaka's example. Felze would deplore this, but it is not clear that Farrère did. Although Felze seems to side with the Chinese position, becalmed by opium and wisdom in the company of Tchéo-Pei, Farrère shows much sympathy as a novelist for the efforts of the Japanese: and thereafter, in his non-fictional essays on the relationships between Japan and China, he continues to work with the national stereotypes he created for his novel. Looking forward to these later works, it would seem that Farrère never really understood the Chinese position (although Felze did), and felt that he – and the West – could identify much more easily with the Japanese attitude towards their own country: patriotism which was not bolstered by action seemed to be an impossibility for him, and therefore he would rule, in *Le grand drame de l'Asie* for instance, that no action meant no patriotism – or indeed, no country to be patriotic about, in the case of China. Indeed, *La Bataille* contains Farrère's most sympathetic portrayal of the Chinese: in his later works, his inability to understand what he sees as their passivity makes them into a true 'other' for Farrère, with whom the Japanese compare, in his eyes, favourably.

Farrère's political essays

Farrère continued in his Japanophile position thereafter, and ex-panded on his thoughts about this Far Eastern country which, unlike China, he felt he understood. *Mes Voyages* (1924) is a book of essays in which Farrère writes about his visits to various Eastern lands, and which ends on two chapters about Japan, 'Le Japon ancien' and 'Le Japon moderne': these chapters are included in a slimmer, edited version of the book (called *Extrême-Orient*) published in the same year. (Farrère's publisher never missed an opportunity for making the most of his marketable author.) The book's main purpose is to give a sympathetic portrayal of Japan, and to explain and demystify Japanese culture for the uninformed reader. Farrère seems to have realised the damage done to the French way of seeing Japan by both Loti and the Yellow Peril, and in *Mes Voyages* he is continually at pains to undo it. In 'Le Japon ancien' he gives an excellent succinct history of the country, interspersed with somewhat clumsy attempts at exposing the mechanisms of exoticism, such as 'Je vous dis tout cela [...] pour que vous découvriez un peu le pays vraiment mystéri-eux où nous sommes!... mystérieux pour nous, s'entend!'[34] Describing the feudal system of Japan in the sixteenth century, he likens the clans, and their geographically charged names, to French families and their names: 'Vous voyez que les noms japonais ressemblent singulièrement aux nôtres! Combien avons-nous eu de Rougeville, de Fontaine, ou d'autres Monts ou Vals analogues!'[35] Such comparisons successfully foster a sense that cultures develop in similar ways, whether in the East or in the West, and a 'transcontinental' analysis – of events in Japan, France, England, Spain and Syria in 1185 – strengthens the credentials of this novelist turned historian, and his attempts at developing an 'objective' view of Japan.

The chapter on 'Le Japon moderne', however, is immediately much more partisan, containing extreme and obviously untrue statements such as 'dans le vocabulaire nippon, il n'y a d'ailleurs pas de mot injurieux' (p. 255). But this chapter is written with a clearly political intent: Farrère's desire to argue the case for a distinctly French policy towards Japan that is different from the Anglo-American one. Farrère predicts greatness for the increasingly powerful Japanese nation, and hopes that France will not invest in any misguided notions of loyalty towards the United States if things come to a head in the Pacific:

> ce n'est pas le pavillon tricolore, c'est le pavillon étoilé qui, en 1854, déclencha sur le monde cette avalanche asiatique, dont le monde aujourd'hui s'épouvante! Après tout, sur ce Pacifique, probable champ de bataille à venir, nous n'avons, nous, que des intérêts bien minimes […] Tant mieux pour nous, cette fois! […] nos sympathies, à l'heure décisive, pourraient bien être du côté de l'Empire du Soleil-Levant, – dont je prédis, dès aujourd'hui, la foudroyante victoire! (p. 284)

It is necessary to put this 'prediction' into historical context. Compared with the time of the Russo-Japanese conflict, there was now little or no fear in Europe of a pan-Asian attack, a Yellow Peril consisting of an immense Chinese army spearheaded by the Japanese, as it had become clear to all that Sino-Japanese relations were much less than cordial. Fears of an economic invasion remained, but Japan was now thought of as a rapidly industrialising power which was nevertheless no direct threat to the West. It is perhaps indicative that, in the West, the only bestseller on a Japanese theme in the period between the First and Second World War was Arthur Whaley's translation of the *Tales of Genji*: the Western reading public preferred to reach back to an ancient Japan, pre-1905 and pre-Loti, averting its eyes from the modern descendants of Lady Murasaki.[36] Yet Japan had been on the Allied side in the First World War, successfully defeating the German forces in China. Farrère, a naval man and one who had popularised the image of a military Japan with his best-selling novel, no doubt felt that it was in the interest of the West not to forget about the unpredictable nation that, less than twenty years ago in 1924, had defeated the Russians so comprehensively. It was certainly the case that Japan was suffering from a lack of recognition and respect: the British had declined to renew the Anglo-Japanese Alliance in 1922, and at the Conference of Versailles, the Western powers had decided to veto the racial equality clause that the Japanese had put up for inclusion in the Covenant of the League of Nations.[37]

In the early 1930s, Japan began its conquest of China, and was immediately condemned for its actions. Farrère's 1937 book, *Forces spirituelles de l'Orient (Inde-Chine-Japon-Turque)*, attempts to analyse the Japanese invasion of China in a favourable light, pointing out the Japanese 'need' for raw materials to feed an expanding population, and the unfairness of the American and Australian bans on Japanese immigration which made it impossible for the Japanese to better their lives elsewhere.[38] The first of these, of course, is an argument for any coloniser: given what the European powers were doing in Africa and South-East Asia, Farrère's point would have been a reasonable one for his times. But the main thrust of his argument was based on a racialist claim, stemming perhaps from his thoughts in *La Bataille*. Having described the Chinese as a wise but super-annuated race in the section devoted to China ('Forces spirituelles de la Chine'), he starts 'Forces sprirituelles du Japon' by dramatically contrasting the Japanese with the Chinese: 'Les Chinois sont tellement loins de nous, par le cerveau, par les nerfs, par le coeur [...] le Japon, au cours des âges, a évolué à peu près comme nous [...] je ne suis pas sûr le moins du monde que le Japon, originellement, ait été une nation asiatique' (*Forces spirituelles de l'Orient*, p. 143). This surprising claim is one that Farrère will stick to until 1939, the hypothesis – derived from 'historical' facts of his choosing – that the Japanese are actually not from the Far East, but the Far West.[39] Although he had granted his character Felze a degree of understanding for China in *La Bataille*, Farrère himself had clearly never understood what he saw as China's passivity when faced by its Western – and now, Japanese – colonisers. The otherness of China afforded him a logical argument to support the Japanese against them. Japan, like the European nations, was an occidental country, and as such could be trusted to colonise and organise China, an oriental one:

J'affirme donc que les Japonais n'ont pas été, primitivement, des hommes jaunes aux pommettes saillantes, formalistes, traditionalistes [...] mais, au contraire, des hommes rouges ou bruns, vifs, entreprenants et souples. [...] Voilà des marins, ou je m'y connais mal. Voilà des soldats, ou je me trompe beaucoup. Résumons tout d'un mot: voilà des hommes. Et leur coeur est solidement enraciné dans leur poitrine. (*Forces spirituelles de l'Orient*, pp. 145–146)

Farrère's racialist (and navalist?) preference for the Japanese had turned into full-fledged support for the country in *Le grand drame de l'Asie*, published in 1939, only a few months after the outbreak of the Second World War. Farrère had accepted an invitation from the Japanese government to visit and to witness at first hand the state of affairs in the country. *L'Echo de Paris* commissioned him to write twenty or so articles about his trip: it was with all the trappings of the journalist, therefore, that Farrère set off for Japan in 1938. Accompanied by government representatives and received by the Franco-Japanese cultural institutions, Farrère spent time in Tokyo, Kyoto, Nara and Osaka, taking in touristic highlights (Nikko, which he already knew through Loti) and cultural exhibitions (*kabuki*, *nô*, *bunraku*); he also met with admirals, members of the cabinet (many of whom were against the war) and several academics who acted as interpreters. He was then taken to Japanese-occupied Korea and Manchuria, where he was welcomed by government officials as well as some French missionaries, whence he returned to Europe via Shanghai, Hong Kong and Saigon. Upon his return he discovered that *L'Echo de Paris* had gone bankrupt, so the text – after being published by a couple of magazines – came out in book form, chez Flammarion, in 1939.

The trip was Farrère's first to Japan since his three days in Nagasaki in 1899, and astonishingly, those three days are still his point of reference as he describes Japan in the 1930s. He needs a reference located in the past, because the first step in his apologia – for, true to the wishes of the Japanese government, Farrère reacted positively to what he saw on this trip – is that Japan, so brave and honourable in 1895 and 1905, has not changed: 'Le Japon a changé? Non, c'est le même. Eternel.'[40] Underneath the factory chimneys, all is still well and Japanese, 'les jardins...'. According to him, what he had valued about the Japanese and sought to depict in *La Bataille*, 'le courage et l'esprit de sacrifice', are still very much present. He then moves quickly towards the argument already essayed in *Forces spirituelles*, that the Japanese are a Western race, with the added twist this time that they are in fact particularly akin to the French: 'l'âme japonaise est intacte. [...] Et j'en suis heureux. Car cette âme-là était la soeur de l'âme française. [...] Toute l'histoire du peuple japonais semble être une répétition de l'histoire du peuple français. A telles enseignes que je me refuse, net, à admettre que le peuple japonais soit un peuple asiatique.'[41] Japan is a Far Western land, and Kobé is like Genoa or Marseille. Having thus aligned Japan on the side of the West again, Farrère goes on to make use of a number of the standard arguments, used by those who wished to legitimise European colonisation, in order to justify Japan's actions in Korea and China.

Farrère's first point is that Japan, lacking arable land, needs to look further afield in order to feed its people: and that what it has done, taking over land in Korea and China that was not being used, is completely justifiable: 'la Corée annexée depuis 1910, et surtout la Mandchourie, protégée depuis 1932, offrent au Japon des ressources minières considérables, *inexploitées antérieurement*'.[42] The fact – if it was indeed a fact – that the Japanese were exploiting previously *unused* land is important to Farrère's argument, as indeed it was for supporters of colonisation in both England and France. Farrère would have been appealing to the commonly held belief, traceable back either to Roman law or to the Bible,[43] that land should not be allowed to stand idle: there is moral merit in cultivating the soil, and the cultivator is entitled to its possession.[44] Three hundred years earlier John Locke, pondering the 'rights' of English settlers and agriculturalists with respect to the 'empty' tracts of Amerindian land in North America, had ruled that

> Whatsoever then [Man] removes out of the State that Nature hath provided, and left it in, he hath mixed his *Labour* with, and joyned to it something that is his own, and thereby makes it his *Property* [...] 'tis *Labour* indeed that *puts the difference of value* on every thing.[45]

Farrère was almost certainly not a student of Locke, but the notion that an energetic, colonising people might have some kind of right over the land of a less 'industrious' one was common currency in his day.[46] Such colonisation might even be considered a kindness to the indigenous peoples: Farrère described the Japanese activity in Manchuria as directly benefiting the Chinese people, as the produce also went into Chinese stomachs: 'il s'agit simplement de mettre en valeur telles ou telles richesses mondiales qui ne soit pas encore utilisées. Et ce, pour le plus grand bien de tout le monde.'[47]

As well as relying on such 'moral' colonialist arguments to do with cultivation and labour, Farrère also used direct comparisons with the West to justify the Japanese presence in Korea. Everything that the Japanese are doing, he points out, is mirrored by what the French and British are doing in other parts of the world: '[les Japonais] eurent l'intention, semble-t-il, de "protéger" l'empire coréen, à peu près comme la France protégeait dès lors la Tunisie, et l'Angleterre certains sultans et maharajahs des Indes. Mais la Corée n'était plus en état d'être protégée. [...] en 1910, le Japon, vainqueur des Russes, annexa net la Corée comme la France avait fait de Madagascar.'[48] Farrère is scrupulously careful to match the Japanese with the French (or British) action for action (he gives a matching instance for the protection, then the annexation of Korea). If it were not for the devastating effects of colonisation on Korea, Tunisia or Madagascar, it would almost be possible to call Farrère an egalitarian thinker, given his even-handed treatment of Japan as a colonial power. The Japanese had rightly accused the European powers of hypocrisy when they condemned Japan for its colonisation of China: they had demanded an equal right to invade other countries for profit, so to speak. Farrère certainly does Japan this justice. Considering the Japanese case within the Western colonial paradigm is, in historical context, an admirably enlightened attitude: it is important to note this, as it is too easy, with hindsight, to feel that Farrère was nothing more than a dupe of the Japanese public relations team that showed him around on his 1938 trip.

Ideologically, therefore, Farrère's championing of Japan was not entirely without its merits, given that it incorporated an attempt to consider Japan on a par with the European powers. On a more visceral level, however, his pro-Japanese attitude reveals him to be conventional at best, racist at worst: his view that the Japanese have 'cleaned up' Seoul and Peking, for instance, is that of a man with a deeply ingrained respect for law and order (perhaps inevitable in a former naval officer), and a tendency to approve unreservedly of progress. 'Séoul, jadis vaste village sans routes d'accès ni chemins, est devenue une capitale moderne fort architecturale, dont les anciens temples, pagodes et palais archaiques ont été respectés et restaurés d'ailleurs, mais dont les édifices récents, gares, usines, banques [...]

sont de matériaux robustes et de bel appareil.'[49] Not even the Japanese can beautify Mukden, however: 'Moukden est [...] une ville très chinoise, rudement assainie par les Japonais, mais demeurée fort laide et peu pittoresque' (p. 74). As for Peking, Farrère evades his narrative responsibility to discuss the Japanese possession of it by saying that it 'appartient à l'humanité. Ceux qui s'en trouvent momentanément les maîtres n'en sont, en stricte justice, que les gardiens' (pp. 86–87). The Japanese, of course, are model 'gardiens', leaving the historical monuments intact whilst cleaning up the unhygienic areas of the city: once more the 'protection' argument for colonisation is invoked, as it will increasingly be where China is concerned, given Farrère's conviction that the Chinese are unable to govern themselves.

Indeed Farrère's way of seeing Japan goes hand in hand with his vision of China, and the two countries define themselves against each other in his eyes. The Chinese, according to Farrère, are not a nation (p. 152): the fact that they have no sense of nationhood justifies foreign intervention. 'Il faut aux Chinois un maître *qui ne soit pas Chinois*' (p. 157). The Japanese, as we know, are not Asian: therefore their government of China is a good thing, a young Occidental people organising and rejuvenating an ancient, wise but weary people, a people whom, as we saw earlier, Farrère found very difficult to understand. He goes so far as to argue that the aim of the Japanese in China is not selfish: Japan wants nothing from China, 'sauf qu'elle soit en ordre, qu'elle sache bien se débarrasser de toute emprise étrangère et qu'elle autorise les étrangers, – les Japonais d'abord, il va sans dire, – à exploiter telles et telles richesses minières dont la Chine ne fait rien du tout pour l'instant et n'a d'ailleurs jamais fait grand' chose en aucun temps' (p. 101). We are back to the labour-brings-possession argument, but then Farrère reveals the weakness of his position by invoking capitalism of an extreme kind, which degenerates into pro-Japanese racism. 'La propriété foncière fut entamée profondément par la propriété commerciale. [...] en France, les occupations d'usines, [...] prouvèrent à l'évidence que charbonnier a cessé d'être le maître chez lui, dès que les gens qui ont froid estiment avoir besoin de charbon. Alors, au nom de quelle exception raciale interdirait-on au Japon, qui étouffe dans son archipel, [...] d'aller chercher hors ses frontières le fer, le charbon, le pétrole [...] d'autant d'avantage qu'ils représentent une élite intellectuelle et morale de l'humanité?' (p. 149). At this point it must be admitted that Farrère has lost control of his arguments: unsure of the outcome of his 'capitalist' theory, he falls back on the moral high ground, at least for him, of praising the Japanese and seeing them as an embattled and much put-upon race.

Le grand drame de l'Asie is dated 'Océan Pacifique, océan Indien, février–mars 1938': perhaps we should make some allowances for the swiftness of composition when examining the structure of his apologia. It concludes, however, with a clinching argument which justifies, in Farrère's eyes at least, all of Japan's excesses: Japan is fighting against communism. Japan may have invaded China, conquered Korea, but this is all in the interest of pushing back the Soviets: 'Si le Japon se bat aujourd'hui, et se bat en Chine, ce n'est pas contre la Chine [...] c'est contre le communisme. C'est pour l'ordre et pour la civilisation, contre l'esclavage et le revolver moscoutaire.'[50] An excuse which has continued to be useful to many a world affairs problem, this anti-communist stance is Farrère's unanswerable argument in favour of the Japanese. Since the time of the Russo-Japanese War, Japan has been valiantly struggling against her enormous neighbour: since it has turned communist, the struggle is an even more important one that eclipses all others in the vicinity. 'Il n'y a pas de conflit sino-japonais, il y a un conflit nippo-soviétique',[51] Farrère proclaims towards the end of his work, and goes on to hope that France, still bound by its old alliance with Russia, might contribute to world peace by seeing a way to developing friendly relations with Japan.

Farrère's non-fictional writings on Japan reveal him to have been a well-intentioned but limited observer of the political situation in the Far East, who scrupulously attempted to see Japan as the equal of the Western powers, but who was only able to do this by turning the Japanese into an 'Occidental' race superior to the rest of the Oriental world. His arguments for the 'sameness' of France and Japan are interesting in the context of the self–other relationships that we have been examining, and the result of a genuine desire to see Japan 'objectively'. Of course, any attempt at objectivity is limited by unconscious prejudices, and Farrère did not transcend those of his time and class: his concept of civilisation was completely European, and closely linked with his love of order and cleanliness, which made it easier for him to accept the Japanese invasion of China. In this he is entirely unlike Henri Michaux, who, although he too had his civilised prejudices, was fully conscious of them, and preferred to adopt the persona of the 'barbarian', not the civilised European. Farrère's novel on Japan is more supple an instrument where pro-

Japanese sentiment is concerned: freed from the national categories that restrict him in his essays, if not from the novelistic conventions discussed earlier, he succeeds in painting an idealistic but alternative portrait of Japan which led to its re-branding, so to speak, from being the land of mousmés to that of noble heroism and sacrifice. The combined effect of his novel and essays is that of a sincere attempt to portray Japan in good faith, to argue for 'the other side' of public opinion and to make judgments and predictions – however erroneous they may have turned out to be – from the observation of human motives and actions: in other words, the activity of a journalist.

Henri Michaux, *Un barbare en Asie*[52]

There was another francophone writer travelling in Japan in the 1930s: Henri Michaux. *Un barbare en Asie* (1933) is an account of Michaux's voyage through Asia in 1931, with sections entitled 'Un barbare en Inde', 'Un barbare en Chine', 'Un barbare au Japon', and so on. Michaux had already written one travelogue, *Ecuador*, in 1928. In this work he had derided the amateur traveller-writer, whose authoritative accounts of foreign countries and peoples were often based on the briefest of acquaintances, and received with far more respect than they were due: 'Les écrivains commencent à se dire de l'univers. Parfois il arrive que l'un d'eux se mette en voyage, pousse jusqu'à Hong-Kong, passe la nuit avec une Jaune. Puis il revient, on le regarde, on l'invite à parler. [...] Il connaît la Chine!'[53] At first sight, large parts of *Un barbare en Asie* appear to contain instances of precisely the kind of travel writing that Michaux had condemned five years earlier, dogmatic statements about the Asian countries that he visits from what seems to be a very obviously Western and personal point of view. Indeed, in places, *Un barbare en Asie* can appear to be a text 'qui ne parvient pas à sortir du discours hégémonique occidental sur les civilisations qui lui sont différentes'.[54] At other points in the text, however, these apparently dualist statements are subverted by certain rhetorical devices: this self-centred traveller is also a self-conscious one, and there is a complex and constantly developing relationship between him and the countries he visits that demands a more subtle explanatory model than the binary one of hegemony. His account of Japan is a particularly interesting instance, partly because his reaction to the country is so extreme. In what follows, I will examine the presentation of Japan in 'Un barbare au Japon', and attempt to show how, in spite of the apparently 'self-centred' viewpoint, Michaux's 'Japan' is the result of a journalistic vision that ultimately attains a high degree of objectivity.

Michaux himself was aware of the negative impressions that this work might give rise to in later years, and tried to counteract them in advance by writing a series of prefaces: a very brief one in 1945, then a much longer apologia, as well as a clarification of his methods and intentions, in 1967, which begins with the following words: 'il date, ce livre. [...] De ma naïveté, de mon ignorance, de mon illusion de démystifier, il date.' 'Un barbare au Japon', moreover, is distinguished by its own, separate preface, written in May 1984. This means that in the Gallimard edition of 1986, 'Un barbare au Japon' is fenced in by no fewer than three apologetic prefaces. It is also the only 'barbare' to contain several footnotes added retrospectively to the text, in each case adding something positive that has come to him in hindsight. Michaux was clearly most uneasy about the postwar reception of this 'barbare', and well he might be, for in it he seems to like nothing about Japan. The 1984 preface seeks to explain how this situation came about, whilst distancing the author in the present from his early text as much as possible:

> Je relis ce barbare-là avec gêne, avec stupéfaction par endroits. Un demi-siècle a passé et le portrait est méconnaissable.
>
> De ces fâcheuses impressions d'un voyageur déçu, reste peut-être par-ci par-là une notation 'historique' pour des lecteurs qui voudront retrouver quelque chose d'une de ces singulières périodes d'avant-guerre [...] Ce Japon d'aspect étriqué, méfiant et sur les dents est dépassé. (*Un barbare en Asie*, p. 196)

Michaux's uncharacteristically diplomatic preface to 'Un barbare au Japon' certainly prepares one for a very different experience from that to be derived from the other 'barbares'. 'Un barbare au Japon' is critical throughout of Japan, both of the people and of the country-side, showing an open dislike of everything the traveller comes across. 'Le Japon a un climat humide et traître. L'endroit du monde où il y a le plus de tuberculeux.' 'Les bambous japonais: de tristes épuisés, gris et sans chlorophylle, dont Ceylan ne voudrait pas pour roseaux.' 'Les hommes sont sans rayonnement, douloureux, ravagés et secs', 'des maisons grises, aux pièces vides et glacées, tracées et mesurées selon un ordre dur et intransigeant'. The unremittingly negative outlook makes this text unique within the book, as well as in the corpus of books on Japan that have been examined in this study so far.

The opinionated character of the traveller is in itself not new, nor is his preferred rhetorical device, the generalisation. Generalisations, usually formulated as aphoristic statements, proliferate in all of the 'barbares': 'Le Bengali naît chanoine'; 'L'Indien ne brûle pas les étapes'; 'Le chinois est artisan et artisan habile', 'L'Hindou apprécie la sagesse, la méditation'. These generalisations, once they have built up a certain momentum, have a complex effect on the credibility of the text. An aphorism, traditionally, is a form that claims authority, 'affirmations précises, tranchantes, péremptoires'.[55] However, aphorisms are also invitations to disagree and dispute:[56] being a statement of practical knowledge, derived from experience rather than logic, an aphorism can invite the reader to oppose it with something from his or her own experience. This is especially true when the aphorism, or a generalisation formulated as an aphorism, is spoken by a visitor about a foreign country: the writer's evident lack of contextual experience, as is the case for Michaux in Asia, can prompt the reader to doubt its veracity and reach for a counter-example.[57] Thus Michaux is making use of a double-edged tool which both encourages and discourages belief in order to talk about his travels. What is more, he weakens its impact as truth through overuse. The first ten pages of 'Un barbare en Inde', for instance, contain seventeen statements starting 'l'Hindou', 'l'Indien' or 'le Bengali', and their proliferation has the effect of undermining their collective credibility.[58]

Why does Michaux use, then sabotage, this device? It has been suggested that these aphorisms, which sound reassuringly authoritative, constitute a defence mechanism: the Western writer, by speaking in forms that denote knowledge, reassures himself in the face of the inconceivable and ungraspable difference of the other.[59] So, by using such an ill-advisedly authoritative form within a foreign context in which he is necessarily vulnerable to error, Michaux *dramatises* the malaise of the traveller-writer. When we witness the failure of the aphorism, we see that the writer's malaise was well founded: it becomes clear that he was never in a position to come to know India through formulating such generalisations, stemming as they do from his own epistemological and phenomenological framework. The failure of these knowledge-statements mirrors the failure of the traveller to attain knowledge of the other. By being provocatively but erroneously dogmatic, Michaux shows the self–other dynamic in action, and represents the other as the site of the failure of his rhetoric.

The road to distrust is paved with generalisations, therefore, in all the sections of *Un barbare en Asie*: through their very boldness they undermine the voice's bravado. On closer inspection, however, the reader will notice that the generalisations in 'Un barbare au Japon' are slightly different in form from those of the earlier 'barbares'. These statements very rarely start with 'le Japonais' as the subject, whereas in 'Un barbare en Chine' or 'Un barbare en Inde', they are almost always simple sentences with 'le Chinois' or 'l'Hindou' (or 'l'Indien', or 'le Bengali') as the subject. By contrast, the subjects in 'Un barbare au Japon' are common nouns, mostly in the plural: 'les hommes', 'les femmes', 'des rues de villes d'eaux'. When the proper noun is used, it is more likely to be 'le Japon' or 'au Japon' than 'le Japonais'. These differences have a striking effect, especially after a reading of the other 'barbares': the statements about Japan sound more *realistic*. Statements starting with 'des femmes' or 'des hommes' are more believable than ones that begin 'l'Indien' or 'le Japonais', because the generalisation that follows applies to a smaller, and less abstractly defined, group of people. Similarly, starting a sentence with 'au Japon' makes what follows much more realistic-sounding than generalisations with 'le Japonais' as subject, because the range of possibilities covered by 'au Japon' is less specifically human, and therefore more credible, than that of the possible predicates of 'le Japonais'. It would seem that using common nouns or 'au Japon' as the subject of the generalisations has the effect of breaking down the abstract entity of 'le Japonais' into smaller, more concrete units, making the tone less jocular, and more believable. The fact that the predicates are usually pejorative may also add to the mood of realism (compare, say, 'l'Indien ne court jamais', a completely absurd – and amusing – statement, with 'des villes égales, sans expression, terriblement klaxonnantes'). There are several possible reasons for this subtle change of form. It may be that Michaux is avoiding the ultimate generalising subject, 'le Japonais', because he is being so negative about Japan, and therefore shrinks from implicating the whole of the Japanese population in his predicates. But this would presume that he believes in the efficacy of his earlier generalisations, about the Chinese or the Indian: and as I hope to have shown above, his generalisations are self-defeating. It is more likely that he has chosen to avoid 'le Japonais' precisely in order to avoid triggering the self-ironising mechanism described above, because in this 'barbare' he actually wants his observations to be taken seriously. The presence of the retrospectively introduced footnotes seems also to suggest that the statements they qualify were, originally, to be read without a smile: if the older Michaux considered them to be in need of clarification and explanation, the younger Michaux can clearly not have been relying on their narrative devices to alert the reader to their exaggeration or falseness.

If Michaux feels so differently about Japan, so much so that he changes the style of his generalisations to make them sound more credible, his reasons are not difficult to fathom: Japan, out of all the Asian countries he has travelled through, is the only nation that is preparing for war. Everything that Farrère found attractive about Japan in the 1930s repulses Michaux: the poet sees order as a lack of freedom ('peuple prisonnier de son île, [...] de sa police, de sa discipline'), the organisation as humourless efficiency ('le plus actif, le moins bavard, le plus efficient du monde, le plus maître de soi', p. 199), and relates their love of hygiene directly to their desire for war (Le Japon a la manie de nettoyer. Or, un lavage, comme une guerre, a quelque chose de puéril, parce qu'il faut recommencer après quelque temps', p. 204). It is especially interesting to juxtapose the contrasting reactions of Farrère and Michaux to this last 'Japanese' characteristic, cleanliness: Farrère, of course, approved of Japan for its hygiene ('un peuple propre'), and described the Chinese city of Mukden with a naval officer's satisfaction as having been 'rudement assainie' by the Japanese. There are as yet no connotations, at this point in history, of 'ethnic cleansing' in this context: in spite of their brutal conquest of Korea and China, the Japanese did not go quite as far as a systematic destruction of a people, although they required the people in their colonies to learn Japanese and become secondary Japanese citizens. However, the instinctive connection made by both Michaux and Farrère between the notions of cleanliness (or tidiness) and conquest is proof of their shared inheritance, that of a deeply colonialist Europe which justified its actions by extolling the merits of the order and cleanliness that European powers imposed on their colonies.

The warmongering atmosphere of Japan overshadows everything for Michaux in 'Un barbare au Japon'. He is merciless, for instance, with the pretty, *japoniste* image of the *mousmé* and her dress, and links it to the politics of the time:

[les femmes ont] un rire fou et superficiel, où l'oeil disparaît comme cousu, un habillement de bossue, une coiffure tarabiscotée (la coiffure de geisha), plein de caculs, de travail, de symbolisme, et d'un ensemble benêt. Une cuirasse comprimant et aplatissant la poitrine, un coussin dans le dos, fardée et poudrée, elle consitue la création malheureuse et typique de ce peuple d'esthètes et de sergents qui n'a rien pu laisser dans son élan naturel. (p. 198)

No one, not even Loti, had described the *obi* – the sash of heavy silk that belts the kimono and is tied into various attractive shapes in the back – as something reminiscent of attire for war, 'une cuirasse'. Michaux is well aware of the stereotype that he is destroying here. Both the *japoniste* stereotype and favourable military image are damned within the space of two sentences: the image of the *obi* is damaged by its comparison to armour while any aesthetically pleasing view of military splendour is dismissed by a clever and effective reference to an officer of low rank, through the juxtaposition of 'esthètes' and 'sergents'. His ill-disposedness extends to Japanese art, that other sacred cow of *japonistes* and well-informed Japan-lovers: his bad-tempered description of *kabuki*, *nô* and *bunraku* (pp. 200– 203) judges them by realist standards, flamboyantly rejecting the explanation that artifice is the point of much of this theatre.[60] Michaux, of course, has the alibi of his 'barbarism' as an excuse for failing to 'understand' such sophisticated art forms, but here again the political leitmotiv is evident: 'Théâtre de rogne, avec Voix du Peuple, Voix de Rappels à l'Ordre et de Remontrances, mais sans grandeur' (p. 201). Japan is the clear exception to Michaux's claim that his vision of Asia in this work was almost entirely apolitical.[61] It is in fact not quite true that Michaux's political sense lay dormant in his other 'barbares': his account of China, for instance, is coloured by his view of it as the peace-loving victim of Japanese and European aggression, which made him describe 'la langue chinoise parlée', for instance, in the following idealised terms in 'Un barbare en Chine': 'la langue chinoise, elle, n'a pas été faite comme les autres, forcée par un syntaxe bousculante et ordonnatrice. Les mots n'en ont pas été construits durement, avec autorité, méthode, redondance, par l'agglomération de retentissantes syllabes, ni par voie d'étymologie'. Tellingly, Michaux's characterisation of Chinese is mostly negative, that is to say that he tells us only what it is not: in other words, his main intention is not so much to describe Chinese as to condemn non-Chinese languages for their repressive structure. 'Comparée à cette langue, les autres sont pédantes, affligées de mille ridicules, d'une cocasserie monotone à faire pouffer, des langues de militaires. Voilà ce qu'elles sont' (p. 153). Putting aside the truth value of the statement, the attraction of the Chinese language for Michaux is obvious: it is peace-loving, unlike everything in Japan.

The militarism of Japan, which makes it so hateful to Michaux, is fundamentally linked to its Westernisation: it is no coincidence that Japan makes him think of Europe, as we see at the end of the 'barbare'. Following an anecdote about a Japanese leave-taking at a station platform, Michaux suddenly offers the reader a metatextual paragraph concerning the validity of his whole project, that of examining the 'mentalité de certains peuples' in his travels. He then enumerates the various features of a people – their dress, their pornography, their theatre – that reveal their character, applying them briefly to the various nationalities that he has encountered in Asia, and concludes thus:

> C'est la façon, le style et non les faits qui comptent. Un peuple, dont on ne sait rien ou qui a tout volé aux autres, idées, religion, institutions, a en propre ses *gestes*, son *accent*, sa *physionomie...* ses *réflexes* qui le trahissent.
>
> Et chaque homme a sa figure qui le juge et, en même temps juge sa race, sa famille et sa religion, son époque.
>
> Y aura-t-il encore une guerre? Regardez-vous, Européens, regardez-vous.
>
> Rien n'est paisible dans votre expression.
>
> Tout y est lutte, désir, avidité.
>
> Même la paix, vous la voulez violemment. (pp. 213–14)

Europe will go to war: so will the Westernised Japan. The sudden, if not unexpected, move back to Europe at the end of 'un barbare au Japon' creates a strong sense that the developed West is at the source of all conflict, exemplified so starkly by Japan. Indeed Michaux's vision of Japan is conceived entirely within the context of its Westernisation: like Europe it is aggressive, having 'conquis, modernisé, battu les records' (p. 199), and its ambition and rapid industrialisation make it 'visiblement destinée à notre mal et à notre civilisation' (p. 200). *Our* civilisation, not civilisation *tout court*: unlike Farrère, Michaux is able to conceive of a civilisation that is not European, and much prefers the non-aggressive, non-European version. 'Un barbare au Japon' is a historically limited vision of Japan, but its political predictions turned out to be accurate, as did the prediction that Japan would continue to become Westernised. In fact the 1984 preface, apologetic and distancing though it may be overall, concludes by emphasising the (now benevolent) similarities between Europe and Japan: 'Il est clair à présent qu'à l'autre bout de la planète, l'Europe a trouvé un voisin. Ses multiples recherches, l'actualité des ses oeuvres, sa curiosité sans borne en tant de domaines de science et d'art – et les plus nouveaux –, où on s'entre-regarde, émules ou admirateurs, suscitent une étrange connivance qui augmente.' There are some slightly worrying expressions in this description: a 'curiosité sans borne' is not necessarily a laudable trait, and 'une étrange connivance' is particularly disturbing. Why 'connivance', and why is it 'étrange'? At the very least the epithet seems to suggest the need for watchfulness, a potential source of worry in both Japan and Europe that does not exist in the other countries of his acquaintance.

Anti-war and anti-European, Michaux the 'barbarian' asserts his independence from contemporary European civilisation as he wanders around Asia. He is egocentric but not Eurocentric, at least not in relation to a colonising and warmongering Europe. It is as a barbarian that he escapes from the dualist discourse of the self and other, where self and other denote opposing civilisations: by refusing, that is, to belong to any civilisation. If there is a gamut of possible positions vis-à-vis the other, with complete allegiance to one's own culture at one end and a total acceptance of the other's culture at the other end, the author of *Un barbare en Asie* refuses both poles, taking refuge in his individuality, out of tune both with Europe and (necessarily) with the Asia that is foreign to him. This is the position, I believe, that Michaux describes as being ideal for the observation of foreign cultures, 'le passant aux yeux naifs'; a barbarian, someone who is as far removed as possible not only from the foreign civilisation but from his own.

Michaux's barbarian may not be ideal journalist material, but the reader of his text ends up being in an excellent position to attain a degree of objectivity, because she is taken through the *process* of his seeing: his bold but erroneous generalisations, designed to help him through the uncomfortable realisation of his ignorance, followed by a delight in and acceptance of the other in China and India, or its violent rejection, in Japan. The barbarian may thus be thought of as a *recorder* – a tool for the reader, who through him can accede to something approximating an objective, journalistic view. The older Michaux says as much with regard to his young self's text, in the first retrospective footnote to 'un barbare au Japon': 'En 1931, ce n'était que combats et, dans les rues, défilés, menaces, commandements. Tout respirait l'irrespirable guerre. Cet état, que peut-être de jeunes Japonais ont peine à se représenter, me paraissait le Japon éternel, intraitable, à quoi il fallait, à quoi je devais tout rapporter.' Michaux here expresses his wish to be of some use to a postwar Japanese generation that will not have breathed the unbreathable air of war. The responsibility of recording – and reporting – a historical reality is that of the journalist, and to gather that 'raw' material Michaux chose as raw a persona as possible, that of the barbarian.

The journalist, as defined in the introduction to this chapter, is sincerely and responsibly committed to reporting the truth, although this truth will always be a limited one. Does this mean that she does not belong in our gallery of travellers and their visions, given that this book is concerned with the creation of *images* of Japan, and not with their truth value? No, because any attempt to represent another culture, even with the most sincere intention of telling the 'truth' about it, necessitates negotiation with contemporary stereotypes and results in the creation of images.[62] The fact that 'real' journalists, such as Charles Pettit or René Pinon, were just as prone to image-making is clear from their writings quoted above. The journalist, even more than the novelist or the poet, is conscious of providing copy for a particular audience, and cannot write in a vacuum. In the period in question, there was a dominant and powerful stereotype – that of the Yellow Peril – that could not be ignored by anyone who wished to write about contemporary Japan: a writer could take refuge from it in the relative 'past' of *japonisme*, but otherwise it was necessary to respond to it, either by agreeing (as Pettit, Driant, and others did) or by providing a counter-image (France's 'le peril blanc'). This is why the journalist is an important member of our troupe of travellers, and the literary journalism that has been examined in this chapter shows how its authors contributed to the creation of an anti-*japoniste*, military image of Japan, a creation inspired not by literary or aesthetic issues or precedents but by political events.

The journalistic vision produces images, but they are nonetheless the result of a different 'way of seeing' from that of, say, Proust or Loti. This is precisely because the intention to tell the truth has a direct impact on the 'way of seeing' involved. In *Sur la pierre blanche*, the desire for objectivity leads Anatole France to adopt a highly abstract style, leading to a correspondingly schematic image of the other; in Michaux, it leads to the assumption of the point of view of a 'barbarian' as being the one furthest removed from the 'partial' vision of a civilised European. In Farrère's *La Bataille*, we have a paradoxical case of a sincere documentary desire embedded within a conventional novelistic framework, and in his political essays a genuine attempt to understand the other which ends in a radical gesture of incorporation, that of occidentalising Japan. In each case the desire to tell the truth dictates the choice of rhetorical devices that go to constitute an objective style of narration, which in turn results in a particular image, and a particular set of conventions to create that image, of Japan. These 'journalists' cannot escape the laws of their narrative tools any more than the novelist or poet can, but at least they can choose the tools that are specifically suited to their conception of the 'truth'.

CHAPTER THREE

Walking towards Japan:
Paul Claudel's *co-naissance* of the East

Paul Claudel's acquaintance with Japan spans the periods covered in the two preceding chapters. Claudel first set foot in Japan in 1898, on a brief visit during his posting to China. He had a further, longer opportunity to deepen his knowledge of Japan during his time as French ambassador there, a post he held from September 1921 to February 1927. Claudel's acquaintance with Japan thus ranges over a thirty-year period, from the age of the *japonaiserie* to that of the Yellow Peril: furthermore, it is intricately interwoven with his religious and aesthetic development. Aesthetic, because his encounter with Japanese art and poetry had a profound influence on his literary output; religious, because in Japan he achieved a certain degree of tolerance and understanding for non-Christian religions that he had failed to reach in the other Asian countries he had visited.[1] In addition to these personal aspects of his relationship with Japan, he was also, of course, required to deal with the country in his capacity as a professional diplomat.[2] It is therefore no wonder that Claudel's vision of Japan is a rich and complex one that comes to us in a variety of genres, ranging from his official reports to the Ministry of Foreign Affairs to the prose, dialogues and poetry collected in *L'Oiseau noir dans le soleil levant*. The diversity and quantity of his writings on Japan, as well as the unusual range of his period of interest, makes him a unique and invaluable figure in our gallery of traveller-writers, deserving – indeed, demanding – a complete chapter to himself.

There will therefore be only one writer in this chapter: but he is one who offers, as mentioned above, a variety of 'ways of seeing' Japan in his texts. Amidst the diversity, however, there is a unifying gesture that characterises their author as a specific type of traveller. This gesture is the trope of *walking*. Walking is the act around which Claudel often structures his travel texts on Japan, although the kinds of walking may vary greatly, from aimless wandering to purposeful plodding. The importance of this activity for Claudel has its basis in fact: a great poet, Claudel was also a great walker,[3] and he frequently linked the act of walking to that of poetry.[4] Within our typology of travellers, therefore, Claudel will be classified as the *walker*, and his way of seeing will be examined as a way of getting to know the other through walking. A lot of walking – of different kinds – goes on in all of the works to be examined in this chapter, and we will see how the activity helps to structure an attitude towards the other that is both refreshingly experiential and humbly temporary.

Although Claudel's many postings abroad had brought him into contact with a number of different countries and cultures, it is generally acknowledged that the Far East, and in particular Japan, was a 'special' case for him, as is evident from the long and impressive list of his 'Japanese' works.[5] *Connaissance de l'Est*, first published in 1900 and written mainly about China, already contained some poems inspired by his brief visit to Japan in June 1898. His years as ambassador in Japan produced, amongst other things, the essays that were later collected in *L'Oiseau noir dans le soleil levant*, as well as *Le Soulier de Satin* and *Cent Phrases pour éventails*. In this chapter, however, I will be focusing on those of his works with specific thematic links to Japan, written between the time of his first encounter with the country in 1898 and his departure from it in 1927. This means that I will not deal, for instance, with *Le Soulier de Satin*, because it is not a work that takes Japan or things Japanese as its subject. The works that we will be examining are *Connaisssance de l'Est*, *L'Oiseau noir dans le soleil levant*, 'La Muraille intérieure de Tokyo' and *Cent Phrases pour éventails*, through which I will be attempting to trace a trajectory of Claudel's developing vision of Japan.

Co-*naissance* and walking

Claudel passed the 'concours' of the Ministry of Foreign Affairs in 1900: China was his first lengthy posting, from 1895 to 1905, during which he was moved between Shanghai, Han-k'éou and Fou-Tcheou. His first visit to Japan occurred during this period, in June 1898. At that time he had already been initiated, by his sister Camille, into *japonisme* and, imbued with her 'admiration sans bornes' for all things Japanese, he appears to have enjoyed his short stay there to the full. True to his time and his sister's enthusiasms, he spent some time in shops selling recognisably *japoniste* wares: 'Dans la rue de

Nihonbashi, à côté des marchands de livres et de lanternes, de broderies et de bronzes, on vend des sites au détail, et je marchande dans mon esprit, studieux badaud du fantastique étalage [...] je me vautre parmi les liasses d'estampes japonaises'.[6] He did not restrict his time to Tokyo, however: he also travelled to Nikko, Nagasaki, Kobe, Yokohama, Hakone, Atami, Kyoto and Shizuoka. The first works by Claudel that have Japan, or things Japanese, as their theme are based on his experiences during this trip, and are to be found towards the end of *Connaissance de l'Est*.

Connaissance de l'Est is a collection of 61 prose poems, inspired by various aspects of the Chinese and Japanese cities and countryside visited by Claudel: titles such as 'Pagode', 'Ville la nuit', 'Vers la Montagne', and 'Halte sur le canal' seem to suggest a degree of mimetic intent. Yet a number of critics would argue that these prose poems are not truly about Japan (or China) at all. It is certainly the case that the poems do not appear to be straightforwardly descriptive of the countries in question:[7] they are dense, lyrical explorations of the poet's *experience* of China and Japan. Some critics have focused on the autobiographical element of *Connaissance de l'Est* as its defining characteristic: 'en nous parlant d'arbres, de temples et de rizières, il ne cesse de nous parler de lui-même'.[8] Even if they are not purely autobiographical, it is possible to see how the vision of the East in these poems is one which places Claudel's 'self' firmly at its centre. Bernard Howells interprets the centredness of the poetic vision as an ideological position:

> *Connaissance de l'Est* [...] is Claudel's attempt to extend the network of analogical relationships and reduce the chaotic 'spectacle' of the East to the homogeneity implied by aesthetic 'understanding'. He was adopting what he described as the typical posture of the Western artist in the face of nature and fighting the dispersal of his personality in impressions.[9]

This interpretation presents the poems of *Connaissance de l'Est* as personal readings of the East by a Western subject, who imposes coherence on the raw materials of experience and organises them around the perceiving 'je'. It is an attitude arguably characteristic of a young and intelligent man of Claudel's personality.[10] Such attempts by a Western writer to explain Chinese customs or Japanese art by 're-unifying' them around himself might be said to constitute an Orientalist attitude to the other, a way of appropriating a foreign culture which ignores its reality. Thus Henri Bouiller compares Claudel unfavourably with Victor Segalen in their respective treatments of China as a literary subject, and claims that Claudel reduced China 'à son univers personnel'.[11]

Another reason why a critic might wish to read these poems as Claudel's personal 'reorganisations' of the East is that in this period Claudel was much influenced by Mallarmé's teachings on the nature of understanding. Understanding, for Mallarmé the Symbolist, was the placing of a perceived object within a system of analogies: things make sense when positioned within a coherent system of the poet's own making. Claudel was certainly well acquainted with this method of 'understanding' the world, and his own theory of knowledge as 'co-naissance', elaborated in *Art poétique*, could be interpreted as a complement to that of Mallarmé. In this work Claudel, rewriting 'connaissance' as 'co-naissance', suggests that 'knowing' is a kind of *rebirth* for the knower into a world which contains the new object of knowledge. If that world is the poet's own system of analogical relationships, as Howells suggests, it is possible to see how *Connaissance de l'Est* could look like an exercise in 'reading' the East from a self-centred, 'Western' point of view.

But the theory of 'co-naissance' seems to suggest something more dramatic than a mere *extension* of 'the network of analogical relationships' in order to 'reduce the chaotic "spectacle" of the East to the homogeneity implied by aesthetic "understanding"'. Birth, even rebirth, is a major event. Describing the effect of coming to know something as a 'rebirth' suggests that the new knowledge is all-transforming, something that precisely fails to fit into former systems of the self. The style of the prose poems of *Connaissance de l'Est* is one that suggests dramatic change: nervous, joyous and above all restless, it is a far cry from the smugly appropriating attitude of the self-confirming analogist. Certainly the poems show a 'will to power' at work, the attempts of a young and idealistic man to dominate and to take charge of what he sees, but these attempts, importantly, *fail*. The result for the poet is a restless and dynamic relationship with the East which is the very opposite of a complacent and dominating Orientalism. Moreover, the poems were written during a difficult and changeful time for Claudel: in 1900 he had sought out – and been rejected by – the monastic community of Ligugé, and in 1901 he met Rose Vetch, 'Ysé' of *Partage de midi*, with whom he was to have a tempestuous affair.[12] *Connaissance de l'Est* is therefore perhaps best read as the record of a dynamic and restless traveller, travelling through geo-graphical space as through his own life. As such, the trope of *walking* is an ideal lens through which to read these poems. Of the various kinds of walking that Claudel puts into practice in his various travel writings, *Connaissance de l'Est* contains instances of the purposeful, determined kind that is directly related to his active desire for knowledge. Many of these poems involve instances of actual walking, but walking is also a powerful metaphor for a certain kind of mental activity. In what follows, I suggest that Claudel adopts the stance of the walker as an ideal, if temporary, position vis-à-vis a foreign country, in that it is a way of measuring (in steps) and coming to know (*co-naître* with) the other, but one which can never lead to perfect knowledge, for the simple reason that the walker always walks on. It is an appropriate activity for a person who would like to domin-ate, but who is also keenly aware that he will never completely succeed.

Connaissance de l'Est contains at least eight poems set in Japan.[13] Most of the poems involve walking of some form or another: when they do not, they are conspicuously immobile ('Le Sédentaire'). 'L'Arche d'or dans la forêt' is an account of a walk through the picturesque grounds of Nikko, situated half-way up a mountain not far from Tokyo. The description is incorporated into the narrative of his walk:

> *j'ai suivi* les voies énormes que barre un torii écarlate; [...] *j'ai gravi* les escaliers; *j'ai*, mêlé aux pèlerins, *franchi* je ne sais quoi d'opulent et d'ouvert, porte au milieu de la clôture comme d'un rêve [...] *j'ai, pieds nus, pénétré* au coeur de l'or intérieur. (my italics)[14]

The reader thus discovers Nikko at the same time as the walker: if we apply the theory of co-naissance to this reading experience, the reader might be said to be *born into* knowledge through encounter, with the various parts of Nikko visited by the poet. 'Ça et là' is also based on a walk, 'dans la rue de Nihonbashi', in which the narrator describes himself as 'un studieux badaud du fantastique étalage'. His commentary on the artwork he finds on sale there turns into a brief aesthetic analysis: 'l'artiste européen copie la nature selon le senti-ment qu'il en a, le Japonais l'imite selon les moyens qu'il lui emprunte; l'un s'exprime et l'autre l'exprime; l'un ouvrage, l'autre mime'.[15] As a result, this poem is sometimes quoted as containing Claudel's con-sidered views on the differences between European and Japanese art, but this is to mistake a happy formulation made 'on the go' for historically accurate truth. It is vital to read the statements made about Japanese culture in these poems, be they about art or Buddhism, as part of the walking experience: they are a traveller's amateur observations during a brief trip to Tokyo, and no more. Otherwise we would have to accuse Claudel of making poorly informed generalisations about ten centuries of Japanese art based on a small sample of *ukiyo-e* prints in Nihonbashi. These statements are all part of his walk of discovery through Japanese art and Tokyo, instances of his knowledge-through-encounter – his *co-naissance* of the many things he sees and witnesses during his walk. As with the visit to Nikko, we the readers discover things with him, in the act of his discovering them: they represent dynamic encounters with otherness, resulting in 'knowledge' that is at times inaccurate but always unfolding.

Walking through Japanese nature, rather than culture, was also one of Claudel's favourite occupations. 'Le Pin', for instance, is about the pine trees he meets along the famous Tokaido road: 'L'Arche d'or dans la forêt' is almost as much about the 'forêt de cryptomères' as about the shrine of Nikko itself.[16] The encounter of the thinking man with nature was an integral part of theories of walking as conceived by earlier walkers in the French canon. Walking has been associated with mental activity since Aristotle and the Peripatetics, but in the modern age it was Rousseau who, claiming that he needed to walk in order to think,[17] first celebrated the experience in some detail in the IVe Livre of *Les Confessions*.[18] Walking becomes one of the many ways in which the self interacts with the world, with the other. Rousseau describes his walks – walks without purpose – as a paradoxical relationship in which the self dominates nature, yet desires to become part of it:

> Je dispose en maître de la nature entière; mon coeur errant d'objet en objet s'unit, s'identifie à ceux qui le flattent, s'entoure d'images charmantes, s'enivre de sentiments délicieux.[19]

In the first instance, nature is at the walker's disposal. Seeing is the first step in his exertion of mastery, stage one in what Sartre calls the 'projet "ontologique d'appropriation" '.[20] The walker can extend his domain by the physical act of walking in and amongst the viewed objects, surrounding himself with the 'images charmantes' that nature has to offer. Another aspect of walking that is conducive to mastery is the possibility of measuring, in steps, the ground covered: 'le promeneur s'approprie le paysage par le martèlement plus plébéien de deux pieds qui mesurent la terre'.[21] Thus it is through sight, touch and intellect that the walker masters his environment.[22] But at the same time, this walker desires to be at one with the objects he sees: 'mon coeur errant d'objet en objet *s'unit, s'identifie à* ceux qui le flattent'. Even when he is not in total communion with the other, the subject enjoys nature in a way that encourages loss of self, surrounding himself with it ('*s'entoure* d'images charmantes'), then becoming intoxicated ('*s'enivre* de sentiments délicieux'). For Rousseau, walking without purpose in nature is the most effective way in which to commune with it, to forget the self–other boundary that he is so aware of vis-à-vis other human beings.[23] He does not fear this communion, nor the subsequent loss of self: indeed the possibility of simultaneously mastering and losing himself in nature, of being both subject and object, appears to be one of the main attractions of walking for him.

In Claudel's 'Le Promeneur', one of the poems from *Connaissance de l'Est* that is set in Japan, the relationship between nature and the poet is much more problematic. The poem shows Claudel engaged on a walk which satisfies the Rousseauist criterion in that it is both 'sans but et sans profit':[24] in other respects, however, Claudel's walker is quite a different species from Rousseau's, or indeed from many a nature walker since, from Chateaubriand through to Loti.[25] Unlike the idly meandering *promeneur*, Claudel starts off as a determined and vigorous walker: 'la main armée d'un bâton tortueux, tel que le dieu Bishamon' (Bishamon is the Shinto god of war). Claudel's discovery of his surroundings – unlike Rousseau's butterfly-like heart, which 'errant d'objet en objet s'unit, s'identifie à ceux qui le flattent' – is that of a conqueror, compared at one point to 'l'entrée d'Alexandre à Jérusalem'.

The conquering poet, however, is an isolated one: he does not fit readily into the human or vegetable landscape. To the 'groupe naïf de paysannes rougeaudes' that he walks past, he is a 'passant inexplicable'. He seems to glory in this solitary independence, scorning 'la piste tracée par le pas ordinaire', but he is just as ill at ease with nature as with human beings:

> *gêné* par la confidence qu'il y a pour faire à la mousse, au coeur de ces bois, une noire feuille de camélia par la chute d'un pleur inentendu, soudain, *maladroit* chevreuil, je fuis, et par la solitude végétale, *je guette, suspendu sur un pied*, l'écho. (my italics)

The otherness of nature embarrasses him, and it is only when he assumes the position of a watchful outsider – 'je guette, suspendu sur un pied' – that he is able to admire and analyse its beauties: 'Que le chant de ce petit oiseau me paraît frais et risible! et que le cri là-bas de ces grolles m'agrée!' He then comes to realise that in nature every creature is meaningfully related to the others, in a harmonious system reminiscent of the Symbolist system of analogies:

> Chaque arbre a sa personnalité, chaque bestiole son rôle, chaque voix sa place dans la symphonie; comme on dit que l'on *comprend* la musique, je comprends la nature, comme un récit bien détaillé qui ne serait fait que de noms propres: au fur de la marche et du jour, je m'avance parmi le développement de la doctrine.

Claudel's walker, unlike Rousseau's, is propelled by a desire to *know*: his vision is governed by a configuration of his aesthetic and cognitive preoccupations. Thus the Mallarméan theory of understanding, in which meanings are created within a coherent system of analogies, underlies the poet's first step towards understanding the nature he is walking through: 'jadis, j'ai découvert avec délice que toutes les choses existent dans un certain accord'. The poet becomes all-important in this system, because he is the primary perceiver – and reader – of the analogies: 'cette secrète parenté par qui la noirceur de ce pin épouse là-bas la claire verdure de ces érables, c'est mon regard seul qui l'avère'. In a Christian context, such a view of nature as a readable system has a precedent in the psalmist's stance, what Albert Beguin describes as a 'medieval' view of nature as allegory.[26] In 'Le Promeneur', nature is found to be divinely, harmoniously ordered, even in the exotic East. Unlike some of his predecessors in foreign climes, Claudel here concentrates on the harmony of nature, rather than on its exuberant difference: there is no list of exotic plant names, no excitement over the profusion of unknown flowers. In the East as in the West, Nature is 'in order', and as such it is to be praised.

Thus the impact of perceiving relationships in nature, although related to the Mallarméan method, is given a distinctly Christian context in 'Le Promeneur': the knowledge does not come solely from the poet, but is a composite creation of God's power, the poet's perception and nature's immanence. The poet is reborn *with* the knowledge of the relationship, and thus helps to recreate it, but it is a re-cognition, and a blessing:

> c'est mon regard seul qui l'avère, et, restituant le dessin antérieur,
> ma visite, je la nomme une revision. Je suis l'Inspecteur de la
> Création, le Vérificateur de la chose présente: la solidité de ce
> monde est la matière de ma béatitude!

There is a second realisation contained in these lines which distinguishes Claudel's position even more clearly from a Symbolist one: that of 'la solidité de ce monde'. The birds and flowers that constitute nature are not symbols of a hidden meaning, at least not of a human meaning, but things in themselves, things that are simply 'there':

> Aux heures vulgaires nous nous servons des choses pour un usage,
> en oubliant ceci de pur, qu'elles soient; mais quand, après un long
> travail, au travers des branches et des ronces, à Midi, pénétrant
> historiquement au sein de la clairière, je pose ma main sur la croupe
> brûlante du lourd rocher, l'entrée d'Alexandre à Jérusalem est
> comparable à l'énormité de ma constatation.

The walker has come to this realisation 'après un long travail', not just of his feet but of his mind, and has arrived at a literal and metaphorical 'clearing' (or clarification). Alexander conquered territory, but Claudel has conquered a difficult knowledge, that of the otherness – the 'there-ness' – of nature.[27] It is not an 'existential' vision of nature in its absurdity, but that of nature as a harmonious system that exists independently of human meanings, answerable only to God's mysterious schemes.

The final two paragraphs of the poem show the poet walking on in thought, wondering about his own species in the light of his discoveries:

> Et je marche, je marche, je marche! Chacun renferme en soi le
> principe autonome de son déplacement par quoi l'homme se rend
> vers sa nourriture et son travail. Pour moi, le mouvement égal de
> mes jambes me sert à mesurer la force de plus subtils appels.
> L'attrait de toutes choses, je le ressens dans le silence de mon âme.
>   Je comprends l'harmonie du monde; quand en surprendrai-je la
> mélodie?

These are difficult lines, but it seems to me that at this point Claudel links the rhythm of walking to that of poetry. Every man has his own walking rhythm, 'le principe autonome de son déplacement', which leads him to his most basic and important needs: Claudel's walking rhythm 'sert à mesurer la force de plus subtils appels'. 'Mesurer' is what walking and poetry share, and the rhythms of

Claudel's poetry are responses to 'l'attrait de toutes choses' which he listens to 'dans le silence de mon âme'. This is an uncharacteristically passive position for Claudel, a state of receptiveness which brings to mind analogous states described by other writers, such as Proust's 'ce "nous" qui serait sans contenu', or Keats' 'thoroughfare for all thoughts'.[28] In each case, the writer empties or silences himself in order to hear other people, other things, the better to reproduce their thoughts or sounds in his work. But Claudel's attitude seems to be slightly but crucially different from Proust's or Keats' 'receptive' states: it is not so much a self-less emptiness as the watchfulness of a silent 'je', a vigil in motion. For Claudel continues to walk, even as he listens in silence: 'et je marche, je marche, je marche!' If a walker is a conqueror, walking becomes a dominating activity: but if, on the other hand, he is silent and observant, walking becomes an activity distinguished by its openness to the other. This is because such a walker actively seeks out encounters, and offers himself to them. This is the attitude of the poet, as we shall see, in *Cent Phrases pour éventails*: in 'Le Promeneur', Claudel's walker seems to arrive at this kind of walking only at the end of the poem.

   The poet thus attains a receptive state of mind, through walking: 'pour moi, le mouvement égal de mes jambes me sert à mesurer la force de plus subtils appels. L'attrait de toutes choses, je le ressens dans le silence de mon âme.' But what is he waiting for? Words such as 'mesurer' and 'appels' give us a clue, as well as the fact that he is a poet: he appears to be listening for the music, the rhythm of the world. The poet's internal rhythm – 'le principe autonome' – allows him to interact with the 'subtils appels' from nature, with the music that it makes: 'chaque arbre a sa personnalité, chaque bestiole son rôle, chaque voix sa place dans la symphonie'. This personal 'measuring' of nature's music takes on new meaning in the context of Claudel's championing of non-traditional metre. In his verse poetry Claudel's favoured type of line was the *verset*, a line derived from the 'verses' of the Bible and extremely variable in length.[29] He preferred it to more regular, traditional lines, believing that it allowed poetry to incorporate the freer, more natural rhythms of breathing and inspiration.[30] Perhaps these last lines refer to Claudel's attempts to 'measure' the subjects of his poems in accordance with his own, personal rhythms, to respond in kind to the music of the world. The desire expressed in the final line, 'je comprends l'harmonie du monde; quand en surprendrai-je la mélodie?' might then refer to the fact that, having understood the harmonious system of God's creation, he now wishes to know the structuring melody beneath the harmony: when, in other words, will his rhythm meet the world's? 'Le Promeneur' thus takes us from the conquering walker to the receptive one, from the self-conscious solitary to the poet who listens to the rhythms of the universe.

The self-conscious subject of 'Le Promeneur', who is of course also the organising 'je' of the whole of *Connaissance de l'Est*, is increasingly revealed to be not only a walker but a writer in the final poems of the collection. In 'Le Point', a poem in the 1900–1905 section, the activity of walking is explicitly related to that of writing: 'Je m'arrête: il y a un point à ma promenade comme à une phrase que l'on a finie'. As the collection draws to a close, the self-consciousness of the writer increases and affects the shape of the whole book as well as that of individual poems. This collection of youthful and idealistic attempts to dominate the landscape both of the East and of the self thus ends in a poem entitled 'Dissolution', which begins not on terra firma but on the sea:

> Et je suis de nouveau reporté sur la mer indifférente et liquide. Quand je serai mort, on ne me fera plus souffrir. Quand je serai enterré entre mon père et ma mère, on ne me fera plus souffrir. [...] Maintenant tous est dissous, et d'un oeil appesanti je cherche en vain autour de moi et le pays habituel à la route ferme sous mon pas et ce visage cruel.

On one level, the speaker's fervent wish for his suffering self to dissolve into nothingness is to be understood in the context of the unhappy end of his affair with Rose Vetch ('ce visage cruel'), but on another level it is about the end of walking: the 'route ferme sous mon pas' has given way to 'la mer indifférente et liquide', and the walker is, in more senses than one, 'at sea'. As we have seen, walking in the East was Claudel's way of taking stock of his surroundings: it was a means of making contact, measuring ('remesurer le chemin qui me rattache à la maison'[31]) and thus getting to *know* his environment in a very physical sense. But on the ship taking him back to France in 'Dissolution', Claudel is in a state of immobility – and therefore ignorance. Immobility makes knowledge impossible in Claudel's scheme of things. 'Co-naissance' is a knowledge based on distinctions, on becoming aware of the difference between the self and other and subsequently being reborn into a world that contains such an other, but in 'Dissolution' separate entities melt into each other and become an undifferentiated flux:

> Tout est dissous et je chercherais en vain autour de moi trait ou forme. Rien, pour horizon, que la cessation de la couleur la plus foncée. La matière de tout est rassemblée dans une seule eau [...] J'aurais beau chercher, je ne trouve plus rien hors de moi, ni de ce pays qui fut mon séjour, ni ce visage beaucoup aimé.

Lack of mobility has led to a loss of self. The act of walking brought out the different rhythms, or melodies, between the self and other, as we found in 'Le Promeneur': every tree, beast and voice had its assigned place in the symphony of nature. But now that he is unable to walk, the poet appears to have lost his ability to distinguish, and therefore also to have misplaced his sense of self as distinct from the other: 'je ne trouve plus rien hors de moi'. Placed as it is at the very end of the collection, this prose poem reminds us that the conquering stance of the Claudelian walker – temporary and incomplete as it was, even in its prime – is now at an end. The prose poem, an experimental and unstable genre that was ideal for Claudel's incursions into the East, could never end in a settling, colonising gesture, and accordingly the final prose poem of *Connaissance de l'Est* literally dissolves the subject into his grief, and into the formless sea.

Walking in circles: 'La Muraille intérieure de Tokyo'

Sixteen years after his 'dissolution' into the sea off the coast of the Asian continent, Claudel returned to Japan as the French ambassador. His arrival seems to have caused some consternation: the informality of his manner, and the imposing nature of his large and robust frame, marked him out as a remarkable presence from the very beginning: 'Claudel bousculait parfois les règles minutieuses du protocole japonais et [...] sa brusquerie et sa rondeur ne lui gagnaient pas toujours, dès l'abord, la sympathie'.[32] But he quickly overcame any initial scruples on the part of his hosts, who were soon disarmed by 'sa bonhomie et sa simplicité paysanne', as well as by his literary career. Known as the French 'shijin-taishi' (poet-ambassador), Claudel made good friends in the academic and artistic milieu, such as the painter Tomita Keisen, the engraver Bonkotsu Igami, and Professor Yamonouchi of Waseda University. Such contacts were useful to him for the publication of a number of his works. *Sainte Geneviève*, for instance, written in Rio de Janeiro in 1918, was first published in Japan, in a luxury edition whose preparation required the skills of his Japanese acquaintances.[33] The end result was a book consisting of a long piece of paper folded accordion-style, with an elegant cover in black lacquer.[34] Its publication was fêted in 1923 at the Tokyo Imperial Hotel, and at this occasion Claudel give a speech detailing how it was only in Japan, where he discovered particular kinds of paper and writing materials, that the poem – which, until that moment, 'ne voulait littéralement pas des moyens que je pouvais mettre à sa disposition' and 'refusait d'exister' – was given 'cette forme personnelle qu'il [the poem] appelait'.[35]

Like many a Western writer, Claudel declared himself seduced by the physical aspects of writing and printing in Japan: he wrote that 'il est impossible pour un poëte d'avoir vécu quelque temps en Chine et au Japon sans considérer avec émulation tout cet attirail là-bas qui accompagne l'expression de la pensée', and took the opportunity to design personally a number of his works.[36] 'Poëmes au verso de Sainte Geneviève, La Muraille intérieure de Tokyo' is the first of his projects which involved properly collaborative work between Claudel and a Japanese artist, and indeed a Japanese academic, as the story of its genesis makes clear. When Professor Yamanouchi asked Claudel to sign his copy of *Sainte Geneviève*, printed on one side only of a long piece of paper folded accordion-style, Claudel turned the book over and handwrote twelve short poems, concerning a walk along the moat surrounding the Imperial Palace in Tokyo, on the back of the single sheet. This was the reason for the full title of the poem. Afterwards, the two poems – *Sainte Geneviève* and 'La Muraille' – were printed in a luxury edition, a veritable *liber scriptus intus et foris*,[37] and published by Shinchosha in 1923.

The walk in 'Poëmes au verso de Sainte Geneviève, La Muraille intérieure de Tokyo'[38] is a very different kind of walk from those described in *Connaissance de l'Est*. The walk of 'Le Promeneur' is described at one point as a 'circuit', but its characteristics are linear and one-directional. The daily walk in 'La Muraille intérieure' is most definitely a circular walk, as its route is predetermined by the wall of the moat. The twelve poems contain a series of reflections, both literal (in the moat) and metaphorical, as the poet walks slowly around the Palace. They are also highly self-reflexive, unusually for Claudel, and meditate on the physical act of writing poetry. The first poem is the longest, comprising thirteen lines, and describes the actual walk around the moat. The second poem remembers the writing of 'Sainte Geneviève' in Brazil, on the same sheet of paper, and Poem III invites the reader to see the physical reality of these poems, written back to back in Brazil and in Japan, as the reality of Claudel's vagabonding existence. Poem IV is a meditation on the work of the poet, comparing him to a fisherman, a hunter and a gardener: Poem V describes the kind of poem the poet wants to write, a 'triple route' spanning the heavens, the earth and the future.[39] Poem VI is about the king who resides within the moat, who wants to cut his castle off from the earth; Poem VII, about the way in which everything that is reflected in the moat appears equally accessible. Poem VIII asks the reader to hold his or her breath so as not to disturb the 'surface magique' of the water/poem; Poem IX describes the consequences of a tiny movement on this surface. Poem X discusses the relationship between an object and its reflection, both in water and in thought. Poem XI comes back to the poet standing at the edge of the moat, and finally Poem XII tells us what the poet has learned from the experience of walking around the moat.

As these brief summaries show, some of the poems are only loosely related to each other, but united by the trajectory of the walk, and by the elements that make it up (the moat, the circle, and its centre beyond the moat). It is a much more meditative walk than that of 'Le Promeneur': also, the poet's 'je' is much less in evidence in 'La Muraille', present in the earlier poems but gradually fading away in the later ones, with the self slowly seeming to dissolve into its surroundings. The poetic structure evolves from poem to poem: roughly speaking, the poems describe a movement from the intricately patterned to the highly irregular, and constitute in themselves a kind of walk through a variety of formal possibilities. Indeed the self-reflexive nature of the subject matter makes this the chronicle of a walk towards a new aesthetic, but it does not, as we will see, reach the furthest limits of its logical conclusion: that achievement is reserved for a later collection of poems, *Cent Phrases pour éventails*.[40] As a result, however, it is in 'La Muraille intérieure' that the tensions between the new and old aesthetic approaches are explored, played out and maintained in a fragile balance. Very broadly speaking, the first five poems, in which the 'je' appears frequently, are set in a context of walking and progress. The poetic 'je' is far less in evidence in poems VI to X, whose context is stillness and timelessness: the last two poems attempt to reconcile the two positions.

The first five poems share a concern with the physical: the movement of the self through space, in the activities of walking and travelling, and the physical aspects of poetry. The first poem features the poet actually walking around the moat, and although it is in free verse the structure is strikingly regular, arranged around a 'rimes plates' rhyme scheme interspersed with a variable refrain:

> Non point la forêt ni la grève, chaque jour le site de ma
> promenade est un mur,   a
> > Il y a toujours un mur à ma droite.   ref
> Un mur que je suis et qui me suit et que je déroule derrière moi
> en marchant et devant moi il y en a encore provision et
> fourniture.   a
> > Un mur continuellement à ma droite.   ref
> A ma gauche il y a la ville et les grandes avenues en partance
> vers toute la terre.   b
> > Mais il y a un mur à ma droite.   ref
> Je tourne (à cette station du tram) et je sais que c'est par là
> la mer,   b
> > Mais le mur est indécollable à ma droite.   ref

The refrain of 'à ma droite' creates a slow, steady rhythm, rendering the wall a reliable physical presence both in the walk and in the poem: it ends with the line 'Et quand je fermerais les yeux, je n'ai qu'à tendre la main/Pour vérifier cette présence à ma droite.' The next four poems are also structurally quite regular. Poems II and III use half-rhyme and rhyme to create a sensation of aural progress in their descriptions of Claudel's travels between Brazil and Japan. These also deal more explicitly with the relationship between movement through space, and poetry. In Poem III, for instance, Claudel likens his vagabonding life to a poem written on the loose pages of a manuscript, floating between the two worlds of Japan and Brazil: 'La vie des autres va son pas dans le paysage continu./La mienne suit sa ligne sur des feuilles interrompues'.

In Poem IV, the poet disappears briefly as we are presented with a discussion of the poet's craft, compared with those of the hunter, the fisherman and the gardener. The gardener even occupies the first-person voice, for the space of a line:

Le pêcheur *attrape* les poissons avec ce panier profondement enfoui au-dessous des vagues.

Le chasseur avec cet invisible lacs entre deux branches *attrape* les petits ois*eaux*.

Et moi, dit le jardinier, pour *attraper* la lune et les étoiles <u>il me suffit</u> d'un peu d'*eau*, – et les cerisiers en fleur et les erables en feu, <u>il me suffit</u> de ce ruban d'*eau* que je déroule.

Et moi, dit le poëte, pour *attraper* les images et les idées <u>il me suffit</u> de cet appat de papier blanc, les dieux n'y passeront point sans y laisser leurs traces comme les ois*eaux* sur la neige.

Pour tenter les pas de l'Impératrice-de-la-Mer <u>il me suffit</u> de ce tapis de papier que je déroule, pour faire descendre l'Empereur-du-Ciel <u>il me suffit</u> de ce rayon de lune, <u>il me suffit</u> de cet escalier de papier blanc.

The lines of this poem do not rhyme, but they are intricately inter-woven by a series of repetitions, internal rhymes and refrain-like phrases that are verbal mirrors of the traps set by the professional hunters. The key word of 'attraper' occurs in every line apart from the last, joining together lines 1 to 4: similarly, the echo of 'eau' in 'oiseaux' and 'd'eau' links lines 2, 3 and 4. But the most insistent repetition is that of 'il me suffit', occuring twice in line 3, once in line 4 and three times in line 5.[41] Repetition at irregular intervals is a characteristic of the *verset*, echoing similar structures in prayers of praise or of request: it creates an incantatory rhythm that is both predictable and progressive. The voices of the gardener and poet are like the voices in a choir, starting up their melodies at different moments but coming together in harmonious chords by singing the same notes at staggered intervals. Furthermore, 'il me suffit de...' is a phrase which has a strangely oxymoronic effect of self-denial ('this is *all* I need') and self-affirmation ('this is all *I* need'), particularly per-tinent in the context of a professional and his craft. Both the gardener and the poet here are strong creative natures with a robust sense of identity, but their energies are poured into the construction of an artefact independent of themselves that will, if successful, outlive them. Indeed, the whole cycle of poems works as a meditation on this relationship between the poet and his poem, as we will see.

The central themes of Poems VI to X seem to be directly opposed to those of the earlier poems. The poet disappears again, and only returns as a diminished presence, nothing more than an observant eye, an alert consciousness that registers images of stillness, eternity, and simultaneity. Poem VI sets the tone by telling the story of a king who detaches his palace from the earth and floats away into a world of sleep and timelessness:

> Autour de mon palais, dit le Roi, j'ai mis un anneau de ciel, déjà il me semble que je ne tiens plus à la terre,
> L'heure du sommeil est venue, déjà il me semble que ça commence à être libre sous moi, comme le ponton à la mer de minuit qui commence à se plaindre et à souffrir.

From this point onwards the poems offer us strangely perfect images, ephemeral yet eternal, of reflections on the water of the moat. The poet's only role is to see them. In fact the poet's 'je' only occurs in one poem of this series, Poem VII, where it sees and – in line 4 – does *not* write:

> Dans l'eau de l'antique fossé toutes les choses se reflètent pêle-mêle, il n'y a aucune différence du près ou du loin.
> J'y vois la chandelle du marchand de nouilles, une grosse étoile lui tient compagnie entre ces deux feuilles de nenuphar.
> La passoire du marchand de beignets y est devenue eternelle et à côté j'y vois la navette de la Tisseuse Céléste; sa main pourrait aller de l'un à l'autre.
> Ainsi dans le poëme que je n'ai pas écrit il n'y a aucune différence de temps ou de lieu, toutes choses y sont réunies par une secrète intimité.
> Tout a cessé de mourir.

The noodle bar's lantern is on an equal footing with a star, the constellation of the Divine Seamstress[42] is within touching distance of the tempura cook's colander: hierarchies and distances are abolished, the temporal is granted the same life span as the eternal, all is equal on the surface of the water. Like a medieval representation of the life of a saint, in which various stages of his or her life are juxtaposed with no regard for chronology, the reflections on the water suspend time and therefore death.

This ideal, timeless world where everything is in harmony, however, exists only in the realm of sleep and illusion (reflection), and in a non-existent poem, 'le poëme que je n'ai pas écrit'. Such perfection does not belong to a life where time passes and human beings breathe away their lives. Indeed breathing is banned briefly in the interests of perfection, although the life-giving breath of the sea creates an abundance of words on the page:

> Lecteur, suspends ton souffle de peur qu'une haleine profane détruise la surface magique.[43]

> Le vent de la mer a soufflé, en une seconde la page etendue devant toi foumille d'une innombrable écriture.

The reader's breath, the human breath brings time and mortality into the world of art, whereas the breath of the sea – perhaps a reference to the Holy Spirit, one of Claudel's favourite breath-related images – is creative and fruitful. Breathing is in fact noticeably more difficult in this second set of poems, in which the rhythmic structures are much less in evidence than in Poems I to V. These poems, although they sometimes make use of repetition to build up momentum, are mainly made up of long, resonating *versets* which vibrate internally but do not encourage forward movement. In a world where stillness is a virtue, these lines exist like artefacts: like the 'mot rond sans aucune tige qui s'épanouit en plein papier' in Poem IX, the polysyllabic words ('les profondeurs superposées de son intelligence') discourage movement in either direction. The rhythm of whole lines is similarly non-progressive:

> Une seule feuille de saule sur le verre de l'étang, et le ciel tout entier avec ses étoiles de la terre et le Palais des Rois et la ville que la vie a quittée
> D'un bout à l'autre de cette etoffe de sommeil se mettent à trembler et frémir.
> La lune au Septième Etage du Ciel est atteinte par la ride imperceptible.

We do not see the leaf in movement: we do not see it falling onto the surface. But its still presence on 'le verre de l'étang' is noted in a solemn line whose sounded 'e's slow it down to a point where it sounds almost immobile. The second half of the line describes the effect of this event, and here again the pace of the line is slowed down considerably by the repetition of 'et'. The vibration of the water, caused by the leaf, appears directionless, described as occurring 'd'un bout à l'autre de cette etoffe de sommeil'.[44] The reference to sleep deadens the movement, which in any case has not yet been noted, as the verbs ('trembler et frémir') only come at the very end of the sentence, after all the clauses and subclauses. The effect is of a movement that is, paradoxically, without motion, perhaps simply because it is 'en plein papier', that is to say in a poem. Taken out of time by being put into the context of art, the wave, frozen on the paper, becomes a wrinkle: 'la lune au Septième Etage du Ciel est atteinte par la *ride* imperceptible'.

Thus the two sets of poems – I–V and VI–X – offer the reader two contrasting states, both emanating from the experience of the walk: the poet in time, and the poem in eternity. Poem XI tries to reconcile the two:

> A ce caractère qui veut dire *l'eau* un point rouge a été mis qui l'arrête pour toujours.
> Comme l'artiste sur une feuille de la pointe de son pinceau a fait un point n'importe où,
> Il rêve et ne sait encore ce qu'il y ajoutera, femme, pin, la mer,
> Ainsi mon regard s'attache à cette marque rouge aux trois quarts de l'étang,
> Non point le soleil d'aujourd'hui, mais témoin submergé et oeil de beaucoup de spectacles consumés,
> Comme la braise d'un hibachi qui n'attendait que moi pour s'éteindre.

As has been pointed out, adding an extra point to the Japanese character for 'water' turns it into the character for 'eternity';[45] varying the location of the point slightly would even transform it into 'ice'. So the poet sees water being frozen, or being made eternal, by art: but as the artist's brush remains poised over his work, the red point appears to spread, for how else would it come to occupy 'trois quarts de l'étang'? This red is not the reflection of the sun, but the colour of the past, 'oeil de beaucoup de spectacles consumés', and is compared with the dying red of the embers in a Japanese brazier (hibachi). Time thus enters the perfect world of the moat surface, but only gently, because the poet's walk is a daily occasion ('chaque jour le site de ma promenade est un mur'): the iterative is not as violent an eruption of time into eternity as a unique event would have been.

The 'lesson' of Poem XII has the gnomic quality of a Zen Buddhist *koan*:

> J'habite l'extérieur d'un anneau.
> J'ai appris que ce n'est point dehors, c'est dedans qu'est le mur dont je suis le prisonnier.
> J'ai appris que pour aller d'un point à un autre il est possible de passer partout excepté par le centre.

We can only speculate on what the 'mur dont je suis le prisonnier' might be, or the significance of the final line. Given the contrast between Poems I–V and VI–X, however, it is possible that the 'internal' wall is the symbol of a mindset: the mindset that believes in the separateness of the self and the world, thereby preventing the reconciliation of time and eternity. If the self can be quelled, if the poet can stop and quietly watch the water of the moat, the melody will blend into the harmony: the self–other dichotomy will fade into the non-aggressive relationship of a consciousness registering an ephemeral world. The self can then disappear into its own creation, and in so doing become part of the other. Another candidate for the 'internal wall' may be the 'Western' mindset that values the centre too much above the periphery. For centuries, Western philosophy has held that meaning is contained in the centre of things.[46] 'La Muraille' itself is a walk along a periphery with the inaccessible Imperial Palace at its centre. To say at its end that the wall is not an external object, preventing his access to the centre, but that his progress is blocked by an internal obstacle, might indicate that Claudel is rejecting – after a final attempt at making it work – the 'centrist' view of the world. In *Cent Phrases pour éventails*, Claudel's first attempt at haiku-like poetry and one which involved a much closer collaboration with a Japanese calligrapher, Claudel abandons a coherent structure based around a centre: the collection is a string of 172 poems, one poem after another with no apparent organising structure, and a negligible presence of the 'je'. 'La Muraille intérieure' may be the first attempt by Claudel to adopt certain characteristics of a non-Western aesthetic.

Walking through art: *L'Oiseau noir dans le soleil levant*

Claudel made full use of his opportunities in Japan to immerse himself in its culture and nature. The entries relating to Japan in his journal give an idea of the frequency with which he attended performances of *kabuki* or *nô* theatre, or went on excursions to touristic attractions in the provinces.[47] In January 1923, for instance, his diary records him travelling to Narita (3rd) and Nikko (12th–14th), going to a *kabuki* play with his friend Yamanouchi (15th), a performance of *nô* in Asakusa (20th) and a sumo wrestling event in Ryogoku just before the end of the month. February 1923 is similarly full of engagements, including a luncheon at the house of a celebrated author with the dancer Nakamura Fukusuki, who was to perform in the première of Claudel's *La Femme et son ombre*.

L'Oiseau noir dans le soleil levant takes its material from these personal experiences of the artistically-minded ambassador. As for the form, it is a truly heterogeneous mixture of discursive texts, dialogues, prose poems and descriptive pieces, written between July 1923 and January 1927. Interviewed in May 1927 after they were published as a single volume, Claudel said of the essays that 'j'ai voulu présenter quelques aspects de l'âme, de la civilisation, de l'art japonais [...] C'est une série de poèmes et de dialogues où j'ai essayé de "proposer" un certain nombre d'idées sur un sujet difficile et essayé encore plus d'expliquer et de faire comprendre que de peindre'. This description of *L'Oiseau noir dans le soleil levant*, which highlights its discursive content, does not do justice to its generic and tonal variety. It certainly includes essays that are more openly discursive than anything in *Connaissance de l'Est*, aspiring to 'connaissance' of a more traditional kind, and as a result critics often refer to *L'Oiseau noir dans le soleil levant* as one of the definitive sources for Claudel's thoughts on, for instance, Japanese art. But the collection also contains highly poetic 'paintings' which, in spite of what Claudel says above, are far more than mere 'vessels' for the transmission of information about Japan.

Indeed, the 'information' offered by the discursive pieces in *L'Oiseau noir dans le soleil levant* often consists of interpretations rather than facts: 'il sélectionne hardiment. Claudel n'hésite pas à solliciter les faits pour les faire entrer dans son système de pensée et pour construire une image cohérente du Japon'.[48] The most overtly discursive piece in the volume, 'Un Regard sur l'âme japonaise: Discours aux étudiants de Nikkô', is a case in point.[49] Spurning an invitation to talk about 'la tradition française', Claudel takes this opportunity to address a group of Japanese students on the subject of their own culture: his excuse is the one that will be used by Michaux ten years later, that the eyes of the innocent foreigner are better at seeing the truth about a country, and that therefore his 'temoignage encore naïf' is worth a hearing. One wonders what these students made of the clearly well-meaning, enthusiastic but very recently arrived French ambassador telling them that, whereas the French language is the key to the French tradition, it is not necessary to understand Japanese in order to understand Japanese culture:

Tout au Japon, depuis le dessin d'une montagne jusqu'à celui d'une épingle à cheveux ou d'une coupe de saké, obéit au même *style*. Pour trouver la tradition japonaise, il n'est pas nécessaire, comme pour les gens de France, de pénétrer jusqu'à ce for intime [la langue française] où se forment les idées et s'essayent les attitudes, il n'y a qu'à ouvrir les oreilles et les yeux à ce concert autour de nous.[50]

Armed with this mode of 'instant access' to the heart of Japanese culture, Claudel goes on to praise what he sees as a quintessentially Japanese attitude, the 'humidité de l'âme', which he has perceived in a variety of cultural artefacts. His examples, however, often show him reaching back to thoughts he had had already at the time of his first visit to Japan in 1898: references to 'ce pin sur la route du Tokkaido tout tordu dans une supplication de paralytique' (p. 177), for instance, or the description of the Japanese drawing that is much more of a sign than a representation (p. 174: cf. p. 113) indicate that, on these subjects at least, Claudel is here simply reproducing theories explored in *Connaissance de L'Est*. It is no crime, of course, to recycle one's own material: asked to give a talk, perhaps at short notice, Claudel clearly did what any busy diplomat (or academic) might have done. But Claudel here was also guilty of being reluctant to part with ideas that had become part of his worldview: perhaps a Symbolist tendency, it nevertheless causes one commentator to write that 'depuis longtemps, Claudel s'est forgé un système d'explication du monde, solide et cohérent: il ne va pas le modifier devant la réalité japonaise, il va au contraire modifier celle-ci'.[51] I will have cause to disagree with this harsh verdict later on in this chapter, but it is certainly the case that this essay, at least, shows how 'les thèmes essentiels de sa vision du Japon sont fixés très tôt, certains dès le voyage de 1898'.

Much more spontaneous, and interesting, are the many 'sketches', for instance 'A travers les villes en flammes', an eyewitness account of the great 1923 Kanto earthquake. Starting with the flat but arresting statement, 'Yokohama est détruit', Claudel's account of the disaster is a masterful mix of factual reporting and evocative description: combining hard figures and place names with personal experiences, he succeeds in giving both immediacy and perspective to the narrative of a historical event. Similarly attractive prose pieces are 'Bougakou', 'Bounrakou' and 'Nô'. In each case Claudel gives a description of an instance of the art form that he has attended, and avoids offering his own theories, certainly any in the style of 'Un

Regard sur l'âme japonaise'. He analyses what he sees, and we thus benefit directly from his dramatist's eye: but generally speaking he does not offer any theories of Japaneseness to explain the dramas, preferring to dwell on their technical aspects with a view to enriching Western theatre from the experience.[52] His aim is clearly instructive, but instruction through instances rather than theories, which therefore necessarily limits the scope of his project. For instance, he cannot and does not offer a theoretically complete understanding of *nô* theatre in his essay on the subject, as what he knows is based only on what he has seen.[53] As if to compensate for the lack of completeness, Claudel has attached 'appendices' by other people to his own account of *nô*: more 'testimonies' for the French reader as part of this empirical approach to gathering knowledge.

Aside from 'Un Regard sur l'âme japonaise', the pieces in *L'Oiseau noir dans le soleil levant* that are most often mentioned by critics are the three dialogues, 'Le Poète et le shamisen', 'Le Poète et le vase d'encens', and 'Jules ou l'Homme-aux-deux-cravates'. These are entertaining but also instructive texts which offer much information on Claudel's aesthetic thinking. Also worthy of note is their form, the quintessentially non-didactic genre that is the dialogue, especially because their subject – Claudel's personal reaction, as a poet and dramatist, to Japanese art – is one about which he could have been authoritative with impunity. Perhaps he chose it in order to avoid a pedantic tone, and to give a vivacious, playful and spontaneous account of his thought processes. In the dialogues, the poet is often shown to be idealistic and prone to pomposity, although also quick to try out new ideas. His interlocutor, be it the *shamisen*, vase or alter ego Jules, is lively and impertinent (to great cost, on at least one occasion: the vase gets thrown out of the window after refusing to give up a particularly bad pun). Of course, both sides of the dialogues are written by Claudel: but even so, the form is one that allows for an admirably open account of his thoughts. The thoughts themselves, when examined, are still recognisably in the style of his earlier, 'comparative' approach to the differences between East and West: a good example of this is the discussion about Japanese gardens in 'Jules ou l'Homme-aux-deux-cravates'.[54] His old arguments against Buddhism are aired again in 'Le Poète et le shamisen', as is his guilty fascination with the notion of emptiness in 'Le Poète et le vase d'encens'. These thoughts do not go as far back as 1898, but it is tempting to agree with Henri Micciollo that Claudel's overall vision of Japan and its art was pretty much 'fixed' by 1923.[55] What continues to develop, however, is his interest in form: and, as I have argued earlier and will argue in the next section, the form in which Claudel's thoughts are offered to us makes a significant difference to our reception of the latter. Rhetorically speaking, also, Claudel's accounts of things Japanese in *L'Oiseau noir dans le soleil levant* seem to move, if we follow the dates of the essays, from the didactic to the impressionistic, the theoretical to the concrete. For instance, in one of the dialogues, an image from nature is offered as part of the conclusion to an argument. Discussing the vanity of introspection, what Claudel calls the 'curiosité impie' that causes men to try to look within themselves,[56] the poet concludes:

> LE POÈTE. La dame de délices au Prado ne se regarde pas, malgré le petite miroir qu'elle tient [...] Elle se compose simplement comme une fleur autour de son mystère.
> LE SHAMISEN. Comme l'une de ces grandes roses que nous avons vues au jardin bouddhiste de Hasédéra et que tu appelles des pivoines.

The verbal discussion is ended by a beautiful and concrete image, that of a peony remembered from a visit to a Buddhist temple: the virtue of woman who does not commit the sin of self-analysis is translated into the beauty of a flower.[57] Indeed the recourse to an image from nature to conclude an abstract discussion occurs in various places in *L'Oiseau noir dans le soleil levant*, for instance at the end of the prose poem entitled 'La Nature et la morale': 'Que la couleur et le parfum délivrent nos sens au lieu de les asservir! Il n'y a qu'une âme purifiée qui comprendra l'odeur de la rose.' Theory thus gives way to the concrete, abstract generalisations to empirical practices.

Less often discussed are the prose poems of *L'Oiseau noir dans le soleil levant*, whose presence links the collection firmly to *Connaissance de l'Est*. Generally speaking, they are less dense in style than those of the earlier volume, and often on more evanescent or imponderable subjects: 'Meiji' and 'L'abdication au milieu des pins', for instance, are poetic evocations of the Japanese reverence for the emperor. There is very little of Claudel's personal reactions in these poems, which distinguishes them from the poems of *Connaissance de l'Est*. More 'personal' in style are 'La Canne', 'Deux Bambous verts', 'L'Arrière-pays' and 'L'abîme solaire'. 'La Canne' is almost a sequel piece to 'Le Promeneur', starting as it does with the words 'Je parle de la canne du promeneur et non pas de la crosse du montagnard'.[58]

At the start, it certainly reads like a 'prolongement' of the earlier poem, just as the stick is to the body of the walker:

> La canne [...] me prolonge et donne en un rythme sans cesse interrompu et changeant le bras comme compagnie et comme contrôle au mouvement régulier des jambes. Elle me devance et elle me suit, elle est le javelot de l'inspiration et le sillage du regret, elle est l'instrument acharné de ma conquête. Elle me permet de toucher, de tâter, de ressentir, de frapper, de retrouver cette route où l'impulsion de ma volonté me transporte, c'est mou, c'est dur, elle est le contact de mon âme avec la route; elle est comme une épée à mon poing, la résolution inflexible de l'étape que j'ai décidée.

The kinship with 'Le Promeneur' from *Connaissance de l'Est* is evident. However, as the poem progresses, it becomes clear that this walker is an older version of the earlier man, and that he is present in his poem *at one remove* from the reader: beyond, or behind, the stick. The older walker, rather than residing in the restless mindset of the young 'promeneur' determined to measure, understand, and conquer the East, is observing himself from a different standpoint. Composed twenty-eight years and one month after 'Le Promeneur', the subject of the poem is not the self-conscious walker, but his appendage: the older Claudel focuses on the *intermediary*, that is to say the object situated in between the man and the ground, 'le contact de mon âme avec la route'. This allows him to observe the whole act of walking from a more detached perspective: from the front and from behind ('elle me devance et elle me suit'), and from a more abstract viewpoint ('cette route où l'impulsion de ma volonté me transporte'). This long, slender object that acts as intermediary between self and other becomes quickly related to another, similar object, the pen:

> Elle remplace pour l'homme en état de rêverie et transfert, ou, comme disent les philosophes, de *puissance*, tous les instruments précis qui lui servent à l'état d'action. [...] Tout ce que l'âme dit à la main, la main le dit à la canne et la canne le répète à la route. Je veux, je dois, je puis, je sais, je vais savoir, je me souviens, ça va, ça ne va pas, il est temps, tout est fini, tout cela s'écrit avec une canne. En avant! j'ai saisi ma canne! Il y a encore un bout de chemin aujourd'hui que je vais faire.

The move from stick to pen is neither clumsy not indeed obvious: it is perfectly possible to carry on reading the poem as being about the stick, even after 'tout cela *s'écrit* avec une canne'. The actual identity of the object is not really relevant as Claudel's writing activity is so clearly related to that of walking: whether he is composing a poem or wandering around Tokyo, he is 'l'homme en état de rêverie et de transfert'. Whether or not the pen is mightier than the stick, Claudel's final cry of 'En avant! j'ai saisi ma canne!' is much more humorous, and self-conscious, than the slightly exasperated 'Et je marche, je marche, je marche!' at the end of 'Le Promeneur'.

Several other prose poems in *L'Oiseau noir dans le soleil levant* seem to echo, or even to conclude, themes first proposed in *Connaissance de l'Est*. The intense communion with light in 'Heures dans le jardin' or 'Le Sédentaire' returns in the experience of a Japanese spring in 'L'Abîme solaire'; the sense of being watched by nature whilst walking in it that occurs in 'L'Arche d'or' and 'Heures dans le jardin' as well as 'Le Promeneur' comes back in 'La Nature et la morale'. And 'Deux Bambous verts', describing a painting by Seiki, seems to offer one possible answer to the final question, 'je comprends l'harmonie du monde: quand en surprendrai-je la mélodie?', of 'Le Promeneur': 'Et de cette double comparaison [of the two bamboos] ne jaillit-il pas pour l'esprit à la fois une harmonie et une mélodie comme des noeuds d'une double flûte?'

Heterogeneous and various, the writings of *L'Oiseau noir dans le soleil levant* are difficult to classify in terms of both content and form. Micciollo ascribes the book's generic diversity to the ambivalent attitude that Japan inspired in Claudel, who was both deeply attracted and worried by the non-Christian country that seemed to contain so much that was pleasing to him. Micciollo goes on to conclude that, in *L'Oiseau noir dans le soleil levant*,

> en raison de cette attitude ambiguë et par le biais d'approches successives et fort différentes, Claudel construit une image du Japon qui à la fois s'intègre dans sa vision du monde, met en valeur la leçon qu'il tire de ce pays et reflète le bonheur qu'il y trouve.[59]

These texts are indeed Claudel's personal visions of Japan, whose contents show that they span a certain period of development in his thinking that links them to both *Connaissance de l'Est* and *Cent Phrases pour éventails*. In terms of the 'walking' trope, they might be thought of as brief promenades taken through Japanese nature and especially art: the essays on *bounrakou*, *kabuki* and *nô* are actual results of day-long excursions into the world of classical Japanese art forms, whereas prose poems such as 'La Canne', 'L'Arrière-pays' and 'L'abîme solaire' are walks through the Japanese countryside during which the walker deepens his acquaintance with a new aspect of Japan. Perhaps it is useful to think about this heterogeneous collection of texts as a collection of walks taken by Claudel with his stick/pen in hand: a stick or pen to find his way through the 'chemin jonché de branches mortes', not to note down a flawlessly formed theory of Japaneseness. As against the isolated instance of coherent but false image-making that Claudel falls into in 'Un Regard sur l'âme japonaise', the majority of the pieces in *L'Oiseau noir dans le soleil levant* show him to be finding his way, in an empirical state of mind, through the meandering paths of his Japanese experience.

The itinerant haiku poet: *Cent Phrases pour éventails*

The true haiku poet is a wandering one,[60] and so *Cent Phrases pour éventails*, Claudel's collection of haiku-like poems, might be described as the apotheosis of his career as an itinerant poet. Both the genre

The fourth fan, 'Autumn', from *Souffles des quatres souffles*, photography: Univ. Sophia Tokyo.

and the subjects of these poems emerge from the act of walking, although a very different kind of walking from that of *Connaissance de l'Est*, and as such they constitute the ideal work with which to conclude our 'dromomanic'[61] analysis of Claudel and Japan.

What is immediately most striking about these poems is their physical appearance. In their original form, they are a combination of Japanese characters, *kanji*, and Claudel's own handwriting – in two columns – for the French text:

花
　　　　　Une
　　　　　rose　　　d'un rouge si fort
酒　　　　　　　　　qu'elle tache
　　　　　　　　　　l'
　　　　　　　　　âme
　　　　　comme du vin

The combination of Japanese and French elements extended to the presentation of the book itself, especially in the original, 'luxury' edition:

> Il s'agit de trois accordéons de papier, étroits et allongés (19cm x 10 cm), imposant qu'on les feuillette à l'orientale, de droite à gauche. Ils sont réunis dans une boîte de toile grise mouchetée d'or à fermeture d'ivoire. Tirée à deux cents exemplaires, sous le titre définitif, Cent phrases pour éventails, elle reproduit lithographique-ment les cent soixante-douze phrases calligraphiées de l'auteur et les idéogrammes choisis par Yamanouchi et Yoshié, calligraphiés par Ikuma Arishima.[62]

As the French and Japanese scripts meet each other in each poem, so the whole of this collection is based around the *encounter*.[63] In what follows, I will show how the poems – or 'phrases' – of *Cent Phrases pour éventails* are instances of encounters between the walking poet and Japan, and how these encounters lead to a new kind of knowledge of Japan for Claudel, one that is fragmented but firmly grounded in reality.

One way in which walking is structurally intrinsic to these poems is the random way in which we encounter their subjects – flowers, trees, mountains, children, *jizô*, rain, insects – which makes the reading experience very much like that of a carefree walk. There is no strong 'self' that holds them together, no master plan that governs their structure. Occasionally the same subject gives rise to a short series of three or four poems,[64] but otherwise the order in which these 172 'phrases' appear seems to be entirely random.[65] They also comprise a variety of different genres. Some, although not very many, are simply descriptive of instances of Japanese culture, for instance phrase 68 which refers to an aspect of Buddhist ancestor worship: 'Je salue en Monsieur Mon Enfant Messieurs les ancêtres de mon mari' (Japanese characters meaning 'ancestors'). Others, even fewer in number, are brief sketches of 'Japanese' scenes: 'Trébuchant sur mes sandales de bois/j'essaie d'attraper le premier flocon de neige' (phrase 55, characters constitute a word meaning 'first snow'). Most numerous, however, are what Michel Truffet calls 'trouvailles métaphoriques', analogical observations based on an encounter with a concrete object, such as this one: 'Cette fleur jaune et blanche/ comme un mélange/ de feu et de lumière' (phrase 131, characters for 'light' and 'flame'). A subgroup of these consists of phrases which are about the writing of poetry. These too are always based around a concrete object, such as ink, paper, or the 'éventails' on which the poems of *Souffles des quatre souffles* were written: 'Eventail/Poëmes é/ crits sur le/ s ouffle' (phrase 77, characters for 'fan' and 'poem').[66]

The 'trouvailles métaphoriques', as well as being the most numerous, are also most significant in that their style embodies a relationship between the self and the other that is both deeply personal and completely contingent. This is because they are not attempts at objective description, but accounts of the poet's perception of, and responses to, chance encounters with aspects of the other. This perception is usually a metaphorical one (traditionally, of course, metaphor is the poet's 'way of seeing')[67] that establishes some connection between one object and another, or one object and an abstract idea. An instance of the former is 'Le camélia panaché / une face rougeaude de paysanne que l'on voit à travers la neige' (phrase 54, characters for 'vermilion' and 'white'): of the latter, 'Le camélia rouge/comme une idée éclatante et froide' (phrase 52, characters for 'camelia' and 'to fall'). 'Le souvenir déjà/ se mêle/ à/ la/ fumé e/ bleu e/ de Kyoto' (phrase 155, characters for 'smoke' and 'Kyoto' or 'city') is similarly poised between the visible and invisible worlds.[68] These metaphorical phrases are thus instances of interaction between the poet and the world he is walking through, moments of insight when he 'sees' a relationship between elements of the visible and invisible world and thereby accedes to an understanding of the other. Indeed *Cent Phrases pour éventails* contains a number of 'metatextual' phrases, so to speak, in which Claudel describes the procedure:

> Vite/ une larme/ qui/ traverse/ un rayon de soleil/ elle a passé (phrase 70, characters for 'tear' and 'sun')

> Entre/ ce qui commence/ et ce qui finit/ l'oeil du poëte a saisi cet/ i/ mperceptible poi/ nt où quelque chose/ p/ ique (phrase 72, characters for 'sting' or 'stab' and 'silence')

Phrase 70 highlights the speed with which the poet must react to these moments of enlightenment. Phrase 72 is a more detailed description of the poet's activity, which requires of him an eye for distinctions, but also an instinctive 'feel' for the 'quelque chose qui pique'. The characters which run alongside the French poem seem to suggest that the poet punctures the silence of the world by turning certain moments into words, and also that this activity is a very physical one. There are many other phrases concerned with demarcations and limits:

> Kwannon/ Au bout de la baguette/ devant l'autel de/ ce point incandescent/ qui est la frontière/ entre la cendre/ et le parfum (phrase 75)

> Le coucou/ localise/ l'endroit/ où nous ne/ sommes p/ as (phrase 80)

> Entre le jour et la nuit/ ce n'est pas encore/ aujourd'hui/ c'est hier (phrase 100)

According to these metatextual phrases, the poet's activity is based in that area 'in between' the concrete and the abstract, or the visible and the invisible: and his intelligence is of that highly analytical, discriminating kind we have already encountered in Claudel's earlier poems.[69]

Given this focus on the distinction between self and other, one might expect the poet in *Cent Phrases pour éventails* to be a clearly defined and markedly individual personality. Significantly, however, he is not: he is much more of a position, a *point of view*, than a persona. In *Cent Phrases pour éventails* the poet is not absent,[70] but when he appears he is very much a subordinate presence, completely unlike the 'je' in, for instance, most of the poems of *Connaissance de l'Est*. He is the I/eye who sees and writes about the flowers, mountains and temples, but not a 'personality' who imposes his individual character on the subjects of the poems: his identity consists almost wholly of his essence as a poet. In other words, although the poet's perception governs the structure and content of all the phrases, he is a minor character, the supporting structure rather than the centre-piece.

Thus the poet is never the subject of the poems, although he may at times (not often) be their grammatical subject: the true focus of each poem is the poet's encounter with instances of Japan, instances of its culture, nature and writing. Indeed one of the major themes of *Cent Phrases pour éventails* is the physical nature of writing in Japan, about which Claudel speaks with much enthusiasm in his preface to the whole book. In Japan, writing is a much more physical affair than in France, involving brushes, ink and beautiful thick paper, 'tout cet attirail là-bas qui accompagne l'expression de la pensée' (*Oeuvre poètique*, p. 691). This, Claudel implies, is how it should be, for the writing of poetry is a physical act that has too often been intellectu-alised, rendered abstract, in the West. In *Cent Phrases pour éventails* Claudel consistently describes writing poetry as an activity not just concerned with the mind but involving the whole body. The follow-ing sequence of phrases, phrases 57 to 59, is a good example of this:

> Plus d'inspiration/ le/ poëte/ pêche/ sans hameçon/ dans/ une coupe de/ saké (characters for 'inspiration' and 'to stop, to cease')
>
> Des deux doigts/ il soulève/ la coupe/ de saké/ et ses lèvres/ s'ouvrent/ peu à peu (characters meaning 'drinking session')
>
> Le vieux poëte/ sent/ peu à peu/ un vers/ qui le gagne/ comme/ un éternuement (characters for 'inspiration' and 'to arrive at')

What is immediately striking is the brevity of the lines, especially in phrase 57: the bumpy rhythm of the single-word lines ('le/ poëte/ pêche') seems to echo the faltering pace of the poet's uninspired composition. The lines in phrase 58 are a little longer, consisting of two or three words each, perhaps mimicking the movement of the poet feebly raising his glass of saké. This gradually lengthening, if always faltering, rhythm slowly grows into the birth of 'un vers' in phrase 59, which is humorously compared with that of an eminently physical phenomenon, a sneeze. Thus this poem is also based on an analogical relationship, but one that shows poetry in an earthy, day-to-day light, which is in accordance with the aesthetic of the haiku: the poet is shown struggling with the difficulties of his task in a most prosaic manner.

The reader's task is comparable to that of the poet, partly because of the graphic representation of the poems in *Cent Phrases pour éventails.* As mentioned earlier, both the French and Japanese scripts are difficult to read, and this necessitates a certain amount of effort on the reader's part:

> Le signe graphique évoque le sujet parlant dans l'effort de l'évocation, de la difficile et incertaine prise de possession de la 'chose' par le signe. Les ruptures graphiques, les variations dimensionnelles des tracés, les diverses épaisseurs d'encrage traduisent les lenteurs, les hésitations ou les précipitations d'une voix devenue invisible, les traits prosodiques de la parole.[71]

The reader is required to adopt the same pace as the poet, occasionally stumbling over 'les hésitations ou les précipitations d'une voix devenue invisible' but which has left its visible mark on the page. And if, like Claudel, he does not read Japanese, he is also required to walk along the path created by the Japanese characters, whilst wondering what they mean. As Truffet writes, 'le lecteur "patient" doit "co-produire" le texte lacunaire qu'il déchiffre', but he is likely not to succeed completely in his 'déchiffrement' because of the Japanese that he cannot read. Thus the combination of Japanese and French writing in these poems offers the non-Japanese-reading reader a unique experience that is at the same time reading and seeing, understanding and ignorance. In this way the poems never become 'invisible' in the way words tend to for a reader who speaks the language, and the experience of reading them retains the nature of an encounter – the meeting of a self and an other – rather than dissolving into the habitual reading experience in which the reader absorbs, fully possesses, that which he has read.

The paradigmatic relationship that governs all of the poems of *Cent Phrases pour éventails* is that of knowledge through encounter: both in the case of the poet meeting his roses, and the reader meeting the French and Japanese signs. The fact that the poems are presented as records of the poet's encounters with the other provides a refreshingly *practical* context for the self–other relationship as it is staged in *Cent Phrases pour éventails*. Furthermore, the contingent nature of the encounters means that the knowledge of the other thus obtained by the self, and contained in the poems, is fragmentary: unlike an abstract system of knowledge, it is made up of odds and ends that do not necessarily cohere. But this fragmentary presentation gives the reader a strong sense that this is a knowledge grounded in reality. That is, the knowledge of Japan in *Cent Phrases pour éventails* gives every impression of having been obtained directly from Japanese flowers, trees, mountains and people, of being a knowledge that has come from physical, unmediated encounters. Roland Barthes, forty-three years later, would praise the same kind of knowledge and prefer it to a more theoretical approach, calling instances of it 'le rendez-vous'. And for the reader, the encounter is a double one: she encounters both the content of the poems and their physical appearance, which itself is double, consisting as it does of two kinds of script. In fact the poems, as they are set out, constitute two columns, which might be thought of as two paths along which the reader can choose to walk.

The two paths are in fact quite distinct: the Japanese characters are always related to the French poem, but taken on their own they consist of two 'words' that do not always match each other. For instance, the two characters alongside 'Le souvenir déjà/ se mêle/ à/ la/ fumé e/ bleu e/ de Kyoto' (phrase 155) are the characters for 'smoke' and 'city'.[72] 'Smoke' and 'city' might well conjure up images of a polluted Tokyo for the Japanese reader who has no French, a million miles from the evocative spirit of the French poem. Similarly, 'Chut!/ si nous/ faisons du bruit/ le temps/ va recommencer' (phrase 101) sets up a relationship between silence and time: the characters indeed mean 'silence' and 'time', but there is nothing in the Japanese to suggest how the two concepts may be linked to each other. At times the two characters constitute a word, as in the case of phrase 153 whose two characters together make up 'droplet', but this does not happen very often.

The poems were clearly not intended for a Japanese reader with no French; but the presence of the Japanese characters means that such a reader could make something of these poems, so it is worth pointing out that the 'Japanese path' created by the characters makes for a very different reading experience from the French one, as can be seen from the following sequence of characters and phrases:

花　　　　Seule　　　　　　　　est
脆　　　　la　　　　　　assez fragile
　　　　　rose　　　　pour exprimer
　　　　　　　　　　　　l'Eternité

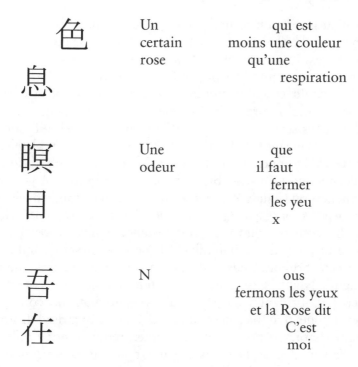

色
息

瞑
目

吾
在

Un
certain
rose

qui est
moins une couleur
qu'une
respiration

Une
odeur

que
il faut
fermer
les yeu
x

N

ous
fermons les yeux
et la Rose dit
C'est
moi

The non-Japanese reader of *Cent Phrases pour éventails* might pardonably assume that, in each case, the meaning of the French poem had been encapsulated in the two characters: there is a prejudicial image of Oriental poetry as being far more concise than Western poetry that might well lead a reader to that conclusion.[73] But this is emphatically not the case in *Cent Phrases pour éventails*. Walking along the French path, so to speak, of these phrases, we might very briefly summarise its route as follows: over the course of the poems the identity of the rose, as fragrance, develops, reaching a dramatic apogee in the fourth phrase when the rose directly addresses the reader.[74] The Japanese path, by contrast, would be a succession of characters meaning 'flower, fragility' (phrase 20), 'colour, breath' (21), one word meaning 'to close one's eyes' (22), and 'I, to be' (23). There are no characters that offer syntactical links: it is nothing but a succession of the above nouns and verbs, highly evocative and perhaps arriving more quickly at the notion of identity that seems to be the theme of this sequence, but not yet poetry.

The question that needs then to be asked is why the characters are there. Is it possible that they are purely decorative, in the *japoniste* tradition? It is difficult to imagine how this might be the case, given the genesis of the characters. As Truffet explains, they were added to the French texts after Claudel had written them, and were chosen by two Japanese academics, friends of Claudel who spoke fluent French and who would certainly not have entertained the idea of using Japanese writing decoratively. In order to answer this question, we should perhaps start from the fact that Claudel himself did not read Japanese. This means that he had to trust his advisers completely, and indeed the calligrapher, given that the result of this collaboration was to render the work unreadable to him, at least in part. A gesture of great boldness on Claudel's part, the arrangement certainly meant that certain aspects of *Cent Phrases pour éventails* are quite clearly beyond his control. Phrase 10, for instance, which reads 'La nuit/ approche ta joue/ de ce bouddha de/ pierre et/ resens combien/ la journée a été/ brûlante', has as its accompanying characters 'summer' and 'night'. Night is certainly there, but summer? Of course, the 'journée [...] brûlante' suggests this season, but the concept of summer is one that has been inferred and summarised from the poem: the characters are therefore an interpretation, not a reflection of the French poem. There is a similar act of deduction in the characters alongside 'Moins/ la rougeur/ de la pourpre/ que le s/ on/ de/ l'or' (phrase 34): they signify 'gold' and 'bell'. The 'sound of gold' is a beautiful, slightly abstract image: turning it into a bell translates it into a concrete instance. Such cases, where the two characters are not strictly within the sphere of meaning created by the French poem, do not occur often, but Claudel must have realised that this might happen, and have wished for the collaborators to take their independent path through his work nonetheless.

Perhaps Claudel hoped that this subsidiary path, unreadable for him, within *Cent Phrases pour éventails* could stand as a symbol of his incomplete knowledge of Japan. This would fit with his choice of a fragmentary form, so inimical to his customary desire for coherence and completeness, and with his preference for practice over theory in this work. Having walked his way from *Connaissance de l'Est* through 'la Muraille intérieure' and *L'Oiseau Noir* to the encounter-based poetry of *Cent Phrases pour éventails*, perhaps Claudel wished to build a margin of ignorance into his final walk in Japan, and that margin was created by his allowing a parallel path of reading to be put into his own work.

The theme of walking has been a useful way of approaching Claudel's 'Japanese' texts, because walking represents a paradigmatic relationship between the self and the other, or the self and the world. For Claudel, it is one way of describing the cognitive, and hence creative, act. In 'Le Promeneur', the walker starts off as a knowledge-seeking conqueror, and ends as a receptive listener who hopes to align his internal rhythms with those of nature. This development is one that is followed by the overall shape of the whole of *Connaissance de l'Est*, and at the end of the collection the walker who is the poetic 'je' dissolves into nothingness, as the poet departs from the East with a broken heart and inability to walk further. In 'La Muraille intérieure', the walk is of a very different kind, but here too the poet's selfhood is challenged: stopping for too long on the edge of the moat can lead to a loss of the self. The results of this walk are both philosophical and aesthetic, and lead Claudel to experiment with decentred form and inertia in his *versets*. In both *Connaissance de l'Est* and 'La Muraille', it is the trope of walking – walking in Japan – that supplies the poet with a model for the necessary yet paradoxical relationship between self and other, the guiding principle behind the perennial oscillation between the individual and creation.

L'Oiseau noir dans le soleil levant contains both concrete and metaphorical walks through Japanese nature and art which are perfected instances of the aimless, meandering walk: they are walks in which 'connaissance' about Japan is gathered on an empirical basis, not through preconceived theoretical systems or generalisations (with the exception of 'Un Regard sur l'âme japonaise'). Here, already, the contingent – things encountered by chance, whether it is a cataclysmic event such as the Kanto earthquake, or a painting of two bamboos by Shiki – has been woven into the structure of the whole, which is why *L'Oiseau noir dans le soleil levant* is so heterogeneous. *Cent Phrases pour éventails*, of course, is structured around the very act of the chance encounter. The wandering poet reacts to each encounter with a brief poem, and in each case his self is subsumed into the encounter with the other: the organising intelligence disappears behind the itinerary of the walk, and becomes a mere recorder of fragments of knowledge and experience.

Yet the fragmentary knowledge of Japan that comes out of the walks in *Cent Phrases pour éventails* is not unrelated to the type of knowledge pursued by the younger walker of *Connaissance de l'Est*. 'Co-naissance', even at its most 'Symbolist' stage, was based on encounters with non-systematised fragments of knowledge: the coherent system was created through the rebirth of the knower into a world that contained the new information. The 'co' of 'co-naissance' signals the fact of living *with* the new knowledge, a co-existence which seems to suggest equality rather than domination. In any case, we saw in *Connaissance de l'Est* that any domination of the other through walking was temporary, uncomfortable (for the walker) and finally unsuccessful (in 'Dissolution'). There does seem to be a development from *Connaissance de l'Est* through 'La Muraille' and *L'Oiseau noir dans le soleil levant* to *Cent Phrases pour éventails*, showing the self becoming more and more accepting of the other: but the awareness of the other is already present in the earliest work. By the time we get to *Cent Phrases pour éventails*, the acceptance of the other into the self's system is at its highest level, with the Japanese characters being incorporated, literally, into the individual poems. But this is not a radically different position from that of the poet in *Connaissance de l'Est*, because the act of walking has always been conducive to the acquisition of fragmentary knowledge, and in all of Claudel's 'Japanese' works this act structures the way in which Japan is seen by the traveller.

Perhaps what develops in Claudel is not so much his attitude towards the other, but his sense of what constitutes knowledge: starting from the Symbolist, systemic version, he journeys to a preference for knowledge left in the fragmentary and contingent state that is obtained through encounter. The history of the twentieth century certainly seemed to favour the latter model as being the only reliable one. The end of the First World War precipitated the demise of systems and structures everywhere, and many a writer turned back to the concrete and personal from the global and abstract.[75] Claudel was certainly able to write fondly about Japan to his Japanese friends after the war, regardless of the country's systematised militarism that had led to such tragedy. Writing to Professor Yamanouchi in 1949, in response to a much-awaited letter from the Japanese academic, Claudel begins his letter thus: 'C'est avec une grande joie que j'ai pris connaissance de votre lettre et constaté que vous avez survécu à l'effroyable épreuve qui a atteint votre cher et beau pays', and ends it on a note of encouragement and sympathy: 'J'ai gardé le meilleur souvenir de notre fraternelle collaboration d'autrefois et c'est de tout coeur que je vous dis, à vous et à tous nos amis: Courage! espérance! Le soleil n'a pas encore fini de se lever! Nippon banzaï!'[76] Boldly disregarding the military connotations of both the rising sun and the exhortation,[77] Claudel reclaims them to refer back to his own experience of Japan, and his personal relationship with members of the now defeated militarist nation. Never one to fall in with a majority opinion, Claudel clearly stuck with his own image of Japan after the war, an image that he had found for himself on his walks, from 1898 to 1927, through Japanese culture and country.

CHAPTER FOUR

Postwar Travellers and Photographic Writing: Roland Barthes, Michel Butor, Gérard Macé

Since the Second World War, Japan has received a multitude of visitors from the West, many times more than the total number who stepped onto its shores between 1532 and 1945. Starting with the American Occupation forces immediately after Japan's surrender in August 1945, they have been of all sorts: academics, journalists, importers, exporters, and countless representatives of that type of traveller ubiquitous in the late twentieth century, the tourist.[1] Like many other countries, Japan has been heavily marketed for tourism in the postwar period, and visited and photographed by tourists from all over the world. But the greater number of travellers, although it has given rise to a greater number of writings on Japan, does not seem to have resulted in any new *types* of traveller. The journalist, the diplomat, even the 'walker' à la Claudel: all have their descendants in the postwar period, as does the amateur art-lover, who numbers amongst his posterity several famous writers – Roland Barthes, Michel Butor, Jacques Roubaud and Marguerite Yourcenar, to name but a few.[2] Indeed the only new kind of traveller, or rather the only new way of seeing that applies to the postwar traveller in Japan, revolves around photography.

There were, of course, photographer-travellers in Japan before 1945: Felice Beato,[3] for instance, as well as Félicien Challaye, returned to Europe with images of Japan that became deeply influential.[4] But it is with the ubiquity and popularity of the photographic image that the camera's point of view has become an integral part of any traveller's way of seeing, whether or not she decides to carry a camera herself. In the late twentieth and early twenty-first century, photography is an inescapable fact in the practice of travel writing. The obvious, but most important effect of the ascendancy of the photograph is its rivalry with writing: wherever there is the possibility of writing about Japan, there is the possibility of a photograph, and this new dispensation has created a fruitful interplay between text and image in the work of a number of these travellers which distinguishes them from earlier instances of their 'type'.

Because of its dominant presence in travel writing of this period, whether or not it is physically present in the texts, I have decided to use photography as my main criterion for selecting and examining images of Japan in this chapter. In other words, I intend to take very literally my original plan to explore different ways of seeing, by concentrating on the different ways in which travellers of the late twentieth century and early twenty-first century have 'seen' Japan through the camera. Photography poses various challenges and problems for the written travelogue. As an illustrative aid it may lead the writer to indulge in a laziness of description, or (in better works) a desire to write what cannot be photographed; it can offer itself as 'proof' of travel, in a way that writing cannot; it can encourage the writer to question the value of writing as a mode of representation when it has to compete (or cooperate) with photography. Many writers are fascinated by the ontological status of photography, and this can become a problematic issue when the accurate representation of the other is at stake. In my discussions of photography in this chapter, I will be starting from the theoretical stance that appears to prevail, namely that the photograph bears a primarily referential, rather than representational, relationship to reality. In so doing I will be in agreement with the Barthes of *La Chambre claire*, but also with a number of more recent theorists of photography and practising photographers.[5] I will also be reaching back to an earlier theorist of art and photography, Walter Benjamin, and making use in particular of his notion of 'aura', indispensable to an analysis of stereotyping vision.

The writers to be dealt with in this chapter, Barthes, Butor and Macé, will not be given equal amounts of space. Indeed the first two writers have been selected to provide a context of postwar French writings on Japan – a prehistory of sorts – for the last, Gérard Macé: they will be visited as significant points on the way to the culmination of the relationship between photography and writing that Macé's writings exemplify. Barthes is a theoretician and connoisseur of photography: he is also a semiotician, an academic traveller who looks to categorise and analyse the other. Butor has written fragmentary pieces reminiscent of Barthes' work on Japan, but he has also collaborated with photographers by composing haiku-like poems, as Macé does, to accompany photographs of Japan. Of the three,

Gérard Macé is the only one who is himself a photographer. He is also a poet, essayist and translator, whose photographs of Japan will be examined in the context of his writings on the same subject. Pursuing the interplay between photography and writing in the works of these and other writers, I hope to arrive at several definitions of what has been called 'photographic writing' in relation to Japan,[6] a genre that includes some of the most interesting travel writing of the late twentieth and early twenty-first century.

Roland Barthes

L'Empire des signes is perhaps the work most neglected by critics in the Barthesian canon, in spite of its publication in what might be considered a 'pivotal' year in Barthes' development: 1970 was also the year of *S/Z*, therefore that of his definitive break with structuralist modes of thought, and his development into the playful patterns of his poststructuralist phase.[7] *L'Empire des signes* is certainly the first of Barthes' works to contain so many photographs, pictures and samples of handwritten text, which link it to the later *Roland Barthes par Roland Barthes* (1975) and *La Chambre claire* (1980). It consists of short chapters on various aspects of life in Japan, such as different kinds of food, the nature of chopsticks, puppet theatre and the practice of gift-giving, analysed in the language of semiotics. The result, at first glance, looks very much like a collection of travel notes and souvenirs by an eminent semiotician: a subjective representation of self-consciously selected aspects of Japanese culture.

As against this impression, however, Barthes makes very clear, from the start, the non-referential nature of his work. The project is a highly complex one, as he explains in detail in the first chapter:

> Je puis aussi, sans prétendre en rien représenter ou analyser la moindre réalité (ce sont les gestes majeurs du discours occidental), prélever quelque part dans le monde (*là-bas*) un certain nombre de traits (mot graphique et linguistique), et de ces traits former délibérément un système. C'est ce système que j'appellerai: le Japon.
>
> L'Orient et l'Occident ne peuvent donc être pris ici comme des 'réalités', que l'on essaierait d'approcher et d'opposer historiquement, philosophiquement, culturellement, politiquement. Je ne regarde pas amoureusement vers une essence orientale, l'Orient

m'est indifférent [...] Ce qui peut être visé, dans la considération de l'Orient, ce ne sont pas d'autres symboles, une autre métaphysique, une autre sagesse (encore que celle-ci apparaisse bien désirable); c'est la possiblité d'une différence, d'une mutation, d'une révolution dans la propriété des systèmes symboliques.[8]

Typically provocative in the best Barthesian tradition, this statement has given rise to a number of critics accusing him of orientalism, egoism or opportunism.[9] How, they have asked, can Barthes claim freedom from the responsibility of mimetic representation, make a patently dubious bid for the fictionality of his creation, at the same time as borrowing 'un certain nombre de traits' from an existing country? Put thus it certainly does look like a case of having one's cake and eating it: at best a self-centred exercise, at worst a colonialist one in that it appropriates the other's features for his own ends.

But this is to misread Barthes' carefully constructed defence of his project, although it is, admittedly, a highly wrought balancing act. Having declared his non-mimetic intentions, he goes on to say that he will avoid the Orientalist fiction that looks 'amoureusement vers une essence orientale': in other words, Barthes is keenly aware that there is a long history of Oriental fantasies behind him.[9] What he seeks is not an alternative world but a differential one: 'la possibilité d'une différence [...] dans la propriété des systèmes symboliques'. That is to say that his fiction will be that of a world that is consciously designed to be different from Europe, a utopia to Europe's dystopia, but which will also challenge the ways in which we think about cultural difference:

> Il faudrait faire un jour l'histoire de notre propre obscurité, [...] recenser le long des siècles les quelques appels de différence que nous avons pu parfois entendre, les récupérations idéologiques qui ont immanquablement suivi et qui consistent à toujours acclimater notre inconnaissance de l'Asie grâce à des langages connus (l'Orient de Voltaire, de la *Revue Asiatique*, de Loti ou d'*Air France*). Aujourd'hui il y a sans doute mille choses à apprendre de l'Orient: un énorme travail de *connaissance* est, sera nécessaire [...]; mais il faut aussi que, acceptant de laisser de part et d'autre d'immenses zones d'ombre (le Japon capitaliste, l'acculturation américaine, le développement technique), un mince filet de lumière cherche, non d'autres symboles, mais la fissure même du symbolique. Cette fissure ne peut apparaître au niveau des produits culturels: ce qui est présenté ici n'appartient pas (du moins on le souhaite) à l'art, à l'urbanisme japonais, à la cuisine japonaise. (*ES*, pp. 10–11)

The languages that Europe has tended to use to describe the East have been, as Barthes tells us here, 'des langages connus', appropriating discourses such as those of Voltaire, Loti or more recently the travel brochures of Air France. Such Orientalist discourses have structured the way in which we describe or analyse the East ('les gestes majeurs du discours occidental'). What Barthes is offering is an antidote to such discourses: not a text that will give us a better description or analysis of the 'real' Japan, but one which will challenge the conventions which structure our ways of thinking about Japan. 'Un mince filet de lumière cherche, non d'autres symboles, mais la fissure même du symbolique' refers to the way in which he will search out not new symbols of the East, but the fault line in the symbolic system which creates our very concepts of 'East' and 'West'. This is the sense in which Barthes' 'Japan' will be a fiction: it will belong to a different ontological order, being not so much a representation of a real place as a differential creation that will expose the codes that Europeans have always made use of when talking about Japan.

The results of this project are as playful as they are subversive. The following description of the *tempura* chef, for instance, is one which undermines a sense-making discourse with which Barthes himself has long been associated, that of structuralism:

> Son activité est à la lettre graphique: il inscrit l'aliment dans la matière; son étal est distribué comme la table d'un calligraphe; il touche les substances comme le graphiste (surtout s'il est japonais) qui alterne les godets, les pinceaux, la pierre à encre, l'eau, le papier; il accomplit ainsi, dans la cohue du retaurant et l'entrecroisement des commandes, un étagement, non du temps, mais des temps (ceux d'une grammaire de la *tempura*). (*ES*, p. 39)

Never has a battered prawn been so thoroughly theorised. Similarly, writing about *sukiyaki* (dubbed 'la nourriture décentrée'!), a family dish cooked at the table with all the diners participating by putting the raw ingredients into the boiling soup, Barthes reaches for the outlandish hyperbole of 'une petite odyssée de la Nourriture que vous vivez du regard: vous assistez au Crépuscule de la Crudité' (*ES*, p. 31). These descriptions are too playfully constructed to be mistaken for serious representations of Japanese culture. Their tone is closer to that of parody than proper description, and indeed they are perhaps best read as little parodies of certain master discourses:

the discourse of Structuralism, as above, or that of exoticism. The sentence following the above-quoted 'Crépuscule de la Crudité' reminds us that 'Cette Crudité, *on le sait*, est la divinité tutélaire de la nourriture japonaise' (*ES*, p. 30, my italics). Dwelling on the one fact about Japanese food that any Frenchman might be acquainted with, that is to say its rawness (*sushi, sashimi*), Barthes offers us a fanciful account of it which ends up drawing attention to the conventionality of the exoticist discourse.

But in *L'Empire des signes*, Barthes subverts another, more fundamental code used by his predecessors to represent Japan hitherto: that of writing itself. He does this partly through making use of the writing paradigm for his parodic descriptions of Japanese artefacts, as seen above, but also by setting up a distinctly egalitarian relationship between writing and the photographs in his text. He explains the relationship between the two at the very start of the book, in a prefatory paragraph:

> *Le texte ne commente pas les images, les images n' 'illustrent' pas le texte: chacune a été seulement pour moi le départ d'une sorte de vacillement visuel, analogue peut-être à cette* perte de sens *que le Zen appelle un* satori: *texte et images, dans leur entrelacs, veulent assurer la circulation, l'échange de ces signifiants: le corps, le visage, l'écriture, et y lire le recul des signes.* (*ES*, p. 7)

It is very much the case that the photographs are separate entities in the book, not illustrations of the text. There is a photograph of a *pachinko* parlour in the chapter entitled 'pachinko', and a close-up of some boys' faces in the chapter called 'la paupière', but otherwise the photographs tend to appear independently of whatever the text is explaining or describing. If there is a relationship between text and photograph, it seems to be one of analogy. In the chapter on *bunraku* (traditional puppet theatre), called 'les trois écritures', Barthes describes how the puppets are manipulated by perfectly visible puppeteers, and how their dialogue is provided by a narrator sitting on the side of the stage: 'le Bunraku pratique donc trois écritures séparées, qu'il donne à lire simultanément en trois lieux de spectacle: la marionnette, le manipulateur, le vociférant' (*ES*, p. 69). Several pages later, there is a photograph of a hand holding a calligraphy brush over a piece of paper: an instance of writing, true, but only analogously related to the 'writings' of *bunraku*. Similarly, following a section in the same chapter on the 'illusory' nature of Western theatre ('dans notre art théâtral, l'acteur feint d'agir, mais ses actes ne sont jamais que des gestes: sur la scène, rien que du théâtre, et cependant du théâtre honteux', p. 71), there is a series of photographs of a *kabuki* female impersonator: one of him playing a female role, and then another of him without make-up, flanked by his two sons. The caption explains the relevance of this incursion of *kabuki* into a chapter on *bunraku*:

> Le travesti oriental ne copie pas la Femme, il la signifie; il ne s'empoisse pas dans son modèle, il se détache de son signifié; la Feminité est donnée à lire, non à voir: translation, non transgression; le signe passe du grand rôle feminin au quinquagénaire père de famille: c'est le même homme, mais où commence la métaphore?' (*ES*, p. 73)

Thus, *kabuki* is also a non-realistic theatre: like *bunraku*, it does not mimic reality, but signifies it. A photograph of a scene from *bunraku*, placed in this chapter, would have been illustrative: the choice of the *kabuki* photograph fulfils a similar explicative function while maintaining the independence of photography vis-à-vis the text. In fact the photograph here might be said to have the same relationship to the text as the *kabuki* actor to the woman: not copying, but signifying.

Thus the status of writing in *L'Empire des signes* is generally 'downgraded' in the book, and shown to be just one code amongst others that has to compete not only with the photograph, but with the drawings and doodles: in particular, with a number of hand-written – or hand-drawn – maps of Tokyo or Kyoto neighbourhoods that Barthes includes in the book. Being combinations of drawing and writing, they seem to have an advantage over writing on its own: also, they function as extremely striking and immediate instances of Japanese reality, having been produced by Japanese friends of Barthes' in order to direct him to specific places in Tokyo or Kyoto. The handwritten comments are also a subtle way of undermining the general reader's unquestioning acceptance of the printed word. Appearing not only in the margins, but in the middle of the page (in 'prime' space, as it were), they offer alternative narratives that appear more 'authentic' because of their handwritten nature. At the end of the chapter on Japanese food, for instance, a mini-chapter entitled 'Le rendez-vous' opens in Barthes' handwriting, whose content as well as its form is subversive of the *printed* book that is *l'Empire des signes*:

Ouvrez un guide de voyage: vous y trouverez d'ordinaire un petit lexique, mais ce lexique portera bizarrement sur des choses ennuyeuses et inutiles: la douane, la poste, l'hôtel, le coiffeur, le médecin, les prix. Cependant, qu'est-ce-que voyager? Rencontrer. Le seul lexique important est celui du rendez-vous. (*ES*, p. 25)

This 'alternative' text continues with a number of little 'lexiques': four words/phrases in the margin on p. 28 (starting with 'rendez vous yakusoku'), a few more in the bottom half of p. 35 (subtitled 'le rendez vous'), and several more again on p. 51. The overall effect is that of graffiti, a playful scribbling on the monument of the printed page that distracts and amuses, inviting us not to take either form of writing too seriously.

There is, however, one kind of writing that Barthes speaks highly of in *L'Empire des signes*, although it does seem, at first sight, to be an impossible writing. In the haiku, Barthes claims to have discovered a form of writing that has, like the photograph, an unmediated relationship with reality. He describes its philosophy, which is to 'suspendre le langage, non de le provoquer' (*ES*, p. 94), and then goes on to claim that haiku not only stops language but offers a way out of the signifying system, in spite of being formed from language. In 'Tel', Barthes argues that the haiku is neither description or definition, 'les deux fonctions fondamentales de notre écriture classique', but designation: 'le haiku s'amincit jusqu'à la pure et seule désignation. *C'est cela, c'est ainsi*, dit le haiku, *c'est tel*' (*ES*, p. 111). A haiku is a poem which simply points at the referent, instead of describing or defining it. In possessing this 'direct' relationship with the real, haiku – in Barthes' account – is very similar to photography: both haiku and photography have privileged access to the referent, bypassing the signifying system:

Le sens n'y est [dans le haiku] qu'un flash, une griffure de lumière: [...] mais le flash du haiku n'éclaire, ne révèle rien; il est celui d'une photographie que l'on prendrait très soigneusement (à la japonaise), mais en ayant omis de charger l'appareil de sa pellicule. (*ES*, p. 113)

This strange choice of 'l'image d'un acte photographique sans photographie' for the haiku is proof, I believe, that Barthes did not ultimately believe that it was possible to escape writing through writing in this way.[11] At the very least, it is not an option available to the Western writer: amidst his enthusiasm for its freedom from language, he notes that the haiku is 'un langage qui nous est refusé'. Although he flirts with the haiku as a possible saviour, the only real way out of the signifying system for Barthes turns out to be photography, a position that he would affirm in *La Chambre claire*. The photographs in *L'Empire des signes* are neither illustrative (descriptive) nor symbolic (metaphorical): they are simple instances of 'tel', *pointings* at Japan, fragments of reality which have been inserted at appropriate points in the text as 'proof' of the real. The photographs, if not the text, are seen as instances of referents rather than signifieds, anticipating the eventual 'recul des signes' mentioned as a utopian ideal in the prefatory paragraph to the book.

Indeed, already in the very first chapter, Barthes acknowledges the failure of his writing to come up to the impossible standards set by photography when it comes to 'pointing' at Japan. At the same time, however, he makes clear his debt to Japan as his initial source of inspiration:

> L'auteur n'a jamais, en aucun sens, photographié le Japon. Ce serait plutôt le contraire: le Japon l'a étoilé d'éclairs multiples; ou mieux encore: le Japon l'a mis en situation d'écriture. (*ES*, p. 11)

L'Empire des signes is a theoretically sophisticated work, but one that was genuinely inspired by its author's visit to Japan, and it shows Barthes at his ludic best. Playful and subversive towards the codes it exposes, including the most basic one of writing itself, the book succeeds in offering a 'presentation' of Japan that is not, in spite of its complicated agenda, Orientalist. Through announcing itself as a fiction, but retaining difference and subversion as its primary objectives, Barthes' work skilfully sidesteps the representational traps into which some of his predecessors have fallen. And intrinsic to this success is the use of photography. The book opens and closes with two photographs of Kazuo Funaki, a Japanese actor: in the first photograph his expression is serious, his fine features composed as he stares directly into the camera. He reappears at the very end of the book, on the final page facing the penultimate page, on which we read the following:

> Incentré, l'espace est aussi réversible: vous pouvez retourner le corridor de Shikidai et rien ne se passera, sinon une inversion sans conséquence du haut et du bas, de la droite et de la gauche: le contenu est congédié sans retour: que l'on passe, traverse ou s'asseye à même le plancher (ou le plafond, si vous retournez l'image), il n'y a rien à *saisir*.

Photographs of the actor Kazuo Funaki, from Roland Barthes, *L'Empire des signes*

These words, the final words of the body of the text, are followed by '*...au sourire près*', placed at the bottom right-hand corner of the page and serving as a caption for the photograph (on the next page) of the actor, who is now smiling faintly. Thus the photograph has the last word over language, and it directly contradicts the conclusion of the text; there is nothing to capture, says the text, but the supplementary words in the caption gesture towards the smile, faint but unmistakeable, that *has* been captured by the camera. The book has progressed from unsmiling to smiling actor, if nothing else, and these 'émanations du référent', referent Japan, are presented to us as proof of its reality.

Michel Butor

Michel Butor's writings on Japan present us with a curious case of the *difficulty* of writing about Japan for the scrupulous late-twentieth-century writer. His works are moulded by the formal, theoretical and historical pressures he clearly feels whenever he takes up his pen to 'parler du Japon', which, if we are to believe the blurb on the back cover of his most recent attempt, is an enduring obsession: 'Comment parler du Japon? Michel Butor s'y essaie depuis toujours.' Perhaps part of his dilemma stems from a professional level of self-awareness only to be expected of a former *nouveau romancier*. By the same token, however, he seems to revel in the formal difficulties he encounters.

Butor first visited Japan in 1967, but hesitated to write about it directly afterwards:

> Ce devait être un voyage d'un mois, mais on m'a demandé d'y ajouter une semaine en Corée et une au Cambodge. C'est ce qui a provoqué les deux textes du second *Génie du lieu*, intitulés 'La boue à Séoul' et 'La pluie à Angkor', écrits dans la station thermale de Cauterets où notre maison donnait sur le gave. La visite a dépassé mes espérances et je savais dès lors que je ferais tout pour retourner un jour dans l'archipel et pour essayer d'en parler.[12]

It was evidently the beginning of a complicated relationship: like a teenager who chats up the girl sitting next to the one he actually fancies, Butor decided he would write first about the Far Eastern countries that were not Japan, in 'La boue à Séoul' and 'La pluie à Angkor'. His first text on things Japanese (in which, according to him, 'j'ai tenté de m'approcher davantage') was 'Archipel Shopping', which appeared in *Génie du lieu 3, Boomerang*. He was then commissioned to write 'Flottements d'Est en Ouest' by a Japanese publisher, which was published in *Avant-Goût 4* and in *Transit*. *Tables d'orientation: Au Japon côte à côte* (1993) was a collaborative work, composed with a pair of photographers, and finally – to date – *Le Japon depuis la France, un rêve à l'ancre*, was published in 1995.

All of these texts display a curiously *mediated* approach to Japan, in stark contrast with Barthes' desire to accede directly to the Other, whether through haiku/photography or more simply through the 'rendez-vous'. Butor approaches Japan obliquely, first through Cambodia and Korea in *Génie du lieu 2*, in which Japan is mentioned tantalisingly on the edges of his journeys: 'J'ai repris le lendemain l'avion des Japan Airlines pour Tokyo, après avoir fait quelques emplettes dans une galerie marchande reliant les deux principaux hôtels de Séoul'. The text on Japan in *Génie du lieu 3* is concerned with *nô* theatre, but all the information comes from a book by Donald Keene, containing photographs of key scenes by Kaneko Hiroshi: Butor tells us that he obtained the book in Japan during his first visit. Not only, then, is he seeing *nô* theatre through the eyes of Keene and Kaneko (he specifies that he had not, at that stage, seen a *nô* play), but his own 'contribution' is merely to *translate* the captions of the photographs: 'j'ai traduit les légendes, comme si ç'avait été des commentaires murmurés à mon oreille par un ami compréhensif lors d'un de ces spectacles qui m'auraient été alors presque totalement obscurs' (*JF*, p. 32). It is as if he is reluctant to 'see' Japan without some form of protective – or interpretive – screen; or at least he is reluctant to *write* about Japan without a support system of references and mediators in place.

In *Transit*, Butor offers his own selective history of the art and architecture of Japan, basing his text on twenty-one 'classics' from the huge array of possible instances. His selection has, he tells us, been determined in part by his access to them and by strong affinities of a personal nature (a number of the works are characterised by themes dear to Butor, such as travel, 'unfinished' works of art, cultural exchange and artistic collaboration). A new feature of his relationship to Japan in this work, however, is that the structure of the book is modelled on certain features of the visual and architectural works he has chosen to examine: 'his selection of 21 Japanese works can be seen as an allusion to the various numbered series produced by Hokusai, Hiroshige and other artists, Butor offering here his own "21 Views of Japan" or his personal "21 Stages of a Journey through Japan".'[13] The bidirectional format of *Transit* is clearly also a homage to the format of the Japanese book, which proceeds in the opposite direction to a Western book, as well as a development of Butor's fascination with the book as object.[14] Butor is thus much more committed to writing about Japan in this book, but here again it is through the medium of artworks – indeed, photographs of artworks – that Japan is approached.

The photograph is a source of continuing fascination for Butor, as is evident from any list of his works and achievements: he has collaborated on many occasions with photographers as well as artists, and has even published a slim volume of his own photographs (although none of these are of Japan).[15] *Tables d'orientation: Au Japon côte à côte* (1993) is perhaps the work in which Butor gets closest to photography in the context of Japan. It is a large book, 20 by 30 centimetres, containing sixty photographs by Gérald Minkoff and Muriel Olesen: the 'côte à côte' of the title refers to the fact that the photographs come in pairs, one taken by each photographer in the same location. This of course does not mean that the photographs are of the same things: the photo of a station front, for instance, might be paired with the close-up of a commuter standing in the same station. Butor's contribution consists in a series of brief poems which are placed underneath each photograph, in the position normally reserved for a caption. The poems are made up of short lines, never more than six or seven syllables per line, and are directly related to the photographs of which they constitute, in a loose sense, the captions. Thus, for instance, under a photograph of a little girl standing next to a temple fountain on which there is a carved dragon, Butor has written: 'Je me souviens que/ dans une existence antérieure/ j'étais moi-même un roi-dragon/ c'est ce qui me donne/ cet air conquérant'. On the facing page is a photograph of the same carved dragon, this time with no little girl. The poem underneath this one is as follows: 'Je me demande si/ dans une existence futur/ je ne deviendrai pas/ un enfant japonais/ c'est pourquoi je m'essaie/ aux sourires narquois'.

These are essentially slight poems, usually showing a certain familiarity with Japanese culture: the sense of the above poems, for instance, is based on the concept of reincarnation, although they are easily comprehensible even to a reader with no knowledge of Buddhism. Just one or two of them are slightly worrying in their assumption of cultural difference: underneath the photograph of a laughing girl, who has placed her hand over her mouth in the customary Japanese fashion, is the following poem: 'Je cache mon rire/ devant l'étranger/ qui ne doit pas savoir/ ce qu'il éveille en moi/ ce que je vois en lui/ derrière son masque' (p. 33). There seems to be some over-interpretation going on here: in Japan it is just 'good manners' for women to cover their mouths when laughing, whereas Butor's poem seems to partake of an Orientalist mystique of the inscrutable Japanese person.

Perhaps these occasional slips into Orientalism are the result of the fact that Butor never set great store by these slender offerings, which he seems to regard as having been a whimsical experiment in Japanese-like poetical forms ('je désirais utiliser des formes courtes, lointaines adaptations de formes japonaises classiques' [*JF*, p. 165]). It is interesting that the lack of seriousness in his formal approach seems to have occasioned a lack of respect towards the other, about which he is normally so circumspect. These poems were certainly intended to be subordinate to the photographs: 'il s'agissait d'agrémenter par quelque inscription leurs doubles pages dans un volume' (*JF*, p. 164). 'Agrémenter' is an interesting choice of word here, in that it is a word often used to describe the relationship of an illustration or photograph to the text: it reverses the classic hierarchy between photograph and text. Butor's poems are 'trimmings', not essential to the book in any way but included to 'brighten up' (another translation for 'agrémenter') the photographs. In this book, Butor seems to be seeking a deliberately marginal status for his poems: written after the photos were taken, they are really no more than captions. That the photographs are their *raison d'être* becomes clear when they are forced to stand on their own, without the photographs, in *Le Japon depuis la France, un rêve à l'ancre*: separated from the photographs on which they depended for their meaning, they are, quite simply, very difficult to understand.

Le Japon depuis la France, un rêve à l'ancre – the latest, to date, of Butor's attempts to 'parler du Japon', however obliquely – is a triumph of the indirect approach that Butor has cultivated towards Japan throughout the works described above. Structured in alternating chapters entitled 'conférences' and 'confidences', it is a playful collage of quotations on Japan from writers across the ages, from Marco Polo through Loti and Claudel to himself. Roughly speaking, the 'conférences' chapters contain quotations from other writers, whereas the 'confidences' chapters contain quotations from his own works. The quotations are identifiable as such because they appear under sub-headings which are the titles of the works from which he is quoting: for instance, many of the 'confidences' chapters have 'Archipel Shopping' and 'Flottements' as regular subtitles, and the later ones include amongst their subtitles 'côte à côte'. Half-way through the book, we learn that even the sections of the 'conférences' which are not presented as quotations are based on a series of lectures Butor prepared in 1989 for a visit to Rikkyo University in Tokyo. As for the quotations from other writers, Butor has given his readers a delightful collection of quotations from Claudel, Loti, Michaux and Goncourt, many of which come from works that have been examined in my own study. Interspersed with selections from his own writings, the total effect is a dissolution of Butor's own voice, a constant con-textualisation that lessens the impact of his own writings on Japan.

Butor's Japanese writings show him to be clearly passionate yet strangely retiring about Japan. His indirect approaches to the object of his desire seem to indicate both a deep reluctance to write about it, and an obvious enjoyment of this constant deferral. Perhaps it is simply that he is afraid to destroy a dream: the blurb on the back cover of *Le Japon depuis la France* describes how the book 'précise comment s'aventurer au plus près d'une fascination sans l'altérer'. Classic Saidian Orientalism, in a word: but if so, the Orientalism is all in the *form* rather than the content, as Butor is well and impartially informed about the aspects of Japanese culture that he writes about (for instance, in *Transit*), when he does actually manage to write about it. Rather than the bad faith of the nineteenth-century Orientalist, Butor's attitude is part and parcel of his personality as a late-twentieth-century experimental writer, whose allegiance to explorations in form does not allow him to commit to a serious and responsible representational ethos. His whole attitude towards 'writing' Japan is a game that he plays with himself, in which the reality of Japan becomes slowly diminished in its role as the eternally inaccessible object of representation.

A theoretical mind nursing a romantic ideal, Butor succeeds in keeping his distance from the object of his fantasy through the practices of quotation, translation, and commentary in the form of captions, or through giving pride of place to photography. And when that does not seem to be enough, he repeats like a mantra the following phrase: 'Et ce n'est pas encore cette fois-ci que j'aurai réussi à parler du Japon.'[16]

Gérard Macé

Gérard Macé is a writer whose varied works span a bewildering variety of genres. The prose poems of *Bois dormant* (1983)[17] com-bine a Surrealist vision with an irrepressible verbal exuberance, whereas *Le Dernier des Egyptiens* (1989), an imagined biography of Champollion and the story of his fascination with the physical aspect of language, is written in sparse and elegant prose. Another favourite theme is that of memory, whence his enduring love of Proust, whose work is discussed in a number of his books, for instance in *Le Manteau de Fortuny* (1987). His love of the non-verbal image is also attested to in various works, such as *L'art sans paroles* (1999), a collection of essays on silent cinema. As for photography, it is only very recently that Macé took up a camera himself ('jusqu'à l'âge de cinquante ans, les seules photographies que j'ai prises [...] sont celles que des passants m'ont demandé de prendre pour eux',[18] if we are to believe the preface to *La Photographie sans appareil*), but he has been interested in photography, and collaborating with photographers, for a much longer period. *Rome, l'invention du baroque* (1997) contains photographs by Isabel Muñoz: the text in *Choses rapportées du Japon* (1993) is accompanied by photographs by Pierre Alechinsky. His first published collections of photographs came out in 2000, one of which was *Un Monde qui ressemble au monde*, his images of the gardens of Kyoto; the other was *La Photographie sans appareil*. Macé has also published his photographs in a collection of texts on his work, *Images et signes: Lectures de Gérard Macé* (2001), and most recently in *Mirages et Solitudes* (2003).

To date, Macé has published a number of works inspired by Japan, which comprise some of his best travel writing, as well as being meditations on language, memory and childhood: *Où grandissent les pierres* (1985), *Choses rapportées du Japon* (1990), *Un Monde qui ressemble au monde* (2000), *Un détour par l'Orient* (2001). In this section I will trace his debt to earlier writers on Japan, and attempt to show how he emerges from the shadow of these influences as the practitioner of a new genre of travel writing peculiar to the late twentieth and early twenty-first century: the interplay between text and image in his books makes him a writer comparable, for instance, to W. G. Sebald. As far as classification in our typology of travellers is concerned, Macé has inherited a veritable wardrobeful of mantles. His fascination with the higher forms of Japanese culture links him loosely to Claudel and Barthes, although he avoids taking on the role of a full-time cultural critic. Indeed he never appears to aspire to the global, or encyclopaedic position (unlike, for instance, Bouvier),[19] preferring to offer his insights in fragmentary, seemingly disorganised form (as stray objects, for instance: '*choses* rapportées du Japon'): in this tendency he allies himself to the *flâneur*, 'botanising on the asphalt' of Tokyo or elsewhere. His stance is at times reminiscent of Michaux (to whose memory *Où grandissent les pierres* is dedicated) or Segalen (another favourite author of his), although he never takes on the mantle of authority integral to their viewpoints. And like Loti, his travels often take him back into his past, into those memories that are closest to him. Travel abroad as a way home, not just to the self's home country but to its very origins, is a theme that is never explicitly dealt with in Macé's works, but which appears to underlie a number of the texts that we will be examining.

In his essays on photography in *L'Image fantôme*, Hervé Guibert characterises Goethe's *Letters from Italy* as instances of what he calls 'l'écriture photographique', prevalent in genres such as letters and journals: 'c'est la trace la plus récente de la mémoire, et c'est à peine de la mémoire: comme quelque chose qui semble encore vibrer sur la rétine, c'est de l'impression, presque de l'instantané.'[20] Guibert here adapts his understanding of the physical process of seeing to photography: writing of this sort is almost as automatic as seeing, with the outside world making a physical impression (in the sense of imprint) that is immediately transformed into writing. Macé also talks about photography as if it were an extension of vision, but he describes the act of seeing as something much less immediate, an act that is never free of thought. He explains that his method of looking at things, with or without a camera to look through, has always been an act of *recognition* rather than an encounter with something completely new:

> Car il s'agit toujours, grâce à un mélange de surprise et de déjà vu, de reconnaître et de saisir au vol les images qu'on portait en soi, suffisamment transposées pour qu'elles soient autre chose que de pâles copies. Des images latentes, surgies de la mémoire ou du musée imaginaire qui n'attendaient qu'une rencontre au grand jour pour se révéler à nous. De ce point de vue, c'est le cerveau qui est la véritable chambre noire, où la mélancolie prend la pose plus souvent qu'on ne voudrait.[21]

If, as Macé suggests here, our vision is always mediated by what we have already seen, in reality or in our dreams and imaginings, his writing in *Où grandissent les pierres* is 'photographic' inasmuch as it is an exact description of his visual experience in Japan. Made up of fifteen short chapters, some of which are no more than two pages long, the text is a collection of 'snapshots' – of objects, people, and Macé's own thoughts – as he wanders around in Japan at the leisurely pace of a *flâneur*. We are given short descriptions of gardens, people's faces, the alphabets and characters, and of stories from Japanese legend and literature: and in almost every case, the Japanese artefact is related, through some form of recognition, to something that is familiar to the French writer. The links made are never simple comparisons (Macé deplores at one point 'le goût abusif des comparaisons; à quoi sert d'aller si loin si nous n'avons pas quitté nos crânes étroits?'), but associations of ideas or fortuitous resemblances that often occur in a dreamlike state. Thus, for instance, Japanese faces remind him of other (Western) faces he knows, 'comme en rêve lorsqu'on reconnaît un parent proche dans un corps étranger' (p. 23); Tanizaki's tale of the 'tatoueur' and his needles slides into a thought about the 'pointed' nature of a writer's style, derived from 'stylus, c'est-à-dire poinçon'. The temple gardens remind him of a cemetery in his natal village, where he 'retrouve la même émotion que devant les jardins de Kyoto'. Most dramatically, this seeing-as-recognition formula can be discerned in the narrative *order* adopted by Macé to tell the story of Urashima Taro, a Japanese fairy tale. The story is about a young fisherman who saves a turtle's life, and is invited down to the palace of the God of the Sea, where he spends three delightful years. When he decides to go back to his village, the princess of the sea gives him a lacquer box, which should only be opened, she tells him, when he has no idea what to do. Upon his return to dry land, he discovers that nobody recognises him, and is told that his parents died hundreds of years ago: in despair, he opens the box, and a cloud of smoke envelops him, turning him into an old, old man. Macé tells the story differently:

> Un nuage de fumée blanche, une volée de cendres au lieu du grand secret, c'est ce qu'aperçoit bien avant l'atroce réalité d'Hiroshima le héros malgré lui d'une légende japonaise, quand il ouvre en dépit de sa promesse le coffret qu'il tient d'un poisson (d'une princesse selon d'autres récits). Au même moment sa peau se ride, ses mains tremblent et sa chair se décompose...
>
> S'il a cédé à ce funeste désir, c'est qu'après trois années d'une vie voluptueuse, passé dans un palais sous la mer, il n'a plus retrouvé à l'emplacement de sa maison qu'un jardin en friche et une vague vision. 'Aussi loin que je me souvienne, lui répond un voisin qu'il interroge, je n'ai jamais vu ici de maison habitée. Mais on raconte au village qu'au siècle dernier, le pêcheur qui habitait là s'enfuit sur le dos d'une tortue de mer.'[22]

Why start with the punch-line, the dreadful ending of the fairy tale? Because the recognisable element for Macé, listening to the legend, is the cloud of smoke that brings great evil ('Hiroshima' is almost certainly the most recognisable place name in Japan for a French reader, certainly as recognisable as 'Tokyo'). The legend has nothing to do with the atomic tragedy, but it serves as a bridge – an evanescent, unreal one, but a bridge nonetheless – across which the French reader can reach into the heart of a foreign tale.[23] Recognition breeds intimacy, even where there is no reason for it (it is possible to feel warmly towards a stranger if she or he resembles a family member, for instance), which means that one's reaction to a new person or object is already determined by the 'images latentes' in the dark rooms of our minds: 'c'est le cerveau qui est la véritable chambre noire'. The importance of recognition in cognition is what makes Macé tell the story backwards, at the expense of suspense, because his priority is to give us his experience of Japan 'photographically': that is to say that his reader must trace the same trajectory, make the same connections, recognise the same cultural landmarks in order to arrive at the same experience.

Many of the thoughts and experiences described in *Où grandissent les pierres* are reproduced, word for word, in *Choses rapportées du Japon*,[24] but in much shorter form.[25] For instance, in *CRJ*, we are offered as a 'chose' the following fragment:

> Pour demander mon chemin, quelques phrases apprises par coeur et répétées comme les formules des contes.

In *OGP*, this formulation appears as part of a narrative:

> [L]'un des passages couverts de Kyôto où j'étais entré par hasard, peut-être attiré par l'illusion de fraîcheur que donne la lumière un peu verdâtre, et surtour trop las pour demander mon chemin encore une fois, grâce à l'une de ces phrases apprises par coeur et répétées comme les formules des contes. (p. 11)

Similarly, in *OGP*, a comment on the *hiragana* character 'no' emerges from an encounter with a book:

> A l'intérieur de l'étui, le tracé limpide et fin de trois feuilles ourlées d'or, sur la couverture bleu nuit d'un de ces livres qui pour nous s'ouvrent à l'envers, me donna le sentiment d'être admis à contempler un secret qui s'offre sans se dévoiler, et qui calme le coeur au lieu de le faire battre: comme si le monde était en ordre grâce au hasard organisé de cette calligraphie dont chaque caractère

s'inscrit dans un invisible carré, et dont je ne devinais à première vue que le *no* du génitif, lien fragile entre les éléments de la phrase et l'enchaînement des causes. (Partout au Japon les liens sont aussi légers que ceux de l'imaginaire: le moindre signe suffit à interdire une entrée – un bambou posé en travers, une pierre entourée d'une corde – partout sauf en famille, et le mariage est dépendance pour la femme: il faut la force de l'homme pour serrer l'*obi* autour de sa taille, et pour le nouer dans son dos.) (pp. 11–12)

In *CRJ*, the character is presented with no context, and the additional information gives it much more of an existence as an object in its own right:

Le *no* du génitif, dont *la boucle inachevée* est un lien fragile entre les éléments de la phrase et l'enchaînement des causes. (Partout au Japon les liens sont aussi légers que ceux de l'imaginaire: le moindre signe suffit à interdire une entrée – un bambou posé en travers, une pierre entourée d'une corde – partout sauf en famille, et le mariage est dépendance pour la femme: il faut la force de l'homme pour serrer l'*obi* autour de sa taille, et pour le nouer dans son dos).

The texts in *CRJ* are not only shorter: they are extracted from both the narrative and personal context, as is evident from the last example. The seeing 'je' disappears, -or at least is pushed into the background, and the story from which the discovery arose – in the last case, the impressionistic narrative (pp. 39–41) which leads eventually to the distinction between two kinds of red – is also abstracted.[26] The effect of their freedom from author and context is that these brief observations stand alone, like independent objects, the 'choses' of the title. The physical appearance of the pieces strengthens this impression: fragments, of rarely more than ten lines, they are centred squarely in the middle of the page. Their singularity and independence, emphasised by the 'frame' created by the white of the page, gives them a status comparable to that of the photographs[27] with which they are interspersed: as they are neither a commentary on nor an explanation of the photographs, they appear to be on an equal footing with them.

In fact the relationship between text and image in this book has developed over the course of several publications. *Choses rapportées du Japon* was first published in 1990 by Fata Morgana, 'à tirage limité, avec lithographies et eaux-fortes de Pierre Alechinsky'.[28] The 1993 edition, which is the most widespread and the one to which I refer throughout this chapter, contains photographs by Pierre

Photograph from Gérard Macé, *Choses rapportées du Japon*

Alechinsky which were taken in 1955, as well as the last chapter of *Où grandissent les pierres*. The text is also reprinted in *Un détour par l'Orient*, the collection of Macé's 'oriental' texts published by Le Promeneur in 2001, without photographs or illustrations (but followed, as in the 1993 edition, by the same extract from *OGP*). I will discuss the significance of this repeated reprinting of the last chapter of *OGP* later on in this chapter: for the moment, I will address the question of Pierre Alechinsky's photographs in the 1993 edition. It seems strange, almost a form of 'cheating', to insert into the text photographs that are almost forty years older: is it not the attempt artificially to create nostalgia, to evoke an older Japan that is more attractive (because no longer present)? The nature of the photographs themselves suggests another explanation, however. Black and white photographs of stone paths, steps into a garden, a stone lantern or a shop sign, their common characteristic is that they are highly abstract: some of them might in fact be unidentifiable to a viewer who knew nothing about Japanese gardens. We might describe these photographs as being referential without being representative:[29] almost abstract arrangements of lines and shapes, they denote a reality that is difficult to recognise.

Perhaps this effect is intended to be similar to that of Japanese signs, or writing. Signs that one cannot decipher present the same kind of challenge as photographs of things that one cannot recognise. If the objects that have been photographed resemble a series of signs, the reassurance of reality that usually accompanies photography dissolves into confusion, a confusion that resembles the effect of being confronted by words that one cannot read. It is as if photography, an art form that has an obvious connection with reality, and writing, an abstract sign system that has very little connection with reality, move closer to each other in this book: these are photographs that ask to be looked at *as* writing, just as the texts demand, through their presentation, to be looked at *as* photographs. Indeed, this kind of interaction between image and text invites the reader to adopt a different way of seeing. Macé suggests as much in the fragment on dreams:

> Les rêves que j'ai vus, car on ne fait pas de rêves en japonais, on se contente de les voir. 'J'ai vu un rêve' (yume o mimashita) dit-on au réveil, comme on voit l'intérieur d'une maison sans toit, une perspective cavalière sur un éventail ou sur un paravent. Ou dans un livre qu'on ne peut pas lire un caractère qu'on reconnaît.

In Japanese one sees dreams, rather than having them: when the verb is translated into French (or English), the dreams acquire a much more objective existence, separate from the dreamer. We see them as simply as we might see real things, such as 'l'intérieur d'une maison sans toit, une perspective cavalière sur un éventail': or we see them as we might see 'dans un livre qu'on ne peut pas lire un caractère qu'on reconnaît'. Seeing photographs, dreams, objects in the real world (as we do when taking photographs), and writing that we cannot read, are all placed by Macé in the same category for the purposes of seeing. Perhaps the ultimate objective of *Choses rapportées du Japon* is to create in the reader an 'egalitarian' approach to seeing phenomena that we believe exist on separate ontological levels, to challenge his or her belief in the solidity of the real: especially when that reality is one which is foreign to us, such as that of Japan.

A number of Macé's texts 'on the Orient' are collected in *Un détour par l'Orient*: *Leçon de chinois*, *Un français orienté*, the text only of *Choses rapportées du Japon*, the final section (once again) of *Où grandissent les pierres*, and *Petites coutumes*. Of these, the last is the only work that seems to have no content relating to either China or Japan. Macé justifies his choice of texts in the blurb on the inside front cover of *Un détour par l'Orient*:

> La lecture de Segalen à la fin de l'adolescence, l'apprentissage rudimentaire et vite abandonné de la langue chinoise, puis trois voyages au Japon ont fini par me donner, autant qu'une connaissance de l'Orient, un autre regard sur ce qui m'était le plus proche. C'est pourquoi prennent place dans un même volume, à la suite de *Leçon de chinois* et *Choses rapportées du Japon*, les tercets de *Petites coutumes*, inspirés par le village d'Ile-de-France où j'ai été enfant.
>
> Hölderlin l'avait déjà formulé, avec d'autres mots: l'une de nos tâches les plus ardues, mais les plus nécessaires, consiste à s'approprier ce qui nous est le plus familier. Chacun à sa façon, avec des détours qui lui sont propres.[30]

The appropriation through travel, not of 'the other' but of 'ce qui nous est le plus familier', has been a constant theme of Macé's travels to Japan, ever since *OGR*: this perhaps explains the reprinting of its last section, both in the 1993 edition of *Choses rapportées du Japon* and in the volume under discussion. It is as if he wants to alert us to the fact that this is an effect of travel that he has been conscious of from the beginning, and therefore wishes to offer us 'proof' in the form of an extract from the earliest of his 'Japanese' publications. Or even earlier: in *Leçon de chinois*, the account of his 'travels' to China through his study of the Chinese language, Macé describes how learning a new language is a sure way of finding your way back to your own:

> Apprendre une langue, c'est avoir du goût pour l'erreur, comme d'autres pour les aléas du voyage; croire qu'on 'avance' alors qu'on est ramené en arrière le plus souvent. Ainsi, en chinois, les signes d'un jardin sec n'étaient que le bois mort d'une enfance. D'où je suis revenu par le sentier qu'il a fallu jadis frayer en français.[31]

Leçon de chinois explores the fascination of the writer with the mechanics of another, very differently constructed language, as does *Un français orienté*: especially, in the latter work, the aspect of Chinese (and Japanese) writing that has been its traditional source of attraction for Western writers since the sixteenth century, the characters. Macé's understanding of Chinese is too sophisticated, of course, to fall into the trap that Ezra Pound frequented, of imagining that the characters have a directly mimetic relationship to the objects that they represent, in the manner of hieroglyphs: they may have started in that way, but for a fluent user of the language the character is as conventionalised a sign as the letter in the Roman alphabet. Macé's stance vis-à-vis Chinese characters in *Un français orienté* is to describe the range of usage that each character covers, which reveals differences in semantic classification between French and Chinese, between the ways in which each language portions out the reality to which it refers.[32] For instance, this is the range of usage for a single character:

> Ce qui n'est pas encore, ou ce qui n'est plus, marque de son absence [...] le nom de la fiancée qui attend un mari comme celui de la veuve qui attend la mort. Et toute affaire en suspens, comme le futur ou la vie antérieure dont on attend le retour.[33]

This more subtle (and correct) observation about the difference of the Chinese language is only one example of the position occupied by the committed 'exote' that Macé seems to be in this work. The 'français orienté' of the title refers to a language in between Chinese and French, a truly exotic language in that it is neither one nor the other. It is the 'French' that is obtained by a literal translation of Chinese, presumably made up purely of substantives:

> Mais ce Dictionnaire [le Dictionnaire français de la langue chinoise] ouvre aussi sur l'espace vacant entre deux langues, où règne un idiome intermédiaire: ce qui, du chinois, s'entend encore à pareille distance, la langue traduite étant à l'originale ce que l'écho est au bruit. Aussi peut-on dans les même pages déchiffrer les caractères chinois [...] et lire un français orienté qui s'apparente, en ses détours le long d'une muraille de signes, à la poésie elle-même.[34]

In these meditations on the Chinese language, Macé's early love of Segalen is apparent, and seems to steer him towards the position of the well-informed Segalenian 'exote' who rejoices in difference. These texts do not contain any of the characters discussed, or indeed any photographs, and this too would seem to fit in with Macé's overall intention in these works: the reader should not be tempted, by the sight of the actual characters, to see them as decorative, or 'exotic' in the derogatory sense, but be guided into thinking of them as a language and nothing else, simply a different one. Macé's position is worthy of note as the culmination of a historically documented interest in the Chinese character, developed over the decades of the nineteenth and twentieth centuries by a number of important Western writers. Pound, Claudel, and Barthes all spent time relating their understanding of this foreign writing system to their particular literary agendas, but Macé builds on this legacy to create a highly evolved and fruitful interaction between the different languages for the purposes of his own meditations.

The presence of the final volume in this collection, *Petites coutumes*, is justified by the caveat at the start of the book: that travel to the East has given Macé 'autant qu'une connaissance de l'Orient, un autre regard sur ce qui m'était le plus proche'. The short poems inspired by the village in Ile-de-France where he went to visit his grandparents are thus a direct result of his travels, and they are preceded by a few pages in prose describing his 'return' to the village. Each poem includes a word in italics which comes from the local patois: 'les mots en italique, ceux qui les prononçaient n'ont jamais eu le souci de les écrire, et la plupart n'auraient pas su'.[35] Their content, therefore, is entirely 'French'. Their form, however, is interestingly reminiscent of the haiku:

> La pudeur d'un homme
> qui tourne le dos
> pour *lâcher l'eau*

> Les *petites coutumes*
> d'une mère et ses filles
> au bord de la forêt

> Et comme un vieux *lit-cage*
> le landau qui grince
> à la naissance

These fascinating cultural hybrids are both haiku-like and not, recognisable yet strange. Many a French poet has been seduced by the haiku, but usually their attempts to adapt the 5-7-5 syllabic form to French have been practised on 'Japanese-sounding' material: the seasons, blossom, and other subjects from nature.[36] But Macé sticks resolutely to French 'content', as if to guard himself against even the inadvertent creation of *japonaiserie*. It is interesting to compare his attitude to that of Claudel in *Cent Phrases pour éventails* (see Chapter 3). In Macé's case, not only is the content French, but it is intensely *non*-literary, in that each poem is arranged around a word or phrase spoken by illiterate members of the village. Thus he avoids the traps of both exoticism (*japonisme*) and 'high' literature, immediately recognisable but conventional discourses, and the result is a refreshingly new kind of poem that can stand independently of its influences. These poems are a real attempt to combine East and West, the self and the other, through a system of self-imposed restrictions that are designed to defeat the intrusion of that enemy of real poetry that Verlaine suggested strangling, 'eloquence'.

The most recent of Macé's works dedicated to Japan, *Un Monde qui ressemble au monde, les jardins de Kyoto*, contains photographs and an accompanying text, both by Macé. The photographs are mostly of the gardens, but the first two in the book are of a geisha, posing in front of a garden. I will start by showing how, by choosing to place this stereotypical image of Japan at the start of the work and by accompanying it with a text that explains the place of Japan in the author's subconscious, Macé succeeds in neutralising both the traditional aura associated with photographs of Japan and his own, personal aura before embarking on his tour of the gardens of the title.

According to Walter Benjamin, an aura is 'a nimbus obscuring an object': it is the weight of significance that an object of art, or a specific person, may acquire for a certain viewer. So my view of the *Mona Lisa*, for instance, might be strongly affected by my knowledge of its traditional status as a masterpiece, and I may not be able to see it for itself as objectively as I might see, say, a painting by an unknown artist. Aura is thus comparable to significance, over and beyond the meaning, in the Fregean sense.[37] Now photographs can have an aura, in spite of what Benjamin himself said of them:[38] as in my example of the *Mona Lisa*, the image in a photograph may acquire a significance from a historical tradition. Thus a photograph of a geisha, to a French viewer, might easily be 'obscured' by the nimbus of 'Japaneseness' that comes from an acquaintance with *Madame Chrysanthème*. That is to say that over and beyond the sight of an Asian woman wearing a kimono, the photograph would denote 'Japaneseness' to the viewer, in exactly the same way as the

Geisha from Gérard Macé, *Un Monde qui ressemble au monde*

name 'Chrysanthème' denoted 'japonisme' as well as 'chrysanthe-mum' to Loti's contemporaries.[39] Why then does Macé choose, for the first photograph of his book, such a loaded subject?

A close look at the photographs gives us some clues to his motives. At first sight, the geisha looks like the symbol of Japaneseness (the Barthesian 'studium') that we expect, a 'mask' rather than a face. Barthes wrote that 'puisque toute photo est contingente (et par là même hors sens), la Photographie ne peut signifier (viser une génér-alité) qu'en prenant un masque'.[40] This first impression may be height-ened by the fact that she is almost literally wearing a mask on her unsmiling face, because she is heavily made up in the traditional white powder and dark lipstick. But if one looks for just a little longer, the 'punctum' appears, her individuality begins to override her sym-bolic function, especially because there is no caption or text directly descriptive of this photograph. For one thing, there are the wrinkles

Geisha from Gérard Macé, *Un Monde qui ressemble au monde*

on her neck; for another, there is the fact that she is more friendly-looking than conventionally beautiful. The second photograph, a shot of the same woman from behind, continues the process of demystification. There is a slightly unsightly pin in her hair: her makeup ends at the back of the neck, in the traditional style, showing the true colour of her skin: and, from behind, it seems that she is smiling. The aura that makes her the 'symbol of Japan' is eroded by these small, contingent but crucial details, and thus we are given to understand (for, importantly, there is no text as yet) that the old stereotypes will not be exploited in this book.

The second photograph is on the page facing the first page of text. The back of the smiling (?) geisha, then, is still within our field of vision as we read the following words:

Minuscule et vaste comme le monde, le jardin japonais de ma mère était posé sur sa table à ouvrage.

[...] Comme cet objet était posé sur la table à ouvrage, il est lié à jamais à l'univers troublant de la féminité, au point que les pelotes de laine, les aiguilles à tricoter, les coussins piqués d'épingles se superposent à l'image des chevelures noires et compliquées des femmes japonaises telles qu'on les voit dans les gravures d'Utamaro, et quelquefois encore, les soirs de fête, dans les rues de Kyôto. Leur chignon savamment noué, traversé de longues épingles et relevé sur la nuque, ressemble à ces ouvrages en cours abandonnés sous la lampe, [...] qui résumaient pour moi l'univers intouchable et proche de la femme, avec ce qu'il comportait de désirable et de si bien défendu.[41]

Here then is the personal significance of Japan for Macé, the aura which obscures it for him: he puts us on our guard against it by demystifying it. This is a crucial gesture for him to have made at the beginning of his text, as we are about to see a series of photographs of Japan taken by him, that is to say from his point of view: he thus establishes his prejudices, his personal 'blind spots', so that we can compensate wherever necessary while entering into his vision.

Most of the other photographs in this book are of gardens, and the text that surrounds them tells us about the art of garden design in Japan, the hermits and *bonzes* who created the most famous ones, and the effect of their stillness and beauty on the observer. In taking these photographs and writing about the gardens, however, there is one further stereotype that Macé must avoid: that of the hunter-photographer, the appropriator of what he photographs. It has often been argued that the photographic act is one of appropriation, whether or not it is successful.[42] When the photography takes place abroad, the stereotype becomes even more aggressive: the travelling photographer inherits the mantle of the great white hunter, who has exchanged his gun for a camera and goes abroad to stalk his prey. This kind of travelling photographer is not the image that Gérard Macé presents to us in any of his books, and certainly not in *Un Monde qui ressemble au monde*: indeed, as we will see, Macé's images seem constantly to be abdicating the appropriating power of the photograph.

As a photographer and writer, Macé is very conscious of the power of the photograph, both its power to deform its object and the power it gains through reproduction and circulation. Discussing the mass-produced photographs of one of the Kyoto temples he visits, Ryôan-ji, Macé writes that

Ryôan-ji from Gérard Macé, *Un Monde qui ressemble au monde*

Une mauvaise photographie n'est pas une catastrophe, sauf quand elle circule dans le monde entier, diffusant un *cliché* qui défigure les lieux en incurvant les lignes, pour introduire de force une perspective d'ailleurs fallacieuse: bref quand elle est une faute contre l'esprit. (p. 33)

The snapshot in the tourist brochure forces the angle in order to create a fake perspective, which in turn creates an illusion of mastery for the viewer. But the garden in question, the 'jardin sec' of Ryôan-ji, is one which resists such domination through its very structure: it is famous for its fifteen rocks of which only fourteen can ever be seen from an individual angle:

Au Ryôan-ji [...] si une pierre est toujours cachée (jamais la même), c'est qu'on ne saurait *dominer* le paysage qui est tout le contraire d'un panorama: plutôt une vision intérieure face à laquelle il faut se taire si l'on veut y entrer. (p. 31)

This fact, for Macé, is one of the garden's chief attractions, and his preference for views that cannot be dominated is reflected in the structure of his own photographs. Unlike the tourist brochure photo, Macé's photographs adopt angles which deliberately reject the panoramic ambition. Going against the grain of landscape photography, his photographs never seek to embrace a wide expanse of space. On the contrary, they always focus on a smaller, more modest part of the whole, such as in this shot of the above-mentioned garden of Ryôan-ji.

What is interesting about this photo is that, in spite of the fact that it is just one part of the garden, it still manages to suggest the whole beyond the part: and it does this through the use of continuous elements. For instance, in this photograph, the rocks are surrounded by objects placed in such a way that they all suggest continuity beyond the frame of the photograph: the raked lines of the pebbles and the line of the wall are horizontal lines that continue to both left and right in our imagination, and the trees, in their living and growing profusion, are equally effective in not stopping the eye. Walls, if used vertically or at an angle, are the perfect choice for a delimiting function, and vertical trees too can be used to frame objects, but Macé's choice of angle ensures that both wall and trees here suggest a *lack* of borders. The photograph of Koetsu-ji contains trees that *are* vertical, but because there are so many of them, and because they are cut off near the top of the picture, they encourage the eye to move into an imagined space, both upwards and horizontally. The photograph of Ohara creates the effect of a continuum by using an object with a recurring pattern – in this case, a *tatami* – which again fosters the sense of things stretching out to the left and the right. The same effect is achieved with the screens in the photograph of Daisen-in: repetition creates continuity, and the eye can imagine the sequence beyond the frame, the expanse of reality beyond the photograph, the *hors-champ*.[43]

Macé thus avoids what we may call the dominating, panoramic ambition. Another effect achieved by Macé, through his use of a structure which gestures beyond the frame, is the avoidance of the symbolic. Mary Price deplores the symbolic aura that surrounds certain photographs, arguing that any aura that a photograph may have should be the aura of reality, the shock that comes from the

Koetzu-ji from Gérard Macé, *Un Monde qui ressemble au monde*

Ohara from Gérard Macé, *Un Monde qui ressemble au monde*

Daisen-in from Gérard Macé, *Un Monde qui ressemble au monde*

realisation that the photographed person or object once existed.[44] But photographs of high artistic merit, because they frame or angle the object, scene or landscape in such a way as to make any other viewpoint unimaginable, can allow the contingent object (or scene, or landscape) to become a necessary one, because it seems to be the only possible one. In Macé's photographs, by contrast, the opposite is true: the overall effect is that the photographed view, however beautiful and intelligently angled, does not become absolute or necessary: the contingent remains contingent, the photo remains just one of many possible views rather than the master view. This may appear to be an unusually modest attitude for a photographer, who usually prefers to impose his creation as a unique moment captured for eternity: but Macé succeeds in giving the impression that his photographs are mere recordings of reality, well-chosen and skilful recordings though they may be.

In the photograph of Entsû-ji, Macé shows us a Japanese land-scaping technique whose effect may be described as the exact equivalent of what he is trying to do in photography.

> Entsu-ji est l'exemple parfait (unique assure-t-on sur place) de ce
> que les Japonais résument par la notion de *shakkei*, autrement dit le

Entsû-ji from Gérard Macé, *Un Monde qui ressemble au monde*

jeu entre le proche et le lointain, grâce à une vue choisie sur la nature environnante, qui semble être née pour produire un effet de l'art. Et de fait, au-dessus d'une haie tout en longueur se détache la silhouette du mont le plus proche, verdâtre ou bleutée suivant l'heure, dont la découpe sinueuse est soutenue verticalement par les fûts de trois grands arbres. (p. 42)

Shakkei literally means 'borrowed view'; a view, in this case of the mountain, around which the garden is constructed so that it will lend itself to becoming part of the garden. In reality, of course, the mountain is much bigger than the garden, so the fact is that while it might seem to be a 'perfect fit', the viewer is looking at something that goes far beyond the frame of the garden. A *shakkei*, in other words, invites the viewer to look and think beyond the view before him, an effect which is much like that of Macé's photographs. The borders of the photograph are defeated in their restrictive purpose: they have become purely functional, a limiting line of convenience rather than necessity, beyond which it is easy for the mind's eye to continue to see.

The choice of gardens as his *subject* also indicates Macé's determination to avoid dominating or colonising what he photographs. As Macé explains, these gardens are spaces that were designed for self-abnegation, contemplation and memory: they were the haunts of those who had exchanged domination for contemplation as a way of life:

> Souverains retirés ou non, convertis le plus souvent; nobles ayant fait fortune, guerriers se préparant à la dernière bataille, cette fois sans escorte et sans armure; moines revenus de Chine, pour rêver devant un arpent de terre à un monde sans impuretés; architectes acceptant de bâtir sur du sable après avoir déplacé des montagnes, de composer avec l'éphémère pour apercevoir l'éternel entre deux nuages; amateurs de plaisir vouant un culte à l'amitié, tous dépositaires d'un grand savoir et prêts à l'oublier au dernier instant pour que circule l'énergie. (p. 51)

This description of the uses of the garden is very much like the photograph that refuses symbolic status: instead of giving the garden a single, characterising view, Macé prefers to offer a long list of different viewers (monks, retired and active sovereigns, warriors). They all have different aspirations and desires, but have in common the tendency to live not in the present, but in the past or the future. These gardens are spaces where people who have retired from 'active' life seek to spend their time in a different manner, often involving the practice of memory. But not only are they designed for memory, they are designed by memory:

> Les jardins que l'on admire aujourd'hui s'inspirent le plus souvent de sites lointains, quand ce ne sont pas des citations de paysages célèbres, qui aident la mémoire de ceux qui ont voyagé ou fabrique- ant des souvenirs à ceux qui ne voyagent pas. (p. 25)

Being modelled on faraway sites themselves, the present existences of these gardens already incorporate an element of memory: like a literary allusion, they signify two things at once, both themselves and the memory incarnate of a distant site. Like a 'portal' in science fiction, perhaps, they are places where the past can be superimposed on the present, or the distant on the nearby. Macé's description of the garden of Ginkaku-ji certainly suggests that it is a tremulous space of possibilities, a 'lieu de mémoire' where temporal and spatial dis- tinctions break down in the moonlight:

> C'est alors [à l'éclairage de la lune] que le jardin est un véritable lieu de mémoire, dans cette lumière incertaine où se confondent le souvenir et le rêve. C'est sans doute vrai de tout jardin sous tous les cieux, mais plus encore au Pavillon d'argent où se côtoient un lac du continent et le mont sacré qui trône au milieu de l'archipel. Exactement comme dans la mémoire quand se rapprochent sans

prévenir, et sous forme d'images, des événements qui ont eu lieu à des années de distance. (pp. 36–38)

'Un lac du continent' refers to a lake in China, much admired by the poets, whereas 'le mont sacré qui trône au milieu de l'archipel' is a description of Mount Fuji in Japan: the garden therefore ignores the rules of space, as well as those of time. The Japanese garden is thus a space that structurally resembles both dream and memory, a space in which illogical juxtapositions can occur 'sans prévenir'. I now propose to develop this notion of the Japanese garden as a memory-space, a place through which Macé can approach, delicately and carefully, those parts of his memory and self that belong to his pre-conscious mind, as if the journey through space has set off an analogous journey through time. But in the same way that he avoids dominating the gardens of Kyoto through photography, Macé is careful to avoid colonising the pre-conscious with his conscious mind: it is only through delicate allusions and periphrastic descriptions that he refers to the ultimate destination of his time-travelling, as we will see.

In *Où grandissent les pierres*, Macé makes explicit the link between the gardens of Kyoto and his own memories:

> Les labeurs sont ici plus prosaïques, mais c'est pourtant dans ce lieu sans artifice [le cimetière] que je retrouve la même émotion que devant les jardins secs de Kyôto: la mémoire où grandissent les morts a le même orient que les jardins où l'on écoute grandir les pierres, – le même immense territoire dans un espace pas plus grand que le coeur. (pp. 98–99)

If in this text it is the Kyoto gardens that remind Macé of the resting-place of his ancestors, and thence of the concept of a tiny space containing a much larger one ('le même immense territoire dans un espace pas plus grand que le coeur'), in *Un Monde qui ressemble au monde* a much bolder link is made between the gardens and Macé's childhood through the evocation of a miniature object that contains a large space, the 'jardin japonais' of his mother:

> C'est grâce à cet objet [le jardin japonais], en apparence insignifiant, que le Japon associé aux jardins est entré dans mon imaginaire. [...] C'est encore cet objet qui m'a donné à mon insu la conviction qu'un espace immense peut tenir dans le creux de la main: bien avant d'avoir [...] lu que 'dans le monde, tout ressemble au monde', selon la formule laconique et vertigineuse de Marcel Granet. (p. 7, p. 9)

Like Proust's madeleine, the miniature 'jardin japonais' contains the whole of Macé's early childhood, which in turn contains the source of his interest in Japan, which is of course the starting point for his travels to the gardens of Kyoto. Indeed Macé's whole trip to Kyoto is, narratively speaking, embedded in this original space, the maternal space evoked by Macé's memory of his mother's working table. I would argue that the maternal space from which Macé sets off towards Japan is also his final destination: that in travelling so far away, from France to Kyoto, he is in fact travelling homewards from the very beginning, to his childhood and indeed to the very limits of his childhood memories, those that verge on the pre-conscious period.

The only other reference to the mother in this text occurs at the very end, when the narrator is returning to France: but his return journey takes him not only through space, but also through time. For the final paragraph of the text leads us not just back to Europe, but to childhood and beyond, to the womb:

> Puis je songerai peut-être au jardin potager d'un village en Ile-de-France, qu'on arrosait le soir venu en le rejoignant par une sente étroite; presque aussi étroite que le chemin dont nous n'avons aucun souvenir, mais que nous avons dû emprunter pour venir au monde.
> (p. 61)

Macé was born in Paris, but often visited his maternal grandparents who lived in a little village in the Ile-de-France, and the garden is clearly that of their home: as for the reference to 'le chemin dont nous n'avons aucun souvenir', it seems to be a reference to the very beginnings of his existence on earth. It appears from this that Macé's travels in Japan as described in *Un Monde qui ressemble au monde* have been a long journey home, back to the place of his origin, of which he has no memory: in other words, the pilgrimage to these 'lieux de mémoire' that are the gardens of Kyoto has led him back to a place beyond memory, a place he cannot take control of with his conscious mind. The writer's preoccupation with that which is just beyond the edge of the consciousness is reminiscent of the photographer's preoccupation with suggesting that which is just beyond the frame of his photograph: a preoccupation which resulted in a non-dominating, non-colonising view of the Japanese gardens. In a similar way, it is possible to see how Macé here *gestures* towards the pre-conscious, but remains reticent on the subject precisely in order to avoid the invasion of this as yet uncharted territory by the conscious stream of thought and words. Dreams (which, as we saw earlier, Macé relates to Japanese gardens) are the classic medium through which the sub- or pre-conscious manifests itself to the conscious mind, but when we try to explain them, or even simply to narrate them, we discover how illogical they are: in other words, the language of dreams (and of the subconscious) does not translate well into the language of the conscious, rational mind. Macé seems to be fully aware of the perils of forcing such translations (perhaps this comes from his experience as an interlingual translator), and leaves much unsaid on the subject of the subconscious memories that have been evoked by his travels to Japan.

He does, however, make delicate suggestions – literary allusions – regarding the similarities between his journey through space, to Japan, and his journey through time, back into his childhood. I will examine just one instance of this. The travels of a child returning home are strongly suggested by an image used at least twice by Macé when referring to his journey, both to and from Japan. This image is that of the 'cailloux', or pebbles:

> Avais-je suivi l'un de ces conseils que l'on recueille avant de partir en voyage, comme autant de cailloux blancs que l'on sème par avance sur l'itinéraire que l'on essaie de tracer? (p. 12)

The white pebbles are of course one component of the 'jardins secs' that Macé will encounter in Kyoto, but here, in the context of something which is 'semé par avance sur l'itinéraire', they constitute a clear reference to the story of 'le petit poucet', one of Charles Perrault's most famous fairy tales. 'Le petit poucet' and his numerous brothers are taken away into a forest during a period of famine by their loving but poverty-stricken parents to reduce the number of mouths they have to feed, and left there to die. But the first time that this happens, the small but intelligent boy 'avait laissé tomber le long du chemin les petits cailloux blancs qu'il avait dans ses poches', in order to be able to find his way home: and indeed the white pebbles, shining in the moonlight, guide him and his brothers back to their house.[45] In other words, the child drops the pebbles as they go *forward*, so that he will be able to find his way *back*. In a similar fashion, Macé 'sème par avance [de cailloux blancs] sur l'itinéraire que l'on essaie de tracer': the reference to the pebbles gives the reader an early hint that this route, wherever it is to take the traveller, will eventually turn out to be a route back to his origins.

The pebbles reappear at the very end of the text, when Macé tells us that he will be following them back to France:

> Sur la route du retour ou plutôt dans le chemin des airs, ce seront les *kami* mes cailloux blancs, puisqu'on trouve un peu partout ces dieux [...]: le *kami* du feu pour commencer, puis le *kami* tranchant de la roche et celui qui tranche la racine; le *kami* du tonnerre et celui des sifflements; [...] le *kami* du long chemin et celui du laps de temps; le *kami* du grand large et du large intermédiaire [...] Ce seront les *kami* mes cailloux blancs, et les noms des temples que je réciterai pour m'en souvenir comme autant de formules magiques, ouvrant sur des espaces qu'on croit avoir rêvés autant qu'on les a vus: Shisendô, Entsû-ji, Ryôan-ji. (p. 57, p. 61)

Here the fairy-tale pebbles have turned into *kami*, the Shinto gods of Japan, but both pebbles and gods are benevolent entities who will guide Macé back home. *Kami* can mean god, but these are perhaps closer to spirits, spirits dwelling in natural phenomena (such as fire, rocks, thunder, and so on) as part of a pantheist universe. Macé here names also the *kami* of the 'long chemin et celui du laps de temps': this is not one of the traditional deities of the Shinto pantheon, but one invented by Macé in order to bring together once again the passage of time and space, alluding to the fact that the two are often as one, both in the gardens and in his travels.

Perhaps Macé's choice, as the object of his photographs and of his writing, of these spaces that resist control – be they the gardens of Kyoto, or the time in our lives preceding consciousness – is an indication of his boldly thoughtful explorations into those dark areas of our minds that are, mostly, beyond our control: or, in his more elegant turn of phrase, it is an instance of 'la mémoire [qui] aime chasser dans le noir'.[46]

In this study of Macé's works on Japan, we have seen how the relationship between text and image is never the simple one of proof or resemblance. In the case of *Choses rapportées du Japon*, the relationship is a challenge to the different attitudes that the reader will have towards photography and writing as modes of representation: in *Un Monde qui ressemble au monde*, both the text and the photographs constitute spaces beyond authorial control, offered to the reader as starting points for his or her own travels back into the subconscious. In Barthes' book, the texts and images are harnessed to his deictic project, pointing at, rather than describing, Japan in a delicately balanced 'non-representational' act. Butor, on the other hand, gives precedence to the photograph wherever possible, restricting his writing to the 'subordinate' genres of commentary, captions or even translations of captions. In all of these oeuvres, it is the relationship between text and image that creates self-consciousness within the texts: the reader, asked to consider what the photographs are doing in relation to the texts, wondering about the significance of a caption or the relevance of an apparently 'illustrative' photo, is brought naturally to an awareness of the methods being used to create an image of Japan. It is a subtle and effective way of foregrounding issues of representation, much less grating than a postmodern author's deliberate use of his own initials to designate a character, for instance, or of a scene depicting the writing process. It is also a crucial part of the luggage for any intelligent traveller-writer of this period, for at least two reasons. First, any writer who is at all aware of the history of previous images of Japan must take their methodologies into account: second, the period in question is one in which issues about the representation of the other have been hotly debated, making it imperative for writers to avoid certain stereotypical ways of seeing. Textual self-consciousness therefore becomes a necessary precaution for the traveller-writer of the late twentieth or early twenty-first century.

The relationship between writing and photography thus foregrounds the perennial issue of representation for the writer, in the specific context of the representation of otherness, and this leads our authors to pursue different agendas in accordance with their instincts. For Butor, perhaps the most self-avowedly experimental of the three, the superiority of photography in the matter of representation is a simple fact that he chooses to enjoy: indeed it suits him where Japan is concerned, given his reluctance to write about it, and accordingly he redistributes his efforts into the lesser genres mentioned above. Barthes and Macé, by contrast, prefer to reassert the primacy of writing, but in an indirect manner, by putting into practice a gradual incorporation of photography into writing: not just by putting actual photographs into the text, but by adopting photography as a metaphor for writing. We already talk about 'snapshots' in a metaphorical sense to designate short texts that represent scenes or incidents of a certain kind, often related to travel in foreign places (thus a television reporter might give us a 'snapshot' of the state of affairs in a war-torn city, for instance). Both Barthes and Macé, however, are committed to the notion of photography as a metaphor for writing through their practice of what I have called 'photographic writing'. For Barthes, haiku is photographic writing, although as we discussed earlier it is an impossible writing. Similarly, in the 1993 edition of *Choses rapportées du Japon*, Macé offers us a kind of writing that competes with the photographs in the book to become a writing that does not represent or depict, but instead presents itself as a 'chose', an object independent of narrative or author like a photograph seen on its own, without a caption or a surrounding text. And in *Un Monde qui ressemble au monde*, both the text and the photographs offer us 'lieux de mémoire', places that resonate with the promise of other places in both space and time. The description of the garden of Ginkaku-ji is an excellent example of such a textual space:

> C'est alors [à l'éclairage de la lune] que le jardin est un véritable lieu de mémoire, dans cette lumière incertaine où se confondent le souvenir et le rêve. C'est sans doute vrai de tout jardin sous tous les cieux, mais plus encore au Pavillon d'argent où se côtoient un lac du continent et le mont sacré qui trône au milieu de l'archipel. Exactement comme dans la mémoire quand se rapprochent sans prévenir, et sous forme d'images, des événements qui ont eu lieu à des années de distance. (pp. 36–38)

Photography thus becomes what we might call a *way* of writing about Japan in both Barthes and Macé. In their very different texts, both Barthes and Macé have invented a photographic writing which not only offers us a new way of seeing the other in this age of mass photography and tourism, but a new way of seeing *writing* about the other: a new way of seeing what writing can do.

Conclusion:
Textual Worlds

The preceding study has taken us through more than one hundred years, from 1881 to 2004, of French writing about Japan. We have seen that during this period, European images of Japan – at least, the stereotypes derived from *japonisme* and the Yellow Peril – remained more or less constant and recognisable. What is more, they are still, to a certain extent, common currency today. Indeed, it has been asserted that the popular images of Japan in the West have not developed perceptibly since its reopening to the world in 1853: 'observations of the amateur European or American Japanologists of the nineteenth century [can] suddenly pop up in late twentieth-century works'.[1] It is certainly the case that the oldest, 'antipodean' view of Japan as an upside-down, contradictory country of surprises and paradoxes was still very much extant in the late twentieth century, having received a new lease of life immediately after the Second World War from Ruth Benedict's *The Chrysanthemum and the Sword* (1946). An American ethnologist who was employed by her government towards the end of the Second World War to 'work out' the Japanese mentality for reasons of war policy, Benedict described the Japanese as an intrinsically contradictory race, confiming and strengthening this stereotype for many successive generations of Americans and Europeans:

> The Japanese are, to the highest degree, both aggressive and unaggressive, both militaristic and aesthetic, both insolent and polite, rigid and adaptable, submissive and resentful of being pushed around, loyal and treacherous, brave and timid, conservative and hospitable to new ways.[2]

Benedict's title characterised the Japanese using pairs of contrasting attributes, thus implying that they were a predictably unpredictable, and therefore reliably strange, race. This trend has carried on through-out the twentieth century. Titles such as *The Lotus and the Robot*

(Arthur Koestler), *Le Sauvage et l'artifice: les Japonais devant la nature* (Augustin Berque), *D'Edo à Tokyo. Mémoires et Modernités* (Philippe Pons) and *The Missionary and the Libertine: Love and War in East and West* (Ian Buruma) all echo Benedict's model and therefore, to a certain extent, its assumptions. Of course, in some of these cases the resemblance to Benedict's title is a conscious, ironic choice on the part of the author, but this still indicates an acceptance, for better or for worse, of the resonances – and, therefore, of the power – of this particular image of Japan. Thus Ruth Benedict's use of this age-old rhetoric in her title and book, a rhetoric which had in fact never gone out of fashion in the writings of Japan-specialists, has perpetuated it well into the late twentieth and early twenty-first century.

The other popular stereotypes, examined in our earlier chapters, also continue to loom large in contemporary attempts to explain and characterise the Japanese. Stereotypical figures from Yellow Peril days, for instance, lurk beneath the exterior of apparently new images invented to fit the modern, hyper-industrialised denizens of Tokyo or Osaka. As late as 1979, the editor-in-chief of *Le Monde* was quoted describing the Japanese as 'a powerful, dynamic, hard-working people [...] having come to admit that nothing can any longer be achieved through war, but knowing that economic competition, in a way, can perfectly mean war continued by another means'.[3] It does not take a sociologist to work out that the postwar stereotype of the Japanese businessman as a maniacally motivated and deeply con-sensual member of the body economic is actually a reincarnated version of the Yellow Peril soldier. The 'business is war' slogan, at least vis-à-vis Japan, is thus built on a powerful historical foundation within the Western imaginary. The success of Amélie Nothomb's novel *Stupeur et Tremblements*, a black comedy recounting the narrator's humiliating experiences in a successful Japanese firm, relies entirely for its effect on her readers' familiarity with this updated stereotype.[4] This 'recycling' of older images is based on the nature of the stereotype, which is that it feeds on recognition. New material, such as that of the hardworking salary-man, is subsumed into the old category of the Yellow Peril soldier as quickly as it appears, in order to maintain the illusion of a continuous knowledge of the other. Familiar, even when erroneous, conviction is always more comfort-ing than confrontations with the unknown or with new ways of thinking, and this accounts for the longevity of stereotypes, some of which survive purely through repeated self-referral.

The *literary* images that we have studied in the preceding chapters have always been related to these popular stereotypes, and at times take advantage of them to attract a readership: Loti's use of the *japoniste* stereotype to appeal to his readers is a case in point. On the other hand, Proust's use of the discourse of *japonisme* to signify the sexually attractive and transgressive is much more idiosyncratic, because by weaving it into his own semiotic system he transforms it into something specific to his work. Farrère, by contrast, does not stray far from another stereotypical image, that of the heroic and soldierly Japanese, in his novel on the Russo-Japanese War. Michaux takes on both of these stereotyping discourses only to reject them. As for our travellers of the late twentieth century, they display in their writings a constant awareness of the stereotypes of Japan that are all around them – images from tourist brochures, the economics section of their preferred newspaper, or TV programmes on Japanese society – and construct their own works so as to avoid, while acknowledging, the power of the stereotypes that they have inherited from both popular culture and their literary forebears.

For the relationship between the literary images and stereotypes is perhaps not as influential as the relationships between the writers themselves. There are patterns of inheritance from writer to writer that complicate the historical and imaginative backgrounds against which the later travellers shaped their own visions of Japan. Here are 'anxieties of influence' that are easier to trace than those of Harold Bloom, because the subject matter is so specific. Adopting Bloom's model, we can see Loti as the original father-figure in the period under discussion, whose influence is present throughout the era in the form of reactions, additions, corrections and rivalries. Proust's use of the word 'mousmé', introduced into French by *Madame Chrysanthème*, proves his awareness of Loti's domination of *japoniste* discourse,[5] and Claudel's revisiting and redescription of sites such as Nikko, 'discovered' by Loti, are conscious attempts to reclaim these places 'back' from Loti's universe into his own. Michaux, by styling himself as the barbarian, explicitly rejects all the examples of his predecessors, although we have already discussed the ambivalent success of such outright rejection. As for the postwar writers, their relationship to Loti is less tense than that of the generation writing between 1881 and 1945: sufficiently removed from the *japoniste* stereotype to be able to look upon it with some indulgence, although still not capable of ignoring it altogether, writers such as Barthes,

Butor and Macé make references to Loti and the images he has perpetuated with a complicit wink at the reader, because they assume – at times, wrongly – that the reader will share with them an ironic awareness of the history of this image. For these later travellers, Loti is not so much an authority on Japan as an old-fashioned point of reference, whereas for writers choronologically closer to *Madame Chrysanthème* Loti's Japan is an image that needs to be defeated, or at least corrected, because of its dominant presence in the social imaginary of the period.

The desire for narrative authority, which causes writers such as those mentioned above to react against Loti and to 'correct' his image of Japan, has a necessarily difficult relationship with the responsibilities of representation. The preceding chapters have all shown how the writers, with their different ways of seeing, ended up representing Japan: the images have been examined not for 'truth' or 'falsity', but as individual visions that are nevertheless presented with authority. The authoritative position of the writer-traveller, not to be confused with the truth-value of his text, has always been a problematic issue in intercultural texts that attempt to represent the other. On the one hand, the traveller-writer wants to write authoritatively about his experiences of the other, which he may rightly feel are more up-to-date than those of his predecessors. But on the other hand, as an outsider, he feels ill-equipped to do so, and suffers from the weight of his responsibility.[6] Accordingly, some of the voices examined in the preceding chapters betray an acute self-consciousness of the unwelcome combination of authority and outsider status. This situation is common to many of our travellers: it may account for the uneasy cockiness of Michaux's voice, for instance, or the 'embarrassment' of Claudel in 'Le Promeneur' (and the compensatory arrogance of his voice in 'Un Regard sur l'âme japonaise'). The problem of authority is more explicitly foregrounded in texts dating from later in the century, by the self-conscious voices of Barthes, Butor and Macé: Butor, as we saw, is so worried by the implications of authority that he avoids talking about Japan directly wherever possible. This increased self-awareness drives writers of this era to seek sources of authority in other media, such as photography, and to incorporate them into their texts. Photography, of course, is potentially an ally but also a threat to writing's autonomy: its dominant presence in late-twentieth- and early-twenty-first-century travel writing on Japan is proof of how writers of this period are grappling, using the tools of their time, with the problem of responsibility and representation.

The self-awareness of these travellers clearly comes from the fact that they are professional writers. Although travel writing 'a pu apparaître comme une forme quasi mimétique du déplacement physique et du discours du sujet'[7] to the traveller-writer, he will ultimately come to the realisation that writing is always writing: sitting down to write about his experiences abroad, the writer has to come to terms with the fact that his tool, language, cannot *reflect* the faraway lands that he has seen. His experience of foreign languages will have gone further towards alerting him to the finite nature of his own linguistic powers. This awareness of his limitations is sometimes built into his text in the form of self-conscious references to the tools of his trade (Farrère's intertextual imitations of Loti in *La Bataille* draw our attention to the textual nature of the Japan of both his and Loti's works; Michaux's use of aphoristic statements alerts us to the flaws in his presentation of Asia). At other times, the writer will try to make creative use of these limits by approaching travel as if it were a kind of writing. Claudel, for instance, describing his physical progress down the road with his stick in 'La Canne', writes: 'ça va, ça ne va pas, il est temps, tout est fini, tout cela *s'écrit* avec une canne' (my italics). Travelling is thus described in the same *terms* as writing. Similarly, Japan becomes a catalogue for Edmond de Goncourt; kimonos, fans and screens become verbal signifiers within Proust's discourse; Macé's Japanese gardens are 'lieux de mémoire' in which the sculpted sand refers to mountains remembered from books. This does not mean that these writers are reducing the world to a text, but that in using a consciously textual discourse to describe their travelling, they are coming closer to a less mediated representation of the act of travel. Travel cannot become writing, but writing can mimic travel by using its particular idiom to describe it. Barthes' whole project, of course, is a perfect example of self-conscious scriptural travel: 'prélever quelque part dans le monde (*là-bas*) un certain nombre de traits (mot graphique et linguistique), et de ces traits former délibérément un système. C'est ce système que j'appellerai: le Japon.' Fully conscious of the limits of verbal representation, Barthes revels in what it still allows him to do.

All of the travellers examined in this book, in their different ways, are aware of the constraints of their medium, but exploit both the constraints and their consciousness of it to the full. The *japoniste* traveller experiences Japan through the discourse of *japonisme*, and signals his awareness of this through his realisation that his possession of the *japonaiserie* (be it a trinket, a woman or a book) comes to signify the absence of the real Japan (or love, or art). The journalist-traveller uses different generic conventions, ranging from political allegory to aphoristic pronouncements, to configure his distance from the 'true' representation of Japan that is his ultimate, if impossible, goal. Claudel the walker-traveller pursues, through the act of walking, a physical knowledge of the world that lies beyond writing's representational grids: and in *Cent Phrases pour éventails*, he attempts to create the impression that he is *transcribing* experiences of reality, rather than translating them into language. In this he resembles the postwar writers we have examined, the photographer-travellers, who also seek to authenticate their writing about their experiences, but by borrowing from another medium. The resources of photography are available to these writers, and we have seen how this possibility inflects their relationship with their original tool.

Thus it might be said that this history of representations of Japan in French literature has also been a history of the different methods, or modes, invented by writers for representing their particular ways of seeing Japan. Writing about travel can only ever create textual worlds, but it also creates metatextual worlds which foreground the writers' experiences as traveller-writers. They cannot give us instances of 'naked', unmediated seeing, but by sensitising us to the conventions of representation they can help to improve the quality of the 'thought' that goes with the 'sight' which, according to Wittgenstein, together constitute the act of seeing.

Notes

Introduction

1 Guido Gozzano, *Un Natale a Ceylon e altri racconti indiani*, Milan, Ed. Piero Cudini, 1984, p. 145.

2 Ludwig Wittgenstein, *Philosophical Investigations* (translated by G. E. M. Anscombe), Oxford, Blackwell, 1958, p. 212e.

3 'Imagology' is a term coined by a number of French literary scholars such as D.-H. Pageaux and J.-M. Moura to describe their own work in comparative literature. It uses methods derived from structural anthropology, and aims to describe the genesis, context and development of representations of foreign countries in the 'home' literature. An exemplary work is D.-H. Pageaux, *Le bûcher d'Hercule: Histoire, critique, et théorie littéraires*, Paris, Champion, 1996.

4 I have borrowed this phrase from John Berger, *Ways of Seeing*, London, Penguin, 1972: 'every image embodies a way of seeing' (p. 10).

5 My decision to investigate types of traveller owes something to Segalen, and also to Todorov's 'portraits de voyageurs' in *Nous et les autres*, Paris, Seuil, 1989. I certainly refer to some of his ten 'voyageurs types' in the course of my study, although my gallery of *écrivains-voyageurs* boasts a smaller head-count.

6 Imagologists also proceed on the assumption that all writings on the cultural other, be they 'récits de voyage' or 'fictions à l'étranger', are false representations: their interest lies in their internal logic and organisation.

7 In spite of the loose ways in which it has been employed by numerous critics since the publication of his ground-breaking work, *Orientalism*, London, Routledge and Kegan Paul, 1978.

8 Said's premiss in *Orientalism* is that 'the Orient' as a whole is an imaginary construct posited as the 'Other' of Europe, rather than an entity in its own right, and that the characteristics assigned to the East are simply the counterparts of those which the West would like to attribute to itself.

9 Emmanuel Levinas, *En découvrant l'existence avec Husserl et Heidegger*, Paris, Vrin, 1982, p. 188.

10 Todorov, *Nous et les autres*, p. 362.

11 Levinas, *En découvrant l'existence*, p. 196.

12 Arthur Koestler, 'Association and Bisociation', in *The Act of Creation*, New York, Macmillan, 1964, pp. 657–60.

13 Michael Cronin, *Across the Lines: Travel, Language, Translation*, Cork, Cork University Press, 2000, p. 139.

14 Mary B. Campbell, *The Witness and the Other World: Exotic European Travel Writing (400–1600)*, Ithaca, NY, and London, Cornell University Press, 1988, p. 6.

15 George B. Parks (ed.), Henry Yule (trans.), *The Travels of Marco Polo, the Venetian, concerning the Kingdoms and Marvels of the East*, New York, Macmillan, 1927, pp. 249–50.

16 Endymion Wilkinson, *Japan versus the West: Image and Reality*, Tokyo, Chuôkôronsha, first published 1980; reprinted with revisions, London, Penguin Books, 1991, p. 100.

17 Even after a number of Europeans had made it to Japan, the antipodean vision prevailed, prejudice colouring immediate experience: their overwhelming tendency was to characterise the country still as an upside-down, topsy-turvy place. Alessandro Valignano gave a classic instance of this view in 1583 when he reported that the Japanese 'have rites and ceremonies so different from those of all the other nations that it seems they deliberately try to be unlike any other people [...] it may truly be said that Japan is a world the reverse of Europe; everything is so different and opposite that they are like us in practically nothing.' Quoted in Wilkinson, *Japan versus the West*, p. 100.

18 Richard Storry, *A History of Modern Japan*, London, Pelican Books, first published 1960; reprinted London, Penguin Books, 1990, p. 44.

19 Endymion Wilkinson, *Misunderstanding: Europe versus Japan*, Tokyo, Chuôkôronsha, 1982, p. 36.

20 See Arnold Toynbee (ed.), *Half the World: The History and Culture of China and Japan*, London, Thames and Hudson, 1973; or Satoru Obara, SJ, 'Acceptance, Rejection and Transformation: Christianity and the Historical Climate of Japan', *Kirishitan Bunko* series, Tokyo, Sophia University, 1994.

21 The Chinese were allowed to enter and leave the country, as before.

22 Although German, Kaempfer published the book in Dutch in 1727: it was translated into French in 1729.

23 Wilkinson, *Japan versus the West*, p. 106.

24 More material on Japan did become available in French in the early nineteenth century. The numerous works of Phillip von Siebold (1796–1866) were published then, as were those of Isaac Titsingh (1745–1812), all translated into French in the 1820s.

25 J.-B. de Guébriant, in Francisque Marnas, *La 'Religion de Jésus' (Yaso Jakyo) ressuscitée au Japon dans la seconde moitié du XIXᵉ siècle*, Paris, Ed. Missions Etrangères de Paris, 2nd edn, 1931, pp. xxx–xxxi.

26 'Nos chers confrères de Nagasaki ont découvert un très-grand nombre d'anciens Chrétiens qui, dirigés par des chefs de prières et par des baptiseurs qui se succèdent régulièrement, ont conservé les traditions chrétiennes avec une certaine organisation. Sans prêtres et sans Sacrements depuis près de deux siècles, ils se sont conservés dans la foi et dans la piété, au point que dans une persécution qui a eu lieu il y a huit ou neuf ans seulement, un certain nombre d'entre eux sont morts dans les tourments, plutôt que d'abjurer notre Sainte Religion et qu'aujour la plupart se montrent disposés à affronter le martyre. Sans doute il s'est introuduit bien des abus, il s'est glissé bien des erreurs parmi eux; [...] mais, depuis environ deux ans qu'ils sont entrés en rapport avec nos Confrères, ils montrent le plus grand zèle et la plus grande docilité pour s'instruire des vérités de notre Sainte Religion, pour corriger leur moeurs et pour recevoir les Sacrements.' From 'Lettre Commune de 1867: Paris, le 25 juillet 1867',

Lettres Communes, 1841–1869, published by the Missions Etrangères de Paris.

27 Although missionaries' reports were certainly more widely read until the early years of the nineteenth century. Contrasting present-day practice with the earlier centuries, Adrien Pasquali writes that 'nous ne lisons plus les équivalents modernes des "missions" en vogue jusqu'au XIXe siècle qui, pour des raisons de spécification et de spécialisation toujours plus aiguës des savoirs, ne font plus l'objet que d'une discrète diffusion publique. Qui songerait aujourd'hui à s'adresser aux archives vaticanes ou à celles des grands Ordres religieux pour lire l'équivalent des *Relations* du XVIIe siècle ou *des Lettres édifiantes et curieuses* du XVIIIe siècle?' Adrien Pasquali, *Le Tour des Horizons: Critique et récits de voyages*, Paris, Klincksieck, 1994, pp. 105–106.

28 As will be discussed in Chapter 1.

1 Travels through Objects

1 Luc Fraisse, *Proust et le japonisme*, Strasbourg, Presses universitaires de Strasbourg, 1997, pp. 13–15.

2 Y. Thirion sets the date a little later: 'Dès 1875 le mot "Japonisme" [...] fut imprimé: il allait signifier tout à la fois la prédilection pour le produits et les oeuvres artistiques du Japon et leur imitation' ('Le japonisme en France dans la seconde moitié du XIXe siècle à la faveur de la diffusion de l'estampe japonaise', *Cahiers de l'association internationale des études françaises*, 13 [1961], pp. 117–30 [p. 124]).

3 For a useful chronology of events, publications and exhibitions relating to the opening of Japan and the rise of *japonisme*, established by Geneviève Lacambre, see *Le Japonisme*, Catalogue d'une exposition au Grand Palais, Réunion des musées généraux, 1988.

4 Cited in André Billy, *Les Frères Goncourt: La vie littéraire à Paris pendant la seconde moitié du XIXe siècle*, Paris, Flammarion, 1954, p. 323.

5 Gabriel P. Weisberg and Yvonne M. L. Weisberg, *Japonisme: An Annotated Bibliography*, New York and London, Garland Publishing, 1990, p. xix.

6 This was to develop, of course, into the Musée Guimet.

7 Gordon Millan, *Mallarmé*, London, Secker and Warburg, 1994, p. 320.

8 Billy, *Les Frères Goncourt*, p. 323.

9 Samuel Bing (ed.), *Le Japon artistique: Documents d'Art et d'Industrie*, numéro 1 (1888), p. 3.

10 Timothy Mitchell, in *Colonising Egypt* (Cambridge, Cambridge University Press, 1988), characterises the primarily visual philosophy of the late nineteenth century by consciously echoing Heidegger, calling it 'the age of the world exhibition, or rather, the age of the world-as-exhibition' (p. 13).

11 As coined by Martin Heidegger in 'The Age of the World Picture', in *The Question Concerning Technology and Other Essays*, New York, Harper and Row, 1977, pp. 115–54.

12 Mitchell, *Colonising Egypt*, p. 17.

13 Thirion, 'Le japonisme en France', p. 126.

14 See Fraisse, *Proust et le japonisme*, p. 36, pp. 47–48.

15 By 1888, when he was writing essays for Bing's journal, Gonse was much more knowledgeable.

16 André Billy claims that Edmond de Goncourt was accused of plagiarising, for his *Hokusai*, large parts of a biography of Hokusai originally written in Japanese and translated by Hayashi, a Japanese member of the collectors' crowd. See Billy, *Les Frères Goncourt*, p. 329.

17 The rise and fall of *japonisme* can be dated quite precisely: indeed it has been argued by Luc Fraisse that *japonisme* is used as a dating mechanism in Proust, as will be discussed later in this chapter.

18 By Thirion, 'Le japonisme en France', p. 130.

19 Roland Barthes, *Mythologies*, Paris, Seuil, 1970, p. 261.

20 Such categories have often been used as a protective mechanism: Stephen Greenblatt argues, for instance, that in Renaissance Europe, the category of the 'marvellous' was used as a means of classifying knowledge of the phenomena from the New World (Stephen Greenblatt, *Marvelous Possessions: The Wonder of the New World*, Oxford, Oxford University Press, 1991, p. 14).

21 Traditionally, 'cabinets expressed a visual image of the inclusiveness of the European view of the world and its facile ability to incorporate and domesticate potentially transgressive worlds and customs'. Anthony Alan Shelton, 'Cabinets of Transgression: Renaissance Collections and the Incorporation of the New World', in Roger Cardinal and John Elsner (eds.), *The Cultures of Collecting*, London, Reaktion Books, 1994, pp. 177–203 (p. 203). We will see how, in both Proust and Loti, objects of desire are put into cabinets both metaphorical and actual.

22 Philippe Sichel, *Notes d'un bibeloteur au Japon*, Paris, E. Dentu, 1883, p. 4.

23 'C'était un énorme brûle-parfums représentant le dieu de longévité monté sur une biche. Bronze noir incrusté d'argent aux armoires de Tokugawa et mesurant 1m,90 de hauteur sur 1m,10 de longueur'. Sichel, *Notes d'un bibeloteur*, p. 18.

24 The neglect of indigenous history in European accounts of the East is, according to Edward Said, a typical trait of Orientalist literature. See Said, *Orientalism*, pp. 234–35, for a discussion of this issue.

25 'In view of the detailed information which can be obtained from the sixteenth and seventeenth century sources, it is surprising that the Westerners returning to Japan in the nineteenth century know so little of the true affairs in that country.' Michael Cooper (ed.), *They Came to Japan: Anthology of European Reports on Japan, 1543–1640*, London, 1965, p. xi.

26 As already related in my introduction. The most famous of these are perhaps Engelbert Kaempfer's *Histoire naturelle, civile et ecclésiastique du Japon* (translated into French in 1729), and C. P. Thunberg's *Voyage au Japon par le cap de Bonne-Espérance* (translated into French in 1796). Phillip de Siebold's numerous works, as well as those of Isaac Titsingh,were published in the early nineteenth century.

27 Charles de Chassiron, noting the beauty of the Japanese pine trees, refers to them as 'ces pins dont Koempher, le savant Hollandais, dit avoir constaté, au Japon, plus de soixante variétés'. Charles de Chassiron, *Notes sur le Japon, la Chine et l'Inde*, Paris, E. Dentu & Ch. Reinwald, 1861, pp. 9–10. His account of his first voyage to Japan, as one of the 1858 French delegation, is a clear-eyed and intelligent narrative in diary form.

28 A typical title is Pierre-François-Xavier de Charlevoix's *Histoire et description générale du Japon*, Rouen, 1736.

29 Albert Jacquemart, *L'Extrême-Orient au Palais de l'industrie: Notices sur les Collections de M. H. Cernuschi* (extraits de la *Gazette des Beaux-Arts*), Paris, J. Claye, 1874, p. 26.

30 *Catalogue de la collection des Goncourt, Arts de l'Extrême-Orient*, Paris, Motteroz, 1897, p. 11.

31 There is, of course, a long tradition of collectors, from the sixteenth to the eighteenth centuries, who collect objects in order to represent the world in miniature: 'cabinets of curiosities became the allegorical mirror reflecting a perfect and completed picture of the world' (Shelton, 'Cabinets of Transgression', p. 185). With regard to Goncourt in this chapter, I argue that his 'representation' of Japan through the *japonaiserie* is not so much the result of the allegorical desire to represent the world (or part of the world), as that of individual decisions regarding taste and scholarship. I will, however, situate his collecting within the context of previous collectorly trends.

32 E. de Goncourt, *La Maison d'un artiste*, Paris, Flammarion, 2nd edition, 1886, vol. II, pp. 169–283. Henceforth, all references to this volume will be indicated in the text, preceded by *MA*.

33 '[Gaston Migeon] ajoutait que la collection de Burty, comme celle de son ami [Goncourt], témoignait d'une excessive confiance en soi et de l'absence de vraie critique. Il fallait convenir toutefois qu'à l'époque où Goncourt et Burty avaient commencé leur collections, presque tous les bibelots venus du Japon étaient relativement modernes [...] Goncourt a donc ignoré les objets vraiments anciens' (Billy, *Les Frères Goncourt*, pp. 326–27).

34 There will be a detailed discussion of Loti's use of 'japonais' or 'japonerie' to describe Japanese objects and people later in this chapter.

35 This is what Loti will transcribe as 'chamécen' in *Madame Chrysanthème*.

36 If this is indeed Goncourt's attitude towards cataloguing, it is one way in which he is in sympathy with the tradition of earlier collectors. 'The published catalogue became synonymous with the high point of achievement: it announced that the collector had reached his objective – completion; it was an attempt to ensure the collection would be preserved from depredations; and it was a means by which the identity of the collector was fused with the collection' (Shelton, 'Cabinets of Transgression', p. 186). Textual immortality (and immortal possession, of a sort) is thus assured. As far as the physical collection was concerned, it should be noted that Goncourt specifically requested that his collection be put on sale after his death (*MA*, postface by Pol Neveux, p. 324).

37 Even his admirers admit the relentlessly personal nature of Goncourt's judgment: 'sa science se limite à des sensations personnelles, à des intuitions souvent extraordinaires' (*MA*, postface by Pol Neveux, p. 324).

38 'Possession [...] applies to [an] object once it is *divested of its function and made relative to a subject.*' Jean Baudrillard, 'The System of Collecting', in Cardinal and Elsner (eds.), *The Cultures of Collecting*, p. 7.

39 S. Kojima and M. Yamaguchi (eds.), *A Cultural Dictionary of Japan*, Tokyo, Kenkyusha, 1979; 13th printing, 1986, p. 188, my emphases.

40 This kind of traveller is akin to 'the profiteer' described by Tzvetan Todorov in *On Human Diversity*, trans. Catherine Porter, Cambridge, MA, Harvard University Press, 1993, p. 343.

41 There is, on the other hand, the possibility of buying objects of little worth in the foreign country, then selling them for a large profit back in one's home country to people who have no idea of their local worth: this is still common practice among a certain kind of exporter today.

42 Charles Ephrussi, editor of the *Gazette des Beaux-Arts* since 1894, was an inveterate collector of Japanese prints; Madeleine Lemaire, the society painter who illustrated *Les Plaisirs et les Jours* for Proust, was an admirer of the Japanese decorative arts who 'barbouillait à l'infini des pétales de rose de mille couleurs sur des éventails' (Elizabeth de Gramont, quoted in Fraisse, *Proust et le japonisme*, p. 10).

43 See Fraisse, *Proust et le japonisme*, pp. 31–32.

44 I owe this point regarding the important part played by *japonisme* as a dating mechanism in *la Recherche* to Fraisse's book: see Fraisse, *Proust et le japonisme*, pp. 29–33.

45 George Painter, *Marcel Proust*, London, Penguin, 1990, 3rd edition, vol. II, p. 15.

46 In 1910, Proust wrote to René Gimpel, a collector and friend: 'connaissez-vous le petit jeu japonais (chinois? lequel?) qui consiste à mettre des petits papiers dans l'eau, lesquels se contournent, devenant des bonshommes, etc. Pourriez-vous demander à des japonais comment cela s'appelle, mais surtout si cela se fait quelquefois dans du *thé*, si cela se fait dans de l'eau indifféremment froide ou chaude, et dans les plus compliqués s'il peut y avoir des *maisons*, des *arbres*, des *personnages*, enfin quoi' (Fraisse, *Proust et le japonisme*, pp. 13–14).

47 Fraisse, *Proust et le japonisme*, p. 15.

48 Fraisse, *Proust et le japonisme*, p. 38.

49 Fraisse, *Proust et le japonisme*, p. 22.

50 Of course, such characters can be (and usually are) gradually denuded of their mystery, as the narrator grows older and loses his naivety: as Margaret Topping puts it, 'in the case of the narrator's vision of Odette, it is significantly the *young* narrator for whom she possesses an eastern mystique [...] only later to be demythologised in a self-ironizing retrospective on the part of the mature narrator' ('Proust's Orient(alism)', *French Studies Bulletin*, 84 [Autumn 2002], pp. 10–13 [p. 12]). Proust's irony thus cuts through both Odette's vulgar adoption of *japonaiseries* and the narrator's adoption of the erotic/exotic *japoniste* stereotype. But the point of mystery is that, however obvious the deception may appear to the disabused narrator/reader, it is 'real' for he who is mystified: and the consequences for the young narrator, confronted by Odette, Charlus or Albertine, are all too real also.

51 Marcel Proust, *A l'ombre des jeunes filles en fleurs*, Paris, Gallimard, 1923, p. 23.

52 Goncourt's description of the louche character of the early *japonaiserie* shops ('rendez-vous des couples adultères') would seem to support this association: see above, note 8.

53 John Brewer, in a discussion of collectors in England in the eighteenth century, describes how collectors themselves, in private, liked to portray 'the collector's gaze as the look of private sexual desire'. John Brewer, *The Pleasures of the Imagination: English Culture in the Eighteenth Century*, London, Harper Collins, 1997, p. 263.

54 The Japanese kimono is both an outdoors and indoors garment. Its transformation into an exclusively indoors garment in the *japoniste* context is indicative of the distorting matrix that is *japonisme*.

55 The Chinese dressing-gown is a simple signifier of dubious sexual attractiveness, to be placed in the same category as the erotically charged *japoniste* kimono (see previous note). Here Proust adopts the historically accurate (if culturally confused) viewpoint of the Odettes of his world, 'confusing' Japanese and Chinese in a rough and ready recipe for exoticism.

56 On Fortuny's creative reinterpretation of the Japanese kimono, see Fraisse, *Proust et le japonisme*, pp. 60–62.

57 Patrick Mauriès, discussing how enclosure and secrecy were at the core of the collector's mentality, descibes cabinets as 'cloistered spaces for solitary and secret pleasures': *Cabinets of Curiosities*, London, Thames and Hudson, 2002, p. 52.

58 Marcel Proust, *La Prisonnière*, Paris, Gallimard, 1923, p. 10 (my italics).

59 Brewer gives an account of the real-life objectification of Emma Hart, a famous beauty who married 'William Hamilton, long a collector' (Brewer, *The Pleasures of the Imagination*, p. 266): frequently asked to dress in various costumes, and to stand within life-size frames, 'she herself recognized [that she] had been completely objectified' (p. 268).

60 Parts of this section are reproduced from my article, 'The Misreading of *Madame Chrysanthème*: Stereotype Formation and Sleeping Women', *Forum for Modern Language Studies*, 38(3) (2002), pp. 278–90.

61 This relationship was not new in the late nineteenth century: indeed, 'by the late eighteenth century the equation of the object desired by the collector and a beautiful woman had become commonplace' (Brewer, *The Pleasures of the Imagination*, p. 264).

62 Quoted by A. Moulis in 'Pierre Loti au Japon', *Cahiers Pierre Loti*, 24 (1958), p. 9.

63 *Le Cahier rose de Madame Chrysanthème*, Paris, Bibliothèque artistique et littéraire, 1894.

64 Wilkinson, *Misunderstanding*, pp. 43–44.

65 'Pierre Loti' was of course the *nom de plume* of Julien Viaud, a fact that complicates the relationship between the author's name, his pseudonym and the narrator's name. Throughout this chapter, I refer to the narrators of *Madame Chrysanthème* and *La Troisième jeunesse de Madame Prune* as Loti, and to their author as Loti (a standard convention in Loti criticism: see Alain Quella-Villéger, *Le cas Farrère: du Goncourt à la disgrâce*, Paris, Presses de la Renaissance, 1989). The narrator of *Japoneries d'automne*, a non-fictional work, will be referred to as Loti. The importance of referring to the author as Loti rather than as Julien Viaud will be become clear towards the end of the chapter.

66 Pierre Loti, *Madame Chrysanthème*, Paris, GF-Flammarion, 1990, p. 45. Henceforth, all page references to this volume will be indicated in the text, preceded by *MC*.

67 This has been noted by a number of Japanese critics, including those mentioned above. There are very few such authentic Japanese names in *Madame Chrysanthème*; most names, like that of the eponymous heroine, are translated into the French, as will be discussed later.

68 For a clear and concise explanation of this phenomenon from a philosophical point of view, see Colin Davis, *Levinas*, Cambridge, Polity Press, 1996, esp. chapter 2 ('Same and Other').

69 See extract from *La Prisonnière*, quoted on p. 37 of this chapter.

70 Pierre Loti, *Japoneries d'automne*, Paris, Calmann-Lévy, 1889, p. 72. Henceforth, all page references to this volume will be indicated in the text, preceded by *JA*.

71 Pierre Loti, *La Troisième jeunesse de Madame Prune*, Paris, Calmann-Lévy, 1905, p. 20. Henceforth, all page references to this volume will be indicated in the text, preceded by *MP*.

72 Segalen would certainly have connected the two forms of exoticism: 'l'exotisme n'est pas seulement donné dans l'espace, mais également en fonction du temps'. Victor Segalen, *Essai sur l'exotisme*, Fata Morgana, 1978; Fontfroide, Bibliothèque artistique et littéraire, 1995, p. 23.

73 The image of nature taking over a remembered site of memory is a very traditional one, going back as far as Virgil at least. It is used here by Loti, but also by Proust, in a passage which directly follows the one quoted previously (in which the young narrator fantasises about an imaginary past, where attractive women in *japoniste* garb take walks in the Bois): 'Hélas! Dans l'avenue des Acacias – l'allée des Myrtes […] La nature recommençait à régner sur le Bois d'où s'était envolée l'idée qu'il était le Jardin élyséen de la Femme […] de gros oiseaux parcouraient rapidement le Bois, comme un bois, et poussant des cris aigus se posaient l'un après l'autre sur les grands chênes qui, sous leur couronne druidique et avec une majesté dodonéenne, semblaient proclamer le vide inhumain de la forêt désaffectée, et m'aidaient à mieux comprendre la contradiction que c'est de chercher dans la réalité les tableaux de la mémoire, auxquels manquerait toujours le charme qui leur vient de la mémoire même et de n'être pas perçus par les sens' (p. 279). In both cases nature's takeover of a former site is a physical symbol of the passing of time. Interestingly, however, both Loti and Proust add an extra feature: that of pathways, 'les avenues' (Loti) or 'l'Avenue des Acacias… l'allée des Myrtes' (Proust) down which the narrators' memories can travel from the present back into the past.

74 John Elsner, 'A Collector's Model of Desire: The House and Museum of Sir John Soane', in Cardinal and Elsner (eds.), *The Cultures of Collecting*, pp. 155–76 (pp. 155–56).

75 See reference to Barthes above, note 19.

76 Segalen, *Essai sur l'exotisme*, p. 23.

77 As it was, he was deeply critical of Loti, labelling him a 'pseudo-Exote' (Segalen, *Essai sur l'exotisme*, p. 34).

78 Letter to E. Pouvillon, quoted in R. Lefèvre, *En marge de Loti*, Paris, Editions Jean-Renard, 1944, p. 158.

79 Loti is quite straightforward about his motives having been financial in his interview with Philippe Gille, 'Un nouveau livre de Pierre Loti: *Madame Chrysanthème*', *Le Figaro*, 10 October 1887.

80 Certain readers of the novel were more sensitive than others to the new knowledge it offered regarding the *japonaiserie*, however. Vincent Van Gogh wrote to his brother: 'Est-ce que tu as lu *Madame Chrysanthème*? Cela m'a bien donné à penser que les vrais Japonais n'ont rien sur les murs. La description du cloître ou de la pagode où il n'y a rien (les dessins et curiosités sont cachés dans des tiroirs). Ah! C'est donc comme ça qu'il faut regarder une japonaiserie, dans une pièce bien claire, toute nue, ouverte sur le paysage'.

81 Albeit not in any detail: see Quella-Villéger, *Le cas Farrère*, p. 122.

82 Her hair has previously been described as 'cette couronne bouclée de violettes

noires' (p. 21).

83 *La Prisonnière*, p. 84.

84 See the discussion of the letters in Albertine's kimono in the section on Proust, pp. 37–38.

85 'Sleep that knits up the ravelled sleave of care,/The death of each day's life, sore labour's bath,/Balm of hurt minds [...]'; William Shakespeare, *Macbeth*, II. ii. 37–39.

86 *Loti* here shows the flexibility of imagination that Goncourt could not (see p. 27), when he came across the Japanese collector of Chinese 'objets d'art'.

87 'Que se passe-t-il dans le coeur de Pierre? Je voudrais savoir. Dans mes insomnies, je vois un mur s'élever entre nous. Que vais-je devenir si cela continue! Je crains de n'être pour lui qu'un accessoire insignifiant. M'a-t-il jamais demandé si je l'aimais, ou seulement si je pourrais l'aimer un jour! Un jour [...] il s'en ira, bien loin, et je ne le reverrai plus jamais, et tout sera fini!' (*Le Cahier rose de Madame Chrysanthème*, p. 39).

88 Ludovic Naudeau, cited in Félix Régamey, 'Le péril jaune – les responsables', *Mercure de France*, 15 September 1905, p. 195.

89 'No other foreign model – except, possibly, those found in primitive art – changed the look of Western art in all its manifestations so drastically.' Weisberg and Weisberg on the influence of *japonisme* on Western art, *Japonisme*, pp. x–xi.

90 As we have seen, this is also what happens when Goncourt describes his *japonaiseries* with reference to his *japonaiseries*.

2 Journalists and Barbarians

1 Of course, as the Heisenberg principle (amongst other things) has amply demonstrated, scientific truth is far from being truly objective. However, in the present context, it may still be considered a relatively objective standard for comparison.

2 See Storry, *A History of Modern Japan*, pp. 126, 136.

3 François de Villenoisy, 'La Guerre Sino-Japonaise et ses conséquences pour l'Europe', Paris, Imprimerie librairie militaire, 1895, pp. 5–6.

4 Sukehiro Hiraka, 'The Yellow Peril and the White Peril: The Views of Anatole France', in Kinya Tsuruta (ed.), *The Walls Within: Images of Westerners in Japan and Images of the Japanese Abroad*, Vancouver, Institute of Asian Research, University of British Columbia, 1989, pp. 347–52 (p. 348).

5 René Pinon, 'La Guerre Russo-Japonaise et l'Opinion européenne', *Revue des deux mondes*, vol. XXI (1 May 1904), p. 213.

6 Pinon, 'La Guerre Russo-Japonaise', p. 219.

7 Wilkinson, *Japan versus the West*, pp. 125–26.

8 Quoted in Wilkinson, *Japan versus the West*, p. 128.

9 André Chéradame, *Le Monde et la Guerre Russo-Japonaise*, Paris, Plon, 1906, p. i.

10 Charles Pettit, *Pays de Mousmés, Pays de Guerre!*, Paris, Librairie Félix Juven, 1905, p. 287.

11 Pettit, *Pays de Mousmés, Pays de Guerre!*, p. 236.

12 'On the whole the establishments of continental European countries favoured Russia, while their left wings either remained neutral or sided with Japan'. Jean-Pierre Lehmann, *The Image of Japan: From Feudal Isolation to World Power, 1850–1905*, London, George Allen and Unwin, 1978, p. 150.

13 Lehmann, *The Image of Japan*, p. 158.

14 John Carey (ed.), *The Faber Book of Utopias*, London, Faber and Faber, 1999, pp. 38–39.

15 Anatole France, *Sur la pierre blanche*, Paris, Calmann-Lévy, 1905, pp. 209–10.

16 Edmond Théry, *Le Péril Jaune*, Paris, Félix Juven, 1901, p. 309.

17 France, *Sur la pierre blanche*, p. 208.

18 France, *Sur la pierre blanche*, pp. 213–14.

19 France, *Sur la pierre blanche*, p. 214.

20 France, *Sur la pierre blanche*, p. 218.

21 France, *Sur la pierre blanche*, p. 218.

22 Even after the Second World War, *La Bataille* underwent another transformation, this time into a *bande dessinée*, by Marc Andry: it was serialised in *France-Soir* during September and October of that year.

23 Quella-Villéger, *Le cas Farrère*, p. 75.

24 Quella-Villéger, *Le cas Farrère*, p. 84.

25 Quella-Villéger, *Le cas Farrère*, p. 75.

26 Claude Farrère, *La Bataille* (first published 1905), p. 4. References will be made to the 'édition définitive', *La Bataille*, Paris, Ollendorff, 1911.

27 *La Bataille*, p. 7.

28 Quella-Villéger quotes Farrère admitting that he had 'jamais eu le don de bien regarder' (*Le cas Farrère*, p. 401).

29 Such tales, of course, derive from a mythologised image of Spain popular in France. See D.-H. Pageaux, 'L'Espagne héroïque de Victor Hugo', in *Le bûcher d'Hercule*, pp. 283–93.

30 For a concise overview of popular fiction in the period, see for instance David Coward, *A History of French Literature*, Oxford, Blackwell, 2002, pp. 290–97.

31 *La Bataille*, p. 270.

32 *La Bataille*, p. 226.

33 *La Bataille*, pp. 293–94.

34 Claude Farrère, *Mes Voyages*, Paris, Flammarion, 1924, p. 206.

35 *Mes Voyages*, p. 207.

36 Wilkinson, *Japan versus the West*, pp. 130–31.

37 Lehmann, *The Image of Japan*, p. 180.

38 Claude Farrère, *Forces spirituelles de l'Orient*, Paris, Flammarion, 1937, p. 170.

39 See preface to Claude Farrère, *Le grand drame de l'Asie*, Paris, Flammarion, 1939.

40 *Le grand drame de l'Asie*, p. 42.

41 *Le grand drame de l'Asie*, p. 48.

42 *Le grand drame de l'Asie*, p. 56: my emphases.

43 'And God blessed them, and God said unto them, Be fruitful, and multiply, and replenish the earth, and subdue it'; Genesis 2.28.

44 From the eighteenth century onwards, variants of the Roman Law argument known as *res nullius* were used by both the British and the French to legitimise their

colonial activities. This law 'maintained that all "empty things", which included un-occupied lands, remained the common property of all mankind until they were put to some, generally agricultural use. The first person to use the land in this way became its owner.' Anthony Pagden, *Lords of all the World: Ideologies of Empire in Spain, Britain and France*, New Haven and London, Yale University Press, 1995, p. 76.

45 'The Second Treatise of Government', in John Locke, *Two Treatises of Government*, ed. Peter Laslett, Cambridge, Cambridge University Press, 2nd edn, 1970, pp. 306, 314.

46 See note 44.

47 *Le grand drame de l'Asie*, p. 151.

48 *Le grand drame de l'Asie*, pp. 69–70.

49 *Le grand drame de l'Asie*, p. 71.

50 *Le grand drame de l'Asie*, p. 113.

51 *Le grand drame de l'Asie*, p. 190.

52 Parts of this section are reproduced from my article 'Barbarian Travels: Textual Positions in Un barbare en Asie', *The Modern Language Review*, 95.4 (October 2000), pp. 978–91.

53 Henri Michaux, *Ecuador*, Paris, Gallimard, 1928, p. 82.

54 Jean-Xavier Ridon, *Henri Michaux, J. M. G. Le Clézio: l'Exil des mots*, Paris, Kimé, 1995, p. 38.

55 Bruno Thibault, 'Voyager contre: la question de l'exotisme dans les journaux de voyage de Heri Michaux', *French Review*, 64 (1990), pp. 485–95 (p. 488).

56 Montaigne is perhaps the most famous example of a writer using the aphor-ism to this effect.

57 Christopher Ricks has described how proverbs also function in this way: 'Proverbs admit contradictions, and leave us to think not about that but about applicability: we are to decide which of two contradictory truths ("Look before you leap"/"He who hesitates is lost", or "Absence makes the heart grow fonder"/"Out of sight, out of mind") applies in any given situation' (*Essays in Appreciation*, Oxford, Clarendon Press, 1996, p. 323). Aphorisms are distinguished by their author-ship, whereas proverbs are anonymous sayings that have passed into folklore or local wisdom, but the same pattern holds inasmuch as they are both authoritative expressions of experiential truths.

58 For further discussion of Michaux's use of generalisations in *Un barbare en Asie*, see Kawakami, 'Barbarian Travels', p. 980.

59 'Les aphorismes qui définissent l'étranger par des propriétés [sont] présentées comme immuables, définitives [...] comme s'il s'agissait, face à une diversité et à une différence si difficiles à concevoir, de trouver une réassurance dans l'affirmation de "vérités" évidentes'. Marie-Annick Gervais-Zaninger, 'L'insoutenable résistance de l'autre', in André Ughetto (ed.), *Analyses et réflexions sur Henri Michaux, 'Un barbare en Asie'*, Paris, Ellipses, 1992, pp. 45–50 (p. 45).

60 As pointed out by both Claudel, before him (see Chapter 3) and Barthes, after him (see Chapter 4).

61 'Faisais-je exprès de laisser de côté ce qui précisément allait faire en plusieurs de ces pays de la réalité nouvelle: la politique?' Henri Michaux, *Un barbare en Asie*, Paris, Gallimard, 1967, p. 14 (1967 preface).

62 See my Introduction, pp. 2–3.

3 Walking towards Japan

1 This was partly due to the extensive reading that Claudel took on during his time in Japan, not just on Japan but on the other Asian countries that he had visited earlier. However, it was also the case that Claudel was more indulgent towards non-Christian religions in Japan than elsewhere: in *Mémoires improvisés*, for instance, he admits that 'sous sa forme japonaise, la forme amidaïste du bouddhisme m'a plu davantage que le bouddhisme chinois' (*Mémoires improvisés*, Paris, Gallimard, 1954, p. 175). For a fuller discussion of Claudel's 'leniency' towards religion in Japan see Bernard Hue, *Littératures et Arts de l'Orient dans l'oeuvre de Claudel*, Paris, Klincksieck, 1978, pp. 145–47.

2 Claudel was chosen to become French ambassador to Japan soon after the end of the First World War, that is to say in a delicate political climate: his instructions were to 'répandre davantage la connaissance de notre langue, de notre littérature et de nos sciences' in Japan, to move the country away from Anglo-American and German influences. His reports to the Ministère des Affaires Etrangères are collected in Lucile Garbagnati (ed.), *Paul Claudel, Correspondance diplomatique, Tokyo 1921–1927* (Cahiers Paul Claudel 14), Paris, Gallimard, 1995.

3 'Chacun sait – on l'a souvent dit – que Claudel fut un grand marcheur'. Claude-Pierre Perez, *Le défini et l'inépuisable: essai sur* Connaissance de l'Est *de Paul Claudel* (Annales littéraires de l'Université de Besançon, no. 557), Paris, Les Belles-Lettres, 1995, p. 133.

4 In 1897, Claudel wrote to Mallarmé that 'Je puis dire que je dois à Rimbaud tout ce que je suis intellectuellement et moralement, et il y a eu, je crois, peu d'exemples d'un si intime hymen entre deux esprits. Son influence maintenant encore persiste sur moi.' (*Cahiers Paul Claudel*, I, p. 54 [letter of 26 July 1897]).

5 'Seuls la Chine et le Japon ont retenu Claudel à ce point. [...] Aucun des pays où il a vécu ne l'a laissé indifférent et de tous son oeuvre garde la trace. Mais il ne leur a point accordé cette attention fascinée ni pris à les décrire ce soin et ce plaisir. L'Orient l'a touché d'une autre manière que ni le pittoresque ni l'exotisme ne suffisent à expliquer'. Jacques Petit, Preface to Paul Claudel, *Connaissance de l'Est suivi de L'Oiseau noir dans le soleil levant*, Paris, Gallimard, 1974, p. 7.

6 *Connaissance de L'Est suivi de L'Oiseau noir dans le soleil levant*, p. 110, p. 113.

7 Bernard Hue describes how, in *Connaissance de l'Est*, Claudel chose to 'abandonner toute poésie descriptive [...] pour lui substituer un poème à tendances profondément spiritualistes'; *Littératures et Arts de l'Orient dans l'oeuvre de Claudel*, p. 353.

8 Marius-François Guyard, 'L'Homme de *Connaissance de l'Est*', *Bulletin de la Société Paul Claudel*, 100 (1985), pp. 39–41 (p. 41). Also see Petit: 'Claudel poursuit moins dans ces textes une interprétation de la Chine ou du Japon [...] qu'il ne se cherche lui-même', Preface, p. 13.

9 B. P. Howells, '*Connaissance de l'Est*: An Introduction to some Prose Poems by Claudel', *Australian Journal of French Studies*, IV (3) (1967), pp. 323–43 (p. 338).

10 Claudel would claim that this was a constant trait of his character, not limited to his youthful years: 'je ne me suis jamais placé devant un spectacle avec la sensation de m'y perdre, mais au contraire de le dominer et de tâcher d'en réunir les éléments';

Mémoires improvisés, p. 131. On the issue of Claudel's presentation of himself as a consistent and coherent character, see Akane Kawakami, 'Claudel's *Mémoires improvisés*, or the Unimportance of Autobiography', *Romance Studies*, 17.2 (1999), pp. 151–61 (p. 154).

11 Hue, *Littératures et Arts de l'Orient dans l'oeuvre de Claudel*, p. 302.

12 For an account of this tumultuous relationship, see Gérald Antoine, *Paul Claudel ou l'enfer du génie*, Paris, Editions Robert Laffont, 1988, pp. 110–35, or Marie-Josèphe Guers, *Paul Claudel, biographie*, Vendôme, Actes Sud, 1987, pp. 89–94.

13 From the 1895–1900 section of the collection, 'Le Pin', 'L'Arche d'or dans la forêt', 'Le Promeneur', 'Ça et là' and 'Le Sédentaire', all dated June 1898, appear to have Japanese themes; of the later 1900–1905 section, 'La Délivrance d'Amaterasu' is the only one that is obviously about Japan, but 'Le Point' and 'Libation au jour futur' may also be set there.

14 *Connaissance de L'Est suivi de L'Oiseau noir dans le soleil levant*, p. 106.

15 *Connaissance de L'Est suivi de L'Oiseau noir dans le soleil levant*, p. 111.

16 Indeed the *natural* aspect of Nikko is an important antidote, for Claudel, to the pagan sacredness of the site, in self-conscious contrast to Loti's description of the same place, entitled 'La *sainte* montagne de Nikko' (my italics): see Loti, *Japoneries d'automne*, pp. 153–257.

17 'Je ne puis presque penser quand je reste en place; il faut que mon corps soit en branle pour y mettre mon esprit.' *Les Confessions*, Paris, Garnier Flammarion, 1968, p. 199.

18 Jacques Plessen, in *Promenade et Poésie* (La Haye and Paris, Mouton, 1967) picks out Rousseau as a 'point de départ' for his study of walking, because he offers 'une description *phénoménologique* de l'expérience de la marche' (p. 67, my italics).

19 *Les Confessions*, p. 199.

20 Quoted in Plessen, *Promenade et Poésie*, p. 68.

21 Plessen, *Promenade et Poésie*, p. 70.

22 These characteristics of walking have been inherited by most latter-day theorists of walking, for instance by the *flâneurs* of late-nineteenth- and early-twentieth-century Paris, who aspired to the aesthete's disinterested mastery of the topography of the city.

23 'J'ai remarqué souvent que, même parmi ceux qui se piquent le plus de connaître les hommes, chacun ne connaît guère que soi, s'il est vrai même que quelqu'un se connaisse; car comment bien déterminer un être par les seuls rapports qui sont en lui-même, et sans le comparer avec rien? Cependant cette connaissance imparfaite qu'on a de soi est le seul moyen qu'on emploie à connaître les autres. [...] j'ai résolu de faire à mes lecteurs un pas de plus dans la connaissance des hommes, en les tirant s'il est possible de cette règle unique et fautive de juger toujours du coeur d'autrui par le sien; tandis qu'au contraire il faudrait souvent pour connaître le sien même, commencer par lire dans celui d'autrui. Je veux tâcher que pour apprendre à s'apprécier, on puisse avoir du moins une pièce de comparaison; que chacun puisse connaître soi et un autre, et cet autre ce sera moi.' Rousseau, *Oeuvres complètes*, Paris, Editions de la Pléiade, 1959, vol. I, pp. 1148–49.

24 All quotations from this poem are taken from Paul Claudel, *Oeuvre poétique* (Paris: Editions de la Pléiade, 1957), pp. 84–85.

25 Perez notes a 'lointaine parenté' between the poems of *Connaissance de l'Est*

and descriptions of nature in 'les grands récits de voyage du XIXème siècle', but sees this relationship as being not much more than 'l'habileté de Claudel à utiliser à ses propres fins une tradition littéraire' (Perez, *Le défini et l'inépuisable*, p. 35).

26 See for instance Psalm 19: 'Les cieux racontent la gloire de Dieu/Et l'oeuvre de ses mains le firmament l'annonce;/Le jour au jour en publie le *récit*/Et la nuit à la nuit transmet la connaissance' (my italics).

27 Claudel is not often seen as a particularly 'modern' poet, but *Connaissance de l'Est* contains many an instance of an identifiably modern tendency to accept, and even exult in, the independent existence of objects, at times reminiscent of an otherwise very different 'modernist' poet such as Ponge. Compare, for instance, Claudel's 'La Pluie' with Ponge's 'Pluie' in *Le parti pris des choses* (1942).

28 Quoted in Malcolm Bowie, *Proust Amongst the Stars*, London, Harper Collins Publishers/Fontana Press, 1998, pp. 20–21.

29 Clive Scott defines the verset as follows: 'a verse-line of the late-nineteenth and twentieth centuries, deriving from the short numbered paragraphs ("verses") of the Bible and from similar paragraphs in other sacred books. It is the most elastic of rhythmic units [...] it owes its rhythmic cohesion to a variety of possible sources: to patterns of parallelism and repetition, to the combination of familiar metrical entities, to the ordered variation of respiratory spans, to a recurrent number of accents per line, or to a blend of these elements.' Clive Scott, *Vers libre*, Oxford, Clarendon Press, 1990, p. 309. This definition will be referred to again in my analysis of 'La Muraille intérieure', later in this chapter.

30 Claudel is scornful of the even-numbered alexandrine in his *Journal* (although he is not always so dismissive of it): 'l'alexandrin est bien le vers d'un peuple qui sait compter' (*Journal*, I [1904–32], Paris, Editions de la Pléiade, 1968, p. 524).

31 'Le Point', *Connaissance de L'Est*, p. 152.

32 Jacques Bésineau, 'Claudel au Japon: souvenirs et documents inédits', *Etudes* (December 1961), pp. 345–46 (p. 346).

33 'A mon éditeur, M. Nakamé, à mon ami M. Yamanouchi, qui m'a apporté le concours de son intelligence et de son dévouement, au peintre fameux, M. Tomita Keisen, qui a bien voulu mettre au verso de mon poème l'empreinte de son talent, au graveur M. Bonkotsu Igami à qui les procédés japonais utilisés par la plus savante pointe ont permis la reproduction absolument exacte et savante de mes croquis, est due ma reconnaissance.' Paul Claudel, *Oeuvre poétique*, p. 1140.

34 The precise circumstances in which this 'arrangement' came into being have been described by Bésineau, 'Claudel au Japon'.

35 The complete speech is reproduced in Paul Claudel, *Oeuvre poétique*, p. 1138.

36 From the preface to *Cent Phrases pour éventails*, in *Oeuvre poétique*, p. 717. In the section on *Cent Phrases* of this chapter, I will be discussing the possibility that, in becoming involved with these projects, Claudel was succumbing to a *japoniste* temptation.

37 Claudel's fascination with the topos of the book 'written within and on the back side' (Rev. 5.1) is documented by André Espiau de la Maëstre in Michel Malicet (ed.), *Claudel et l'Apocalypse 2*, Paris/Caen, Lettres Modernes Minard, Série Paul Claudel 17, 1998. For some reason, however, he omits any mention of the poem to be discussed here.

38 Henceforth to be referred to as 'La Muraille intérieure'. There are very few

commentaries on this fascinating but difficult poem: see Réjean Robidoux, 'Claudel, poète de la connaissance, "La muraille intérieure de Tokyo"', in *Formes et Figures* (1967); also Maurice Pinguet, 'Paul Claudel et la Muraille intérieure', *Nichifutsu Bunka*, 23 (March 1968), pp. 39–47. The following analysis owes much to an article in Japanese by Takashi Naito, 'Uchibori Jyûnikei shiron', *L'Oiseau Noir: Revue d'études claudéliennes*, 7 (1995), pp. 41–52, although I am not always in agreement with his readings.

39 All quotations from this poem are taken from *Oeuvre poétique*, pp. 654–59.

40 This is noted in Naito, 'Uchibori Jyûnikei shiron', p. 42.

41 The repetition of both 'attraper' and 'il me suffit' is discussed in Naito, 'Uchibori Jyûnikei shiron', p. 46, although what follows is my own analysis: Naito prefers to see them as a 'motif' which shapes the poem, and which suggests obsession in the 'je'.

42 *Itohimé* in Japanese, a constellation with a romantic legend.

43 This is almost certainly a reference to a work of art Claudel records seeing back in 1898, 'un paysage fait de poussières colorées; on l'a mis, de peur qu'un souffle ne l'emporte, sous verre.' (In 'Ça et là', *Connaissance de l'Est*, *Oeuvre poétique*, p. 88).

44 Naito's analysis of the effect of the repeated 'et' ('Uchibori Jyûnikei shiron', pp. 46–47) is diametrically opposed to mine: he argues that the repetition creates a centrifugal force which, slowly but surely, draws everything into itself, like a whirlpool. This is an effect that is sometimes achieved by repetition, but in my opinion it does not occur in these lines.

45 Naito, 'Uchibori Jyûnikei shiron', pp. 47–48.

46 This is the tendency that Jacques Derrida dubs logocentrism: see *De la grammatologie*, Paris, Editions de Minuit, 1967, pp. 21–31.

47 The entries relating to Japan are to be found in the years 1921–27 in his *Journal*, I (1904–32). See for instance his accounts of touristic excursions to Narita, 3 January 1923 (p. 569) or to Nikko, 12–14 January 1923 (p. 571).

48 Henri Micciollo, *L'Oiseau noir dans le soleil levant de Paul Claudel. Introduction: variantes et notes* (Annales littéraires de l'Université de Besançon, 246), Paris, Les Belles-Lettres, 1981, p. 12.

49 It was written very early on in his ambassadorship, in July 1923.

50 *L'Oiseau noir dans le soleil levant*, p. 166.

51 See Micciollo, *L'Oiseau noir*, p. 64.

52 See Micciollo, *L'Oiseau noir*, p. 70.

53 In one theoretical area, however, he is guilty of a conscious omission: it has been pointed out that his description of *nô* theatre ignores its Buddhist elements. Claudel, as mentioned earlier (see note 1), was most receptive to Japanese forms of Buddhism, but he also tended to underplay or even ignore the influence of Buddhism on Japanese culture, preferring to emphasise the part played by Shintoism. Now in the case of *nô* theatre, 'les ouvrages de G. Renondeau en particulier (notons que Claudel ne pouvait pas ignorer les recherches de Renondeau qui était son attaché militaire à Tôkyo) établissent clairement que la trace du shintoïsme dans le nô est beaucoup moins importante que celle du bouddhisme' (Micciollo, *L'Oiseau noir dans le soleil levant de Paul Claudel*, p. 61).

54 *L'Oiseau noir dans le soleil levant*, pp. 305–307.

55 In support of this claim, Micciollo shows how the later texts – such as the

dialogues – were often based on earlier sketches: see Micciollo, *L'Oiseau noir*, p. 33.

56 For a discussion of Claudel's dislike of introspection (and introspective writers), see Kawakami, 'Claudel's *Mémoires improvisés*'.

57 This particular image occurs again in *Cent Phrases pour éventails*, but this time – as we will see – not as part of a recognisable rhetorical trope.

58 Claudel said of *L'Oiseau noir dans le soleil levant* 'qu'il forme diptyque avec *Connaissance de l'est*' (quoted in Petit, Preface to *Connaissance de l'Est suivi de L'Oiseau noir dans le soleil levant*, p. 7): in the case of these poems, this certainly appears to be the case.

59 Micciollo, *L'Oiseau noir*, p. 71.

60 Matsuo Basho (1644–94) set the precedent for wandering haiku poets: his most famous collection, *Oku no Hosomichi* (translated variously, but one English title is *The Narrow Road to the Deep North*), is based on his travels on foot in north Japan.

61 From Plessen (*Promenade et Poésie*), who diagnoses Rimbaud as having been something of a victim of 'dromomania', a fanatical walker.

62 Michel Truffet (ed.), *Cent phrases pour éventails: édition critique et commentée avec la reproduction en fac similé de l'édition japonaise*, Paris, Les Belles-Lettres, 1985, p. 18.

63 I discuss some of these poems in greater detail in my article on *Cent Phrases pour éventails*, 'Claudel's Fragments of Japan: "Connaissance de l'autre" in *Cent Phrases pour éventails*', *French Studies*, 50.2 (April 1999), pp. 176–88.

64 See for instance the sequence of phrases on the rose (phrases 19–29), or on the *jizô* (phrases 9–12).

65 With one exception, the last one, which is about Claudel being separated from Japan upon his departure.

66 *Souffles des quatre souffles* (*Shifu-cho* in Japanese), published in 1926 by Santo Shoin in Tokyo, was a luxurious edition of four poems about the four seasons. They were handwritten by Claudel and illustrated with paintings by Tomita Keisen on four fan-shaped pieces of heavy *washi* (Japanese paper). These poems were later incorporated into *Cent Phrases pour éventails*, becoming phrases 16, 106, 132 and 137. Similarly, twenty of the poems from *Cent Phrases* were published separately, also with paintings by Tomita Keisen, as *Poëmes du Pont des Faisans* (*Chikyo-shu* in Japanese) by Nichifutsu Geijutsusha, also in 1926. For a detailed history of these publications, see volume IV of *L'Oiseau Noir: Revue d'études claudéliennes*.

67 As argued by Aristotle in his *Poetics*.

68 For an introduction to Claudel's lifelong preoccupation with the relations between these two worlds, see Claude-Pierre Perez, *Le Visible et l'Invisible: pour une archéologie de la poétique claudélienne* (Annales littéraires de l'Université de Franche-Comté, no. 648), Paris, Les Belles-Lettres, 1998, pp. 10–11.

69 Claudel's consistency of character was a characteristic recognised by both his friends and enemies, noted by both himself and by biographers: 'Dans le vieillard, l'homme en crises et l'adolescent de Villeneuve n'ont cessé d'exister. Claudel patriarche restait ce passionné, le croyant qu'il avait été'; Guers, *Paul Claudel, biographie*, p. 223) For a critical discussion of this issue, see Kawakami, 'Claudel's *Mémoires improvisés*'.

70 In the course of 172 phrases, 'le poète' appears in seven: the personal pronoun 'je' (as used to designate the poet) occurs in 27.

71 Truffet (ed.), *Cent phrases pour éventails*, p. 140.

72 This character for 'city' can also denote 'Kyoto'.

73 A prejudice propagated by the Imagists, who admired Japanese haiku, among other Eastern poetic forms. See William Pratt and Robert Richardson (eds.), *Homage to Imagism*, New York, AMS Press, 1992, for modern-day descendants who still hold this view.

74 My article 'Claudel's Fragments of Japan' contains an extended analysis of these phrases (pp. 184–85).

75 Imagism, for instance, was a movement that extolled the concrete: T. E. Hulme, one of its founding members, taught that 'verbal images were the only true communicators of meaning, because they were formed in the mind before speech and gave speech its concreteness'. See William Pratt, 'Imagism and the Shape of Eastern Poetry', in Pratt and Richardson (eds.), *Homage to Imagism*, pp. 75–86 (p. 78). A more famous Imagist poet, Ezra Pound, exhorted his followers to 'go in fear of abstractions'; T. S. Eliot (ed.), *Literary Essays of Ezra Pound*, London, Faber, 1954, p. 5.

76 Quoted in Bésineau, 'Claudel au Japon', pp. 349–50.

77 'Banzaï', literally, means 'ten thousand years', so 'Nippon banzaï!' would be translated roughly as 'Hooray for Japan!' Like the symbol of the rising sun, the exhortation has a much longer history than that of the militaristic patriotism with which it became associated. It was quite bold of Claudel to use these images in his letter, as the American GHQ in 1949 would – as Yamanouchi makes clear, in his letter to Claudel – still have been opening and censoring letters from abroad

4 Postwar Travellers and Photographic Writing

1 The tourist has become an important figure in travel writing, and in studies of travel writing, of the twentieth century. See, for instance, Todorov, *Nous et les autres*; Pasquali, *Le Tour des Horizons*; Jean-Marc Moura, *Lire l'exotisme*, Paris, Dunod, 1992.

2 Roland Barthes, *L'Empire des signes*, Geneva, Skira, 1970; Michel Butor, *Le Japon depuis la France, un rêve à l'ancre*, Paris, Hatier, 1995; Jacques Roubaud, *Mono no Aware, le sentiment des Choses*, Paris, Gallimard, 1970; Yukio Mishima, *Cinq Nô modernes*, translated by Marguerite Yourcenar, Paris, Gallimard, 1984.

3 Felice Beato was an Italian photographer who became a naturalised British citizen, whose photographs of Japanese subjects were much admired: Macé refers to one of his iconic shots in *Où grandissent les pierres*.

4 *Le Japon illustré* (1915) contains many photos by Félicien Challaye, which, as we will see below, continued to be used throughout the twentieth century as images of Japan.

5 Such as Philippe Dubois, Denis Roche, Mary Price; Alfred Stieglitz, Stanley Cavell and Rudolf Arnheim.

6 By Hervé Guibert, for instance, amongst others: see my section on Gérard Macé below.

7 Diana Knight discusses the significance of the publication year of *L'Empire des*

signes in 'Roland Barthes in Harmony: The Writing of Utopia', *Paragraph*, 11.2 (1988), pp. 127–42 (129).

8 Barthes, *L'Empire des signes*, pp. 9–10. Henceforth references to this book will be given in the text, prefaced by *ES*.

9 See for instance Jacques Ehrmann, 'L'Emprise des signes', *Semiotica*, 1 (1973), pp. 49–76; or Tom Beebee, 'Orientalism, Absence, and the poème en prose', *The Rackham Journal of the Arts and Humanities*, 2.1 (1980), pp. 48–71.

10 Said's *Orientalism*, of course, was published ten years after Barthes' work; but in 1967 in *Mythologies* Barthes had already categorised racially motivated exoticism as a petit-bourgeois failing.

11 Bernard Comment, *Roland Barthes, vers le neutre*, Paris, Christian Bourgeois, 1991, p. 192. I am indebted to Comment's comentary on *L'Empire des signes* for this insight: see pp. 192–93.

12 Butor, *Le Japon depuis la France*, pp. 23–24. Henceforth, all page references to this work will occur in the text, preceded by *JF*.

13 Jean H. Duffy, *Signs and Designs: Art and Architecture in the Work of Michel Butor*, Liverpool, Liverpool University Press, 2003, pp. 248–49. Much of what follows is based on her section on Butor's relationship with Japanese art: see pp. 245–50.

14 Of course, this is a common fascination among Western writers in Japan, as we have seen in the case of Claudel, for instance: see the section on *Cent Phrases pour éventails* in Chapter 3.

15 Michel Butor, *Butor photographe*, Neuchâtel and Paris, Editions Ides & Calendes, 2002. See the bibliography of this work for a complete list of Butor's collaborative works with artists as well as photographers, such as Pierre Alechinsky, Serge Assister, Maxine Godard, Catherine Noury and Bernard Plossu.

16 This sentence occurs twice in *Archipel Shopping*: see Michel Butor, *Boomerang. Génie du lieu III*, Paris, Gallimard, 1978, p. 391 and p. 399. It is also repeated at the end of the quotations from *Archipel Shopping* in Confidences 9, 10, 11 and 12 (but not 13) of *Le Japon depuis la France*.

17 *Bois dormant*, Paris, Gallimard, 1983. Recently translated into English by David Kelley and Timothy Mathews, a bilingual edition: *Wood Asleep*, Newcastle, Bloodaxe, 2003.

18 Gérard Macé, *La Photographie sans appareil*, Paris, Le temps qu'il fait, 2000, p. 9.

19 Nicolas Bouvier was a travel writer and photographer whose *Chronique japonaise* (1989) is an account of his stay in Japan, interspersed with an authoritative and idiosyncratically presented history of Japan, from its beginnings until the present day.

20 Hervé Guibert, *L'Image fantôme*, Paris, Editions de Minuit, 1981, p. 75.

21 Macé, *La Photographie sans appareil*, p. 22.

22 Gérard Macé, *Où grandissent les pierres*, Paris, Fata Morgana, 1985, pp. 42–43. Henceforth references to this book will occur in the text, preceded by *OGP*.

23 The bridge is one of Macé's favourite and most developed metaphors. It occurs to effect, for instance, in *Où grandissent les pierres*: 'le pont flottant des rêves, à la charpente aussi mal ajustée que les jours incertains, les mois inégaux qui nous permettent pourtant de passer d'une année à l'autre'.

24 Henceforth, *Choses rapportées du Japon* will be abbreviated to *CRJ*.

25 Macé has told me in conversation that he has not allowed *Où grandissent les pierres* to be reprinted because he thought it was 'trop didactique': what he liked of it was recast into the different formula of *Choses rapportées du Japon*, as we have seen.

26 In some cases, the style is reminiscent of Michaux's aphorisms in *Un barbare en Asie*, especially as some of them seem to be fragments of wisdom, brought back from the East in the time-honoured fashion, in spite of the self-deprecating 'choses' of the title.

27 At least, this is the case in the 1993 edition. I will describe the complicated publishing history of this text later in the chapter.

28 The *eaux-fortes* were painted by Alechinsky using, for inspiration, objects from Japan that Macé brought to him in a basket: Alechinsky reproduced the pattern of the basket in some of the works.

29 For a discussion of realism and photography, see Philippe Dubois, *L'Acte Photographique et autres essais*, Brussels, Labor, 1990, chapter 1.

30 Gérard Macé, *Un détour par l'orient*, Paris, Le Promeneur, 2001, front cover.

31 *Un détour par l'orient*, p. 57.

32 This is comparable, for instance, to the way in which the Eskimos have a multitude of words for snow, whereas English makes do with just the one: the two languages divide up the same reality into different parcels of meaning.

33 *Un détour par l'orient*, p. 64.

34 *Un détour par l'orient*, pp. 69–70.

35 *Un détour par l'orient*, p. 121.

36 Paul-Louis Couchoud and Julien Vocance were among the first French poets to attempt the writing of haiku, soon after the First World War: in the twenties, when the form became well known in literary circles, Maurice Gobin and Paul Eluard were among those who tried their hand at this short form. On the history of haiku in French, see Patrick Blanche, 'Simple coup d'oeil sur le haiku en France', in André Delteil (ed.), *Le Haiku et la forme brève en poésie française*, Aix-en-Provence, Université de Provence, 2001.

37 The distinction made by Gottlob Frege between 'Sinn' and 'Bedeutung', often translated into English as 'meaning' and 'significance'. See Gideon Makin, *The Metaphysicians of Meaning: Russell and Frege on Sense and Denotation*, London, Routledge, 2000.

38 Benjamin felt that photographs were too *modern* to have aura: they lacked the 'mystery of the past' that ensures nostalgia and attraction (see Mary Price, *The Photograph: A Strange, Confined Place*, Stanford, CA, Stanford University Press, p. 147). It was therefore its modernity, not the fact of its reproducibility that disqualified the photograph from Benjamin's list of objects that could produce aura. For a convincing argument against this position, see Price, *The Photograph*, chapter 7.

39 For a discussion of the denotative power of names, see Chapter 1, note 67.

40 *La Chambre claire*, Paris, Gallimard/Seuil, 1980, pp. 60–61. Barthes' example is the photograph of a black man, entitled 'William Casby, Born a Slave': he argues that this photograph becomes a symbol of slavery, rather than being simply the photograph of an old black man.

41 Gérard Macé, *Un Monde qui ressemble au monde*, Paris, Marval, 2000, p. 7, p. 9. Henceforth, all quotations from this book will be indicated in the text.

42 'To photograph is to appropriate the thing photographed.' Susan Sontag, *On Photography*, London, Penguin, 1977, p. 4.

43 'L'espace photographique [...] [est] un espace à prendre, un prélèvement dans le monde, une *soustraction* qui opère *en bloc*', which, by implication, excludes the rest of the world, referred to as 'le hors-champ, le hors cadre'. Dubois, *L'Acte photographique*, p. 169.

44 'If the specific has resonance, it is in subservience to a larger referential scheme. The question in photography is how to substantiate a claim that such a scheme may exist, when the limiting condition of the photograph is that its subject matter cannot be the invention of the photographer'; Price, *The Photograph*, p. 175. Barthes, of course, is eloquent on the subject of the realisation that '*la chose a* été *là*'. See *La Chambre claire*, pp. 120–22.

45 Albert G. Latham (ed.), *La Belle au Bois dormant, le chat botté et le petit poucet par Charles Perrault*, London, Macmillan, 1911, p. 25.

46 *La Mémoire aime chasser dans le noir* (Paris, Gallimard, 1993) is one of Macé's titles.

Conclusion

1 Wilkinson, *Japan versus the West*, p. 30.

2 Ruth Benedict, *The Chrysanthemum and the Sword*, first published 1946; London, Routledge and Kegan Paul, 1967, p. 2.

3 From a *Japan Times* questionnaire, 26 June 1979. Quoted in Wilkinson, *Japan versus the West*, p. 137.

4 Amélie Nothomb, *Stupeur et tremblements*, Paris, Livre de poche, 1999.

5 Fraisse, *Proust et le japonisme*, pp. 16–21.

6 'S'agissant de caractériser à grands traits l'évolution historique des récits de voyage, la critique a mis en évidence la transformation [... de] la relation pseudo-objective d'un narrateur-personnage-témoin [...] au récit pseudo-subjectif d'un narrateur-personnage-acteur: son propos serait moins de présenter un univers plus ou moins neuf et inconnu, que de rendre compte des échos de cet univers dans l'individualité qui voyage et observe.' Pasquali, *Le Tour des Horizons*, p. 91.

7 Pasquali, *Le Tour des Horizons*, p. 102.

Bibliography

Primary sources

Barthes, Roland, *Mythologies*, Paris, Seuil, 1970.
——, *L'Empire des Signes*, Geneva, Skira, 1970.
——, *Le Plaisir du texte*, Paris, Seuil, 1973.
——, *La Chambre claire*, Paris, Gallimard/Seuil, 1980.
Butor, Michel, *Boomerang. Génie du lieu III*, Paris, Gallimard, 1978.
——, *Le Japon depuis la France, un rêve à l'ancre*, Paris, Hatier, 1995.
——, *Butor photographe*, Neuchâtel and Paris, Editions Ides & Calendes, 2002.
Claudel, Paul, *Oeuvre poétique*, Paris, Editions de la Pléiade, 1957.
——, *Journal*, I (1904–32), Paris, Editions de la Pléiade, 1968.
——, *Mémoires improvisés*, Paris, Gallimard, 1954.
Duras, Marguerite, *Hiroshima mon amour* (first published 1959), Paris, Gallimard, 1960.
Farrère, Claude, *La Bataille* (first published 1905), Paris, Ollendorff, 1911 ('édition définitive').
——, *Mes Voyages*, Paris, Flammarion, 1924.
——, *Forces spirituelles de l'Orient*, Paris, Flammarion, 1937.
——, *Le grand drame de l'Asie*, Paris, Flammarion, 1939.
France, Anatole, *Sur la pierre blanche*, Paris, Calmann-Lévy, 1905.
Goncourt, Edmond de, *Outamaro, Hokusaï, l'Art japonais du XVIIIe siècle* (1891 and 1896), reprinted as one volume with preface by Hubert Juin, Paris, Union Générale des Editions, 1986.
——, *La Maison d'un artiste*, Paris, Fasquelle, 1881.
Loti, Pierre (pseudonym of Louis-Marie-Julien Viaud), *Madame Chrysanthème*, Paris, GF-Flammarion, 1990.
——, *Japoneries d'automne*, Paris, Calmann-Lévy, 1889.
——, *La Troisième jeunesse de Madame Prune*, Paris, Calmann-Lévy, 1905.
——, 'Un nouveau livre de Pierre Loti: *Madame Chrysanthème*' (interview with Philippe Gille), *Le Figaro*, 10 October 1887.
Macé, Gérard, *Leçon de chinois*, Paris, Fata Morgana, 1981.
——, *Bois dormant*, Paris, Gallimard (poésie), 1983. Translated by David Kelley and Timothy Mathews, *Wood Asleep*, Newcastle, Bloodaxe, 2003 (bilingual edition).
——, *Le Manteau de Fortuny*, Paris, Gallimard, 1987.
——, *Le Dernier des Egyptiens*, Paris, Gallimard (folio), 1989.
——, *La Mémoire aime chasser dans le noir*, Paris, Gallimard, 1993.

——, *L'art sans paroles*, Paris, Le Promeneur, 1999.

——, *Un Monde qui ressemble au monde*, Paris, Marval, 2000.

——, *La Photographie sans appareil*, Paris, Le temps qu'il fait, 2000.

——, *Images et signes: Lectures de Gérard Macé*, Paris, Le temps qu'il fait, 2001.

——, *Un détour par l'orient*, Paris, Le Promeneur, 2001.

——, *Mirages et Solitudes*, Paris, Le temps qu'il fait, 2003.

Macé, Gérard and Pierre Alechinsky, *Choses rapportées du Japon*, Paris, Fata Morgana, 1993.

Michaux, Henri, *Ecuador*, Paris, Gallimard, 1928.

——, *Un barbare en Asie*, Paris, Gallimard, 1933.

Mishima, Yukio, *Cinq Nô modernes* (1960); translated by Marguerite Yourcenar, Paris, Gallimard, 1984.

Proust, Marcel, *A la recherche du temps perdu*, Paris, Gallimard, 1919–1927.

Roubaud, Jacques, *Mono no aware, le sentiment des choses: Cent-quatre poèmes empruntés au japonais*, Paris, Gallimard, 1970.

Yourcenar, Marguerite, *Nouvelles Orientales*, Paris, Gallimard, 1963.

——, *Mishima ou la vision du vide*, Paris, Gallimard, 1980.

Secondary sources

Allen, Louis and Jean Wilson (eds.), *Lafcadio Hearn: Japan's Great Interpreter*, Folkestone, Kent, Japan Library Ltd, 1992.

Antoine, Gérald, *Paul Claudel ou l'enfer du génie*, Paris, Editions Robert Laffont, 1988.

Bancquart, Marie-Claire, *Anatole France, un sceptique passionné*, Paris, Calmann-Lévy, 1984.

Beebee, Tom, 'Orientalism, Absence, and the poème en prose', *The Rackham Journal of the Arts and Humanities*, 2.1 (1980), pp. 48–71.

Beillevaire, Patrick, *Le Japon en langue française: ouvrages et articles publiés en France de 1850 à 1945*, Paris, Société française des études japonaises, Editions Kimé, 1993.

Benedict, Ruth, *The Chrysanthemum and the Sword* (first published 1946), London, Routledge and Kegan Paul, 1967.

Berger, John, *Ways of Seeing*, London, Penguin, 1972.

Bésineau, Jacques, 'Claudel au Japon: souvenirs et documents inédits', *Etudes* (December 1961), pp. 345–51.

Billy, André, *Les Frères Goncourt: La vie littéraire à Paris pendant la seconde moitié du XIXe siècle*, Paris, Flammarion, 1954.

Bing, Samuel (ed.), *Le Japon artistique: Documents d'Art et d'Industrie*, numéro 1, Paris, Marpon et Flammarion, 1888.

——, *Catalogue de la collection des Goncourt, Arts de l'Extrême-Orient*, Paris, Motteroz, 1897.

Bongie, Chris, *Exotic Memories: Literature, Colonialism, and the Fin de Siècle*, Stanford, Stanford University Press, 1991.

Bouvier, Nicolas, *Chronique japonaise*, Paris, Payot, 1989.

Bowie, Malcolm, *Proust Amongst the Stars*, London, Harper Collins/Fontana, 1998.

Brahimi, Denise, *Un aller-retour pour Cipango: Essai sur les paradoxes du japonisme*, Paris, Noël Blandin, 1992.

Brewer, John, *The Pleasures of the Imagination: English Culture in the Eighteenth Century*, London, Harper Collins, 1997.

Brody, Elaine, *Paris: The Musical Kaleidoscope, 1870–1925*, London, Robson, 1988.

Buruma, Ian, *Wages of Guilt: Memories of War in Germany and Japan*, London, Vintage, 1995.

——, *The Missionary and the Libertine: Love and War in East and West*, London, Faber and Faber, 1996.

Campbell, Mary B., *The Witness and the Other World: Exotic European Travel Writing (400–1600)*, Ithaca, NY, and London, Cornell University Press, 1988.

Cardinal, Roger and John Elsner (eds.), *The Cultures of Collecting*, London, Reaktion Books, 1994.

Carey, John (ed.), *The Faber Book of Utopias*, London, Faber and Faber, 1999.

Cercle d'études claudéliennes au Japon, *L'oiseau noir: Revue d'études claudéliennes* (vols. 1–11), 1977–2001.

Chamberlain, Basil Hall, *Things Japanese*, London, Kegan Paul, 1891.

——, *Japanese Poetry*, London, John Murray, 1910.

Champfleury [Jules Husson], 'La Mode des japonaiseries', *La Vie Parisienne*, 1868.

Charlevoix, Pierre-François-Xavier de, *Histoire et description générale du Japon*, 6 vols., Paris, Giffard, 1754 (Rouen, 1736).

Chassiron, Charles de, *Notes sur le Japon, la Chine et l'Inde*, Paris, E. Dentu & Ch. Reinwald, 1861.

Chéradame, André, *Le Monde et la Guerre Russo-Japonaise*, Paris, Plon, 1906.

Comment, Bernard, *Roland Barthes, vers le neutre*, Paris, Christian Bourgeois, 1991.

Cooper, Michael (ed.), *They Came to Japan: Anthology of European Reports on Japan, 1543–1640*, Berkeley, London, University of California Press, 1965.

Couchoud, Paul-Louis, *Sages et poètes d'Asie*, Paris, Calmann-Lévy, 1916.

Coward, David, *A History of French Literature*, Oxford, Blackwell, 2002.

Cronin, Michael, *Across the Lines: Travel, Language, Translation*, Cork, Cork University Press, 2000.

Davis, Colin, *Levinas*, Cambridge, Polity Press, 1996.

Delteil, André (ed.), *Le Haiku et la forme brève en poésie française*, Université de Provence, 2001.

Derrida, Jacques, *De la grammatologie*, Paris, Editions de Minuit, 1967.

Dower, John, *Japan in War and Peace*, London, Fontana, 1996.

Dubois, Philippe, *L'Acte Photographique et autres essais*, Brussels, Labor, 1990.

Duffy, Jean H., *Signs and Designs: Art and Architecture in the Work of Michel Butor*, Liverpool, Liverpool University Press, 2003.

Duret, Théodore, *Critique de l'avant-garde*, Paris, Ecole Normale Supérieure des Beaux-Arts, 1998.

Ehrmann, Jacques, 'L'Emprise des signes', *Semiotica*, 1 (1973), pp. 49–76.

Eliot, T. S. (ed.), *Literary Essays of Ezra Pound*, London, Faber and Faber, 1954.

Etiemble, René, *Comment lire un roman japonais? Le Kyoto de Kawabata*, Paris, Fanlac, 1980.

Fenollosa, Ernest, *Review of the Chapter on Painting in Gonse's 'L'art japonais'*, Boston, James R. Osgood, 1885.

Fraisse, Luc, *Proust et le japonisme*, Strasbourg, Presses universitaires de Strasbourg, 1997.

Garbagnati, Lucile (ed.), *Paul Claudel, Correspondance diplomatique, Tokyo 1921–1927* (Cahiers Paul Claudel 14), Paris, Gallimard, 1995.

Gautier, Judith, *Fleurs d'orient*, Paris, Armand Colin, 1893.

Gonse, François, *L'Art japonais*, 2 vols., Paris, Ernest Grund, 1885.

Gozzano, Guido, *Un Natale a Ceylon e altri racconti indiani*, Milan, Ed. Piero Cudini, 1984.

Guers, Marie-Josèphe, *Paul Claudel, biographie*, Vendôme, Actes Sud, 1987.

Greenblatt, Stephen, *Marvelous Possessions: The Wonder of the New World*, Oxford, Oxford University Press, 1991.

Guibert, Hervé, *L'Image fantôme*, Paris, Editions de Minuit, 1981.

Guimet, Emile, *Promenades japonaises*, Paris, Charpentier, 1878.

Guyard, Marius-François, 'L'Homme de *Connaissance de l'Est*', *Bulletin de la Société Paul Claudel*, 100 (1985), pp. 39–41.

Heidegger, Martin, *The Question Concerning Technology and Other Essays*, New York, Harper and Row, 1977.

Hokenson, Jan Walsh, *Japan, France, and East-West Aesthetics*, Madison/Teaneck, Fairleigh Dickinson University Press, 2004.

Howells, B. P., '*Connaissance de l'Est*: An Introduction to some Prose Poems by Claudel', *Australian Journal of French Studies* (1967), pp. 323–43.

Hsieh, Yvonne Y., *Victor Segalen's Literary Encounter with China: Chinese Moulds, Western Thoughts*, Toronto, University of Toronto Press, 1988.

Hue, Bernard, *Littératures et Arts de l'Orient dans l'oeuvre de Claudel*, Paris, Klincksieck, 1978.

Humbert, Aimé, *Le Japon illustré*, Paris, Hachette, 1870.

Ishikawa, Yoshiko, *Tabi no écriture*, Tokyo, Hakusuisha, 2000.

Jacquemart, Albert, *L'Extrême-Orient au Palais de l'industrie: Notices sur les Collections de M. H. Cernuschi* (extraits de la *Gazette des Beaux-Arts*), Paris, J. Claye, 1874.

Kaempfer, Engelbert, *Histoire naturelle, civile et ecclésiastique du Japon* (2 vols.), The Hague, P. Gosse and J. Neaulme, 1729 (French translation).

Kawakami, Akane, 'Claudel's Fragments of Japan: "Connaissance de l'autre" in *Cent Phrases pour éventails*', *French Studies*, 53.2 (April 1999), pp. 176–88.

——, 'Barbarian Travels: Textual Positions in Un barbare en Asie', *The Modern Language Review*, 95.4 (October 2000), pp. 978–91.

——, 'Claudel's *Mémoires improvisés*, or the Unimportance of Autobiography', *Romance Studies*, 17.2 (1999), pp. 151–61.

Khatibi, Abdelkébir, *Figures de l'étranger dans la littérature française*, Paris, Denoël, 1987.

Knight, Diana, 'Roland Barthes in Harmony: The Writing of Utopia', *Paragraph*, 11.2 (1988), pp. 127–42.

Koestler, Arthur, 'Association and Bisociation', in *The Act of Creation*, New York, Macmilla, 1964, pp. 657–60.

Kojima, S. and M. Yamaguchi (eds.), *A Cultural Dictionary of Japan*, Tokyo, Kenkyusha, 1979; 13th printing, 1986.

Lacambre, Geneviève, *Le Japonisme* (Catalogue d'une exposition au Grand Palais), Paris, Réunion des musées généraux, 1988.

Latham, Albert G. (ed.), *La Belle au Bois dormant, le chat botté et le petit poucet par Charles Perrault*, London, Macmillan, 1911.

Lavers, Annette, *Roland Barthes, Structuralism and After*, London, Methuen, 1982.

Lefèvre, R., *En marge de Loti*, Paris, Editions Jean-Renard, 1944.

Lehmann, Jean-Pierre, *The Image of Japan: From Feudal Isolation to World Power, 1850–1905*, London, George Allen and Unwin, 1978.

Levinas, Emmanuel, *En découvrant l'existence avec Husserl et Heidegger*, Paris, Vrin, 1982.

Locke, John, *Two Treatises of Government*, ed. Peter Laslett, Cambridge, Cambridge University Press, 2nd edn, 1970.

Lowe, Lisa, *Critical Terrains: French and British Orientalisms*, Ithaca, NY, Cornell University Press, 1991.

Makin, Gideon, *The Metaphysicians of Meaning: Russell and Frege on Sense and Denotation*, London, Routledge, 2000.

Malicet, Michel (ed.), *Claudel et l'Apocalypse 2*, Paris/Caen, Lettres Modernes Minard (Série Paul Claudel 17), 1998.

Mauriès, Patrick, *Cabinets of Curiosities*, London, Thames and Hudson, 2002.

Micciollo, Henri, *L'Oiseau noir dans le soleil levant de Paul Claudel. Introduction: variantes et notes* (Annales littéraires de l'Université de Besançon, 246), Paris, Les Belles-Lettres, 1981.

Millan, Gordon, *Mallarmé*, London, Secker and Warburg, 1994.

Millet-Gérard, Dominique, *Claudel: La Beauté et l'Arrière-Beauté*, Paris, Sedes, 2000.

Minear, R. H., 'Orientalism and the Study of Japan', *Journal of Asian Studies*, 39 (1980), pp. 510–16.

Mitchell, Timothy, *Colonising Egypt*, Cambridge, Cambridge University Press, 1988. Moulis, A., 'Pierre Loti au Japon', *Cahiers Pierre Loti*, 24 (1958), p. 9.

Moura, Jean-Marc, *Lire l'exotisme*, Paris, Dunod, 1992.

Naito, Takashi, 'Uchibori Jyûnikei shiron', in *L'Oiseau Noir: Revue d'études claudéliennes*, 7 (1995), pp. 41–52.

Nothomb, Amélie, *Stupeur et tremblements*, Paris, Livre de poche, 1999.

Obara, Satoru, SJ, 'Acceptance, Rejection and Transformation: Christianity and the Historical Climate of Japan' (Kirishitan Bunko series), Tokyo, Sophia University, 1994.

Okaya, Koji, *Pierre Loti no yakata*, Tokyo, Sakuhinsha, 2000.

Pagden, Anthony, *Lords of All the World: Ideologies of Empire in Spain, Britain and France*, New Haven and London, Yale University Press, 1995.

Pageaux, D.-H., *Le bûcher d'Hercule: Histoire, critique, et théorie littéraires*, Paris, Champion, 1996.

Painter, George, *Marcel Proust*, London, Penguin, 1990.

Parks, George B. (ed.), Henry Yule (trans.), *The Travels of Marco Polo, the Venetian, concerning the Kingdoms and Marvels of the East*, New York, Macmillan, 1927.

Pasquali, Adrien, *Le Tour des Horizons*, Paris, Klincksieck, 1994.

Perez, Claude-Pierre, *Le défini et l'inépuisable: essai sur Connaissance de l'Est de Paul Claudel* (Annales littéraires de l'Université de Besançon, no. 557), Paris, Les Belles-Lettres, 1995.

Perez, Claude-Pierre, *Le Visible et l'Invisible: pour une archéologie de la poétique claudélienne* (Annales littéraires de l'Université de Franche-Comté, no. 648), Paris, Les Belles-Lettres, 1998.

Petit, Jacques, Preface to Paul Claudel, *Connaissance de l'Est suivi de L'Oiseau noir dans le soleil levant*, Paris, Gallimard, 1974.

Pettit, Charles, *Pays de Mousmés, Pays de Guerre!*, Paris, Librairie Félix Juven, 1905.

Pinguet, Maurice, 'Paul Claudel et la Muraille intérieure', *Nichifutsu Bunka*, 23 (March 1968), pp. 39–47.

Pinon, René, 'La Guerre Russo-Japonaise et l'Opinion européenne', *Revue des deux mondes*, 21 (1 May 1904), p. 213.

Plessen, Jacques, *Promenade et Poésie*, La Haye and Paris, Mouton, 1967.

Ponge, Francis, *Le parti pris des choses*, Paris, Gallimard, 1942.

Pratt, William and Robert Richardson (eds.), *Homage to Imagism*, New York, AMS Press, 1992.

Price, Mary, *The Photograph: A Strange, Confined Place*, Stanford, CA, Stanford University Press, 1994.

Quella-Villéger, Alain, *Le cas Farrère, du Goncourt à la disgrâce*, Paris, Presses de la Renaissance, 1989.

Reckert, Stephen, *Beyond Chrysanthemums: Perspectives on Poetry East and West*, Oxford, Clarendon Press, 1993.

Régamey, Félix, *Le Japon pratique*, Bibliothèque des Professions Industrielles, Paris, J. Hetzel et Cie, 1891.

——, *Le Cahier rose de Madame Chrysanthème*, Paris, Bibliothèque artistique et littéraire, 1894.

——, 'Le péril jaune – les responsables', *Mercure de France* (15 September 1905), p. 195.

Revon, Michel (ed.), *Anthologie de la littérature japonaise des origines au XXe siècle*, Paris, Delagrave, 1910.

Ridon, Jean-Xavier, *Henri Michaux, J. M. G. Le Clézio: l'Exil des mots*, Paris, Kimé, 1995.

Ricks, Christopher, *Essays in Appreciation*, Oxford, Clarendon Press, 1996.

Robidoux, Réjean, 'Claudel, poète de la connaissance, "La muraille intérieure de Tokyo"', in *Formes et Figures*, special issue of *Cahier Canadien Paul Claudel* (No. 5), Ottawa, Editions de l'Université Ottawa, 1967.

Roubaud, Jacques, *Mono no aware, le sentiment des choses*, Paris, Gallimard, 1970.

Rousseau, Jean-Jacques, *Oeuvres complètes*, Paris, Editions de la Pléiade, 1959.

——, *Les Confessions*, Paris, Garnier Flammarion, 1968.

Said, Edward, *Orientalism*, London, Routledge and Kegan Paul, 1978.

Segalen, Victor, *Essai sur l'exotisme*, Fontfroide, Bibliothèque artistique et littéraire, 1995.

Schwartz, William Leonard, *The Imaginative Interpretation of the Far East in Modern French Literature, 1800–1925*, Paris, Champion, 1927.

Scott, Clive, *Vers libre*, Oxford, Clarendon Press, 1990.

Sichel, Philippe, *Notes d'un bibeloteur au Japon*, Paris, E. Dentu, 1883.

Sontag, Susan, *On Photography*, London, Penguin, 1977.

Storry, Richard, *A History of Modern Japan*, London, Pelican Books, 1960; reprinted London, Penguin Books, 1990.

Thibault, Bruno, 'Voyager contre: la question de l'exotisme dans les journaux de voyage de Heri Michaux', *French Review*, 64 (1990), pp. 485–95.

Thirion, Y., 'Le japonisme en France dans la seconde moitié du XIXe siècle à la faveur de la diffusion de l'estampe japonaise', *Cahiers de l'association internationale des études françaises*, 13 (1961), pp. 117–30.

Titsingh, Isaac, *Mémoires et Anecdotes sur la dynastie régnante des Djogonus, souverains de Japon. Publié avec des notes par M. Abel Rémusat*, Paris, 1820.

Théry, Edmond, *Le Péril Jaune*, Paris, Félix Juven, 1901.

Thunberg, C. P., *Voyage au Japon par le cap de Bonne-Espérance* (translated into French in 1796).

Todorov, Tzvetan, *Nous et les autres: la réflexion française sur la diversité humaine*, Paris, Seuil, 1989.

——, *On Human Diversity*, trans. Catherine Porter, Cambridge, MA, Harvard University Press, 1993.

Topping, Margaret (ed.), *Eastern Voyages, Western Visions: French Writing and Painting of the Orient*, Bern, Peter Lang, 2004.

——, 'Proust's Orient(alism)', *French Studies Bulletin*, 84 (Autumn 2002), pp. 10–13.

Toynbee, Arnold (ed.), *Half the World: The History and Culture of China and Japan*, London, Thames and Hudson, 1973.

Truffet, Michel (ed.), *Cent Phrases pour éventails: édition critique et commentée avec la reproduction en fac similé de l'édition japonaise*, Paris, Les Belles-Lettres, 1985.

Tsuruta, Kinya (ed.), *The Walls Within: Images of Westerners in Japan and Images of the Japanese Abroad*, Vancouver, Institute of Asian Research, University of British Columbia, 1989.

Ughetto, André (ed.), *Analyses et réflexions sur Henri Michaux, 'Un barbare en Asie'*, Paris, ellipses, 1992.

Villenoisy, François de, 'La Guerre Sino-Japonaise et ses conséquences pour l'Europe', Paris, Imprimerie librairie militaire, 1895.

Weisberg, Gabriel P. and Weisberg, Yvonne M. L., *Japonisme: An Annotated Bibliography*, New York and London, Garland Publishing, 1990.

Wilkinson, Endymion, *Misunderstanding – Europe versus Japan*, Tokyo, Chuôkôronsha, 1982.

——, *Japan versus the West: Image and Reality*, London, Penguin Books, 1991.

Wittgenstein, Ludwig, *Philosophical Investigations*, trans. G. E. M. Anscombe, Oxford, Blackwell, 1958.

Index